DATE DUE

Democratizing Foreign Policy?

Democratizing Foreign Policy?

Lessons from South Africa

Edited by Philip Nel and
Janis van der Westhuizen

LEXINGTON BOOKS
Lanham • Boulder • New York • Toronto • Oxford

LEXINGTON BOOKS

Published in the United States of America
by Lexington Books
An imprint of The Rowman & Littlefield Publishing Group, Inc.
4501 Forbes Boulevard, Suite 200, Lanham, Maryland 20706

PO Box 317
Oxford
OX2 9RU, UK

British Library Cataloguing in Publication Information Available

Library of Congress Cataloging-in-Publication Data

Democratizing foreign policy? : lessons from South Africa / edited by Philip Nel and
Janis van der Westhuizen.
    p. cm.
  Includes bibliographical references and index.
  ISBN 0-7391-0585-X (cloth : alk. paper)
    1. South Africa—Foreign relations—1994- 2. Democratization—South Africa. I. Nel,
Philip. II. Van der Westhuizen, Janis, 1969-

    DT1975 .D46 2003
    327.68—dc21

                                                                    2002040689

Printed in the United States of America

♾™ The paper used in this publication meets the minimum requirements of American
National Standard for Information Sciences—Permanence of Paper for Printed Library
Materials, ANSI/NISO Z39.48–1992.

Contents

Preface

The year 2002 is a crucial year in the evolution of democracy in Africa. This is the year that the New Partnership for Africa's Development (NEPAD) is being promoted globally and implemented continent wide. NEPAD signals a commitment on the part of participating African governments to institute good governance, to take collective responsibility for the behavior of one another, and to implement economic policies that will encourage domestic and foreign direct investment. In turn, Africa expects the leading nations of the world to help it create the macroconditions that will promote economic growth and prosperity for Africa's people. Despite many unanswered questions, and despite concern that the macroeconomic precepts of NEPAD may not be the most appropriate for Africa's current developmental needs, many observers agree that "NEPAD is the only game in town."

The African Union (AU) has also been launched in 2002. This successor to the Organization of African Unity is intended to encourage closer economic and political integration on the African continent and makes provision for ambitious projects such as an African Parliament, a common market, and a shared currency and central bank. Although this project will take years, if not decades to implement, it is based on a vision of shared responsibility and a commitment to make Africa work that hold good promises for the future.

Apart from all the other potential benefits of NEPAD and the AU, the most important from our perspective is that it provides the citizens of Africa with a normative framework against which they can judge the acts of their leaders. The norms entrenched in the founding documents of NEPAD and the AU are self-imposed, and African leaders can expect that not only the international community, but also their own citizens will in future want to evaluate policies and behavior in view of these norms. These documents in themselves are thus tools of empowerment.

That does not mean that the citizens of Africa will effectively and concertedly make use of this opportunity, nor that they will be given the opportunity by the leadership to do so in any sustained and systematic way. If we have to go on past practice, then we probably should not have too high hopes in this regard. If citizens do not deliberately seek and pry open opportunities for effective democratic public participation, the normative potential of NEPAD and the AU will soon be repressed by a political and economic elite who stands to lose more than they will gain from being called upon to be accountable to their fellow citizens. The only way to prevent this from happening is by institutionalizing democratic public participation in the making and implementation of policy. Despite the fact that the AU and NEPAD emerged from processes that could hardly be described as participatory, these initiatives do open some scope, but all depends on how strongly citizens want to exploit this scope.

Although this book focuses on foreign policy making in only one African country, its overall aim is to contribute to an African debate about the prospects and challenges of institutionalizing democratic participation on the continent. For us, democratic participation means more than the holding of elections and parliamentary oversight, although it does also include these elements. It consists also of opportunities for Africans to systematically and in a sustained manner deliberate about their interests and about policy options to secure these interests. Given South Africa's central role in the NEPAD and AU initiatives, and the fact that South Africa will be the first Chair of the AU, the degree to which democratic participation in this broader sense is a reality in South Africa is quite crucial. So also is the terrain of foreign policy, broadly defined. As we argue in the introductory chapter, policies that transcend the boundaries of states have a determinate impact on the daily lives (and deaths) of people. Hence, our biggest challenge in effecting democratic participation in Africa lies in the field of foreign policy making and implementation in general. Again, a South African case study could provide important pointers to the challenges that we face in this regard.

This book is the result of a cooperative research project that was initiated by Philip Nel and funded by the Research Committee of the University of Stellenbosch. As editors we would like to acknowledge the hard work and patience of the contributors to this volume.

Philip Nel
Janis van der Westhuizen

Introduction

Democracy and "Policies beyond the State"

Philip Nel and Janis van der Westhuizen

Does it matter whether policies geared toward an environment beyond borders of the state are formulated and conducted in a democratic manner? In this book we present evidence that it does, and we make a case that it represents a normative ideal worth pursuing more than we as South Africans have done so up until now. We believe that the prevailing narrow definition of what democracy is, and the current erosion of public participation in the making of South Africa's foreign policy do not only impair the quality of that policy, but also represent a departure from ideals and values that lie at the heart of what post-apartheid South Africa is all about.

The danger of excluding or marginalizing those very people who should be the subjects of foreign policy—the citizens—is already present if one opts for the traditional, state-centric conception of foreign policy. Foreign policy is usually conceived of as the sum total of the official plans and initiatives taken by a country with respect to its external environment, plus the values and attitudes that underlie these plans and initiatives. In the approach adopted here, we steer away from relying solely on this meaning, although it will inevitably be found in some of the analyses that make up this book. But this state-centric concept of foreign policy has never and increasingly cannot capture all the dimensions of how citizens of a country respond to and try and shape their global environment, whether through official or through other collective means. While citizens look to the state to provide them with security against transnational threats to their safety, wealth, and happiness, they increasingly also make use of a variety of other collective means outside of state practices to respond to challenges that span national borders, and to relate to their external environment. For that reason we want to make it clear that foreign policy also has this broader meaning for us,

1

referring to all the collective actions that citizens take with respect to the environment beyond borders of their state. By raising the question of democracy in this broader context of societal responses to global economic and political patterns, mediated or unmediated by the state, we want to fathom the extent of participation, and the quality of that participation in terms of both procedural and substantive norms.

After all, South Africa's democratization was fundamentally driven by the power of international norms. In her contribution to this book, Audie Klotz shows how these 'democratic' attributes of South Africa have been constructed by the interplay of global and domestic normative processes. She illustrates how the apartheid State—despite its disavowal of the norm of racial equality—nevertheless sought to justify apartheid on normative grounds by creating tribal 'homelands' in step with decolonisation. Similarly, the international system continued to shape the contours of a postapartheid state, given that both governmental and nongovernmental antiapartheid forces prodded rivals toward the argumentation phase of South Africa's socialization.

To the extent that states still manage to maintain their monopoly on a fairly broad range of these collective responses, especially those that rely on violence or the threat of violence, and other coercive means, state-based 'foreign policy' continues to be a basic feature of our world. In raising the notion of democracy within this narrower context, we have in mind a mode of conduct that recognizes and institutionalizes the right of the citizens of a country individually and collectively to participate in the making of government policy that affects them directly or indirectly; that makes provision for public contestation about different publicly known policy options; and that ensures that the policies chosen address the 'real interests' of the citizenry (in contrast to presumed, perceived, or proscribed interests). Note, therefore, that we combine a procedural understanding of democracy with a substantive one. We accept that 'to define democracy is a political act' (Saward, 1994:7), and so we place our normative cards on the table right here at the start of this book. Although not all contributors would necessarily agree with us that the substance of policies could be used as a measure of democracy, we believe that it should be. We believe that any coherent usage of key normative indicators of democratic practices, such as autonomy, equality, and accountability, must make provision for the extent to which the practices that purport to be democratic (a) enable the agents of democracy (the people) to identify all forms of social domination and to take action against it, (b) provide the people with adequate subsistence levels so that they are physically and socially capable of demanding and exercising their equal rights; and (c) empower citizens politically to hold officials and politicians accountable for their deeds.

The reason why most contributors to this book underline the degree to which they see democracy in substantive, economic terms (see Ian Taylor's contribution for an extensive substantiation of this argument) and more than merely the occasional "two-minute democracy" exercised by voters, bears upon the tendency (especially since the late 1970s) to resuscitate the nineteenth-century separation of economy and politics, and thus to shield key aspects of economic management from politics and by extension, popular pressures (Cox, 1994:50). By the late twentieth century pluralist notions of democracy—"emptied" of economic concerns—effectively depoliticized the public realm at the onset of a process of profound dislocation with the expansion of the market well beyond the kind of regulatory framework provided by the postwar Keynesian state.

John Ruggie called the underlying logic of this relatively interventionist state a form of "embedded liberalism" which sought to promote the pursuit of Keynesian growth strategies at home without disrupting monetary stability abroad, through institutional mechanisms that would limit the impact of the clash between international liberalization and domestic stabilization. In practice this meant isolating some elements of economic life while promoting other aspects of the market at the same time. In short, it was decidedly seen as part of political "modernization" for the state to expand its social and economic functions along these lines.

From the 1960s onward, however, domestic structural costs, the consequences of growing external trade, and the increasing salience of international financial transactions, made it difficult for welfare states to insulate national economies from the global economy in which they were located. When governments tried to do so, the arrival of stagflation in the 1970s suddenly started to turn the tables. Inflation, which had hitherto been seen as a stimulus to growth and as benefiting both business and labor alike, came to be seen as inhibiting investment. As Robert Cox (1994: 46) has noted, "governments were made to understand that a revival of economic growth depended on business confidence to invest, and that this confidence depended on 'discipline' directed at trade unions and government fiscal management."

Moreover, both governments and corporations had increasingly relied on debt—and particularly *foreign debt*—to finance the massive projects with which welfare states provided mass employment. Because this meant that such loans were negotiated in foreign currencies, governments had to become more sensitive to their international credit ratings. And as the proportion of state revenue going into debt payments increased, governments often became more accountable to external bond markets than to their own constituents (Cox 1994:47). These new structural constraints and the growing global centralization of policy making have led to the "internationalisation of the state," as Cox (1994:49) has described it:

> Its common feature is to convert the state into an agency for adjusting the national economic practices and policies to the perceived exigencies of the global economy. The state becomes a transmission belt from the global to the national economy, where heretofore it had acted as the bulwark defending domestic welfare from external disturbances. Power within the state becomes concentrated in those agencies in closest touch with the global economy—the offices of presidents and prime ministers, treasuries, central banks. The agencies more closely identified with domestic clients—ministries of industry, labour ministers, etc., become subordinated.

Besides the word "globalization," 'competitiveness' became a part of a powerful and near-universal discourse through which governments could easily justify a multitude of initiatives and public policy changes. Arguing that such decisions merely reflected the realities of globalization and the need to be competitive, leaving them with "no other choice"—education programs, health, taxation, social security, transport—all traditionally considered to be "domestic" issue areas—have increasingly become subject to the degree to which they enhance the state's 'competitiveness'.

Facing the full force of "*un*embedded liberalism" trade liberalization intensified the global division of both labor and class: workers in American steel, Zimbabwean textile or Malaysian semiconductor plants shared the same fate if they could not move up the ladder of value added or "compete." No longer were corporations exclusively subject to the discipline of credit rating agencies, but governments had to ensure that fiscal and monetary policy would elicit the kind of support upon which good credit ratings were contingent. Indeed, not only were the lives of middle-class consumers determined by their credit record, but even university professors' career prospects depended upon their international research rating.

Yet the process of globalization triggered an odd paradox: despite the unprecedented degree of global informational, communicative, and transport access, perceptions of powerlessness and democratic impotence have become as common among the working and middle classes of Washington, Brussels, and Tokyo as they have in Buenos Aires, Pretoria, and New Delhi. As Walker (1988) noted, power has gone "elsewhere, untouchable." With the onset of very public displays of dissatisfaction since Seattle aside, these perceptions may explain a certain level of political apathy expressed in different forms in the paradoxical emergence of a kind of revisionist reaction on the one hand and disengagement on the other. For some of the most marginalized in the world economy, be they American antigovernment "Patriots," xenophobic South Africans, or Muslim extremist guerilla groups in the Phillipines, such displays of parochialism may be one way to cope with the perceived loss of influence. For the world's middle class (and relatively affluent working class) indulging in the material gratification of a global consumer culture is quite another. A steady decline in voter interest and participation in national elections even in the established democracies may reflect the concern of the contented: "whether I vote or not, does it matter?" Similarly, for younger generations in the world's emerging democracies (often marked by religious or ethnic cleavages) the allure of a consumer culture casts a pale shadow over a political life marred by religious or ethnic concerns best avoided at all costs.

Fortunately, such periods of "limited" or "thwarted" democracy are not unique inasmuch as globalization is seen as a historic process of market expansion and accompanying social turmoil. Relating this process to industrial transformation, Craig Murphy (1994) has shown how a series of stepwise changes in the scale of industrial economies from the subnational economies of the early

Industrial Revolution to the current Information Age was precipitated by a period of "relatively slow economic growth in which rapid marketization takes place, the state seems to retreat, and uncompromising versions of *laissez-faire* liberalism triumph." A second phase usually follows, marked by a heightened role for 'a more socially oriented liberalism' fueled by the increasing success of egalitarian social movements as well as the consolidation of a variety of "governance" institutions—be they interstate or work-driven institutions aimed at creating a certain level of stability, relative prosperity and thus space for the development of the next and larger industrial complex (Murphy, 2002:1).

It would seem as if we have entered into such a second phase globally, in the wake of the series of antiglobalization and antineoliberal episodes of resistance since Seattle 1999. These episodes may be harbingers of a re-embedding of the economy within a more egalitarian social context, but there are no guarantees that this outcome will inevitably flow from these episodes of resistance. For one, many questions about the representivity and social embeddedness of the groups responsible for these episodes can be asked. Are these so-called social movements really "people's movements," or are they simply an alternative elite who hope to replace the prevailing hegemony with a counterhegemony? Should we be content with such a counterhegemony, or is this the time to strive for a *post*hegemonic moment, that is, a dispensation in which economic and transnational policy making in general are not only socially embedded, but in which the citizens of the world become their own liberators?

This is the broader, admittedly populist context in which we want to raise questions about the degree to which South African's citizens are (a) recognized by the power elite inside (and outside) South Africa as the real subjects of policies that go beyond the borders of the state, and (b) are provided with the opportunities and means to shape these policies. However, we ask these questions not only because of our normative commitment to the vision of a global posthegemonic order, but also because of the legitimizing role that notions of democracy and public participation are playing in the political make-up of South Africa's postapartheid government. The self-understanding that this government has of itself and of the legitimacy of its foreign policy is based on the assumption that the current foreign policy is based on democratic practices, is attuned to the will and interests of "the people," and is therefore far superior to what went before. This claim lies at the heart of the recently released 'Special Report back to the Nation' document *Integrated Democratic Governance: A Restructured Presidency at Work* (Chikane, 2001) in which the Mbeki presidency explains and justifies the various attempts that they have taken to "put people first" also in the making and conduct of South Africa's foreign policy. We will return to this crucial document in some of the chapters to follow, but it is instructive to cite some sentences from the first few paragraphs of the concluding section of this document, to illustrate what we say above about the self-understanding of the South African government:

> The old South African Office of the President was not accountable to the majority of the people, whereas the new Government and President are. The old order was militaristic; the new Government is not. Instead it is participatory and democratic. It was secretive, whereas this Government is committed to the transparency and accountability that is required by the Constitution and other relevant legislation. The old government squandered resources on a gargantuan scale in defense of the indefensible: an unwanted apartheid system. The new Government seeks to conserve and extend resources for the benefit of all South Africans, particularly the historically disadvantaged. (Chikane, 2001:50)

This claim for legitimacy is based also on the presumed democratic quality of the government's foreign policy. This claim was already a feature of the new government even before it came to power in 1994,[1] but it has gained in importance during the Mbeki presidency. On a declaratory level, the Mbeki presidency has been characterized by a strong commitment to "putting the people first" (*Batho pele*), and this slogan has indeed become a main theme of the Mbeki presidency. Much of the emphasis of his administration has been to speed-up and generally to improve the delivery of services to the South African population, especially the poor and the needy.

The principle of putting people first also extends to the conception that the South African government has of its foreign policy and international role. A foreign policy role conception can be defined as, in Holsti's well-known words, "the policy makers" definition of the general kinds of decisions, commitments, rules, and actions suitable to their state and of the functions their state should perform in a variety of geographic and issue settings' (Holsti, 1988:110-111). This remains a useful working definition, as long as one does not interpret it in a methodological-individualist fashion to mean that explanations of role conceptions have to dwell no deeper than the psychological profiles, the operational codes, and the bureaucratic settings of the relevant decision makers.

As has been related in detail elsewhere,[2] President Mbeki and his foreign policy team has continued with the heavy emphasis that the Mandela presidency had already placed on multilateral diplomacy as the "cornerstone" of post-apartheid South Africa's foreign policy. Despite some early "heroic," but largely unsuccessful attempts to use multilateralism to effect significant change in the human rights practices of certain states, during the latter part of the Mandela presidency SA's multilateral role increasingly became one of a "bridge builder" between competing global forces. This role suited the "normal" middle-powership profile that observers attributed to the South African state, and was coterminous with South Africa's ascension to leadership positions in bodies such as the United Nations Conference on Trade and Development (UNCTAD, the Southern African Development Community (SADC), the Non-Aligned Movement (NAM), and the Commonwealth.

Despite much continuity with the Mandela era, significant foreign policy changes became noticeable when Mbeki took over in mid-1999, though. Most noticeable among these is the explicit reformist profile that has been given to

South Africa's foreign policy in general, and multilateral diplomacy in particular. As we use the concept, "reformism" is a foreign policy role conception that relies on established institutions and diplomatic practices to effect change in the dynamics of international interaction, without altering the ordering principles of that interaction. We thus place emphasis on the superficial level of change pursued by reformism, but it is important to distinguish the *level* of change from the *degree* of change. A specific incidence of change may be large and significant—for instance, if bilateral and multilateral creditors would decide to write off the debt of the poorest countries in one swoop—without affecting the basic power differentials structuring international relations. Reformism pursues change, including large degrees of change, but should be distinguished from transformism, which is concerned self-consciously to pursue change at an appropriate level in order to secure, firstly, changes in the fundamentally shared understandings governing and maintaining the international/ transnational order. These shared understandings have to do with whom are regarded as legitimate participants in the order, with the way violence is organized, and with the role of private property and market principles in producing wealth. Secondly, transformism would aim at a fundamental re-ordering of the structure of global politics, that is, the patterns in which actors are arranged in terms of their capabilities and power.

As has been pointed out by a number of observers, one cannot claim that the Mbeki presidency is pursuing either (a) or (b). What can be said is that Mbeki has introduced and has taken part in a vigorous reformist program, aimed at improving the fortunes of developing countries in general, and Africa in particular. That this program is based on a self-conscious role conception is clear from this extract from President Mbeki's speech during the budget vote of the president in the National Assembly, 13 June 2000:

> At the center of all (our multilateral) engagements I have mentioned is the critical question of our time, of how humanity should respond to the irreversible process of globalization while addressing the fundamental challenges that face the bulk of humanity. These include poverty, underdevelopment, the growing North-South gap, racism and xenophobia, gender discrimination, ill health, violent conflicts and the threat to the environment. These problems cannot be solved except in the context of the global human society to which we belong. We must and will actively continue to engage the rest of the world to make whatever contribution we can to ensure that the process of globalization impacts positively on those, like the millions of our people, who are poor and in dire need of a better life. This engagement must necessarily address, among other things, the restructuring of the United Nations, including the Security Council, a review of the functions of such bodies as the International Monetary Fund and the World Bank, the determination of the agenda and the manner of the operation of the World Trade Organization and an assessment of the role of the Group of Eight major industrial nations (G-8). Central to these processes must be the objective of reversing the marginalisation of Africa and the rest of the South, and therefore compensating for the reduction of national sovereignty by increasing the capacity of the South to impact on the system of global governance.[3]

The motto of putting people first thus clearly also has a foreign policy dimension to it. As the earlier cited Chikane document puts it:

> Since 1999 the Presidency (together with the Department of Foreign Affairs and other Ministers and Departments), has moved to consolidate and extend the country's international role in the interests of all South Africans, as well as the people of the region, the continent and the developing South. This is part of South Africa's vision of a better life for all at home, alongside a better world for all on the continent and beyond. (Chikane, 2001:44)

The same commitment also characterizes the New Partnership for Africa's Development (NEPAD), a document largely drafted by South Africa and agreed to by the Organization of African Unity at its annual summit in 2001. This document commits African leaders to what are termed "people-centered and democratic" policies, and holds forth a new model of cooperation between Africa and leading members of the Organization for Economic Cooperation and Development (OECD) for the sake of Africa's political, economical, and social renaissance. In its conclusion, the NEPAD document summarizes this vision thus:

> The objective of the *New Partnership for Africa's Development* is to consolidate democracy and sound economic management on the continent. Through the program, African leaders are making a commitment to the African people and the world to work together in rebuilding the continent. It is a pledge to promote peace and stability, democracy, sound economic management and people-centered development and to hold each other accountable in terms of the agreements outlined in the program. (NEPAD, paragraph 204).

There can hardly be any doubt, therefore, about the seriousness of the Mbeki presidency to portray itself as deeply committed to make democracy work to the benefit of the people of South Africa (and of Africa). We choose our words carefully here: in the absence of clear evidence pointing in a specific direction, it is inadvisable to form any hasty conclusion about the inherent commitment on the part of the Mbeki presidency to putting people first. Some skeptics may want to dismiss it as simply a device to popularly legitimize a style of rule that has in effect benefited only a narrow elite group of the people, and has in effect imposed unnecessary hardships on the vulnerable. Others would want to point out that a serious and deep "commitment to the People" is indeed an ingrained part of the very normative fabric of the ANC and its allies in the tripartite alliance and that, independently of the wishes of any ruling elite within the ANC, it acts as a powerful populist constraint and incentive in policy formulation. We expect that the truth of the matter lies somewhere between these two assessments, and that commitment to the people probably plays a much more complicated and ambiguous role within the ANC than what these two positions assume. We are therefore prepared to keep an open mind on the matter, and hence our careful conclusion that at best we can be certain of the Mbeki presidency's *declaratory* commitment to putting the people first.

This commitment on the part of Mbeki raises five important questions The first is a very general, even philosophical question, but is implied in all that we attempt to do in this book: *is it appropriate to associate the concept of public or people's participation with the notion of foreign policy?* What does public participation mean, and is it something that is desirable in the making of foreign policy? The chapter by Nel, van Wyk, and Johnson provides a conceptual framework within which these questions can be addressed, and they conclude that there are solid theoretical and practical reasons why the citizens of a democratic country must be centrally involved in the making of foreign policy. One of the means to give effect to this is by asking the public to regularly express their opinion on foreign policy issues—something that is hardly ever done in South Africa today.[4] To counter arguments that the public is often ill-informed and a poor judge of complicated foreign policy issues, the authors review recent findings from secondary opinion-poll studies in the United States that shows that the public in the United States is "pretty prudent," at least with respect to certain foreign policy issues at least. There is no reason to assume that this would not be true in South Africa as well. However, Nel, van Wyk, and Johnson also point out that public opinion polls are an extremely anemic form of "democratic participation," and that one therefore has to investigate also more robust mechanisms, such as those suggested by the participatory and deliberative democracy literature.

The second question raised by the government's commitment is *what exactly does President Mbeki mean when he commits himself to putting people first?* Getting clarity on this question will help us a long way toward understanding what the reigning conception of democracy among the government is. This question is also addressed by the chapter by Nel, van Wyk, and Johnsen. They suggest that we should distinguish between two different meanings of the phrase "putting people first," namely "governance by and of the people" on the one hand, and "governance for the people" on the other hand. Their assessment is that the Mbeki presidency has acted only in terms of this second, paternalistic conception, and that this has had considerable implications for the way in which foreign policy in particular is made in South Africa today.

Does the factual record with respect to foreign policy making support the conclusion that putting people first has not meant 'governance by the people of South Africa'? This links up with a third important question that flows from the declaratory position of the Mbeki presidency: *how much democracy has there been in the making of South Africa's foreign policy?* Most of the chapters in this book, each in their own way, raise this question and suggest different answers depending on the issue or dimension of foreign policy making that is at stake. Nel, Van Wyk, and Johnsen conclude that levels of public participation in policy making is exceedingly low in South Africa, and that this is a function of the nature of the democracy that was established in South Africa after 1994, and the "guardianship" conception that the Mbeki presidency has of its own role. Parliament, potentially a crucial institution for participation, has never had a central role to play in South Africa's foreign policy, but it stands to lose even the peripheral role that it has had. The reasons for this are a mix of factors: it is partly the result of the low level of attention that political parties represented in parliament accord to foreign policy during debates and elections. However, neglect of parliament's foreign policy role by the government and ruling party has also contributed to this. An important subsidiary question is whether this neglect is of the benign or of the malign sort.

Does civil society step into this breach and how successful have South African NGOs been in making foreign policy a more participatory process? le Pere and Vickers analyze the role of think tanks in this regard. Although these NGOs played a decisive participatory role during the transition period under Mandela, their influence gradually waned either due to government establishing its own research capacity in distinct issue areas; differential degrees of receptiveness by individual state ministries or the nature of an issue. Overall, however, South African NGOs—not unlike their counterparts elsewhere—are at best able to raise issues, with their degree of influence ultimately determined by government: short of policy making, the capacity for input appears at least robust. At the same time, the challenges facing NGOs have been to shift gear toward a more "watchdog" oriented role.

Would the democratization of foreign policy allow the labor movement to optimize its potential counterhegemonic role both nationally and internationally? Assessing the role of labor and other social movements in South Africa's foreign economic policy, Patrick Bond paints with broad brushstrokes to highlight five reactions to the global economic crisis especially since the late 1990s Asian crisis. After illustrating the interplay between these sets of forces at the global level, Bond points to Pretoria's high level of susceptibility to the Washington consensus on the one hand, and an attempt—however haltingly—to "reform" neoliberalism in the aftermath of the post-Washington consensus on the other. Such ambiguity accounts for the South African government's presence both *within* Washington's corridors of power and *outside* it as part of an incipient Third World nationalist counterreaction. How South Africa's "global justice movements" thus connect with other transnational social movements remains critical, given Pretoria's interlocutory role between the G-8 and the Group of Developing Nations at the United Nations (the G-77). However, Bond's analysis suggests a great deal of uncertainty regarding outcomes. For despite the Congress of South African Trade Unions' (COSATU) opposition to Pretoria's neoliberal turn, the union movement needs to "lead not lag" the other "global justice movements" and "return to its roots in the independent left" if the hegemony of the Washington consensus is to be challenged.

South Africa's democratic transition created an opportunity for a more gender sensitive and inclusive approach to women, also in the realm of foreign policy. Schoeman and Sadie address whether a more democratic foreign policy enhances the possibility for a more "feminized" foreign policy to emerge. They find that despite increased opportunities for women to participate in decision-making within the Department of Foreign Affairs, there is no evidence that women's contributions are being "maximized." "Maximising" would mean the inclusion of more women in decision making and the paying of more attention to women's issues which would change how the Department of Foreign Affairs functions, with significant consequences for the practice of diplomacy.

Moving the debate from various civil society *actors* and their impact on the making of foreign policy to *issue areas*, we highlight two case studies: trade policy, specifically South Africa's free trade agreement with the European Union (EU) and South Africa's controversial sixty-six billion Rands arms acquisition drive.

Reflecting on the saga of South Africa's protracted negotiations with the European Union on the finalization of a trade and development agreement, Bertelsmann-Scott highlights the degree to which the eventual free trade agreement involved quite a large cross-section of different interest groups. Underlining the significance of structural constraints such as globalization and what the European Union was prepared to negotiate about, Bertelsmann-Scott's chapter suggests that even if foreign policy issues are amenable to a high level of democratization domestically, the eventual decisions taken cannot really escape the crushing weight of asymmetrical global power relationships. In the concluding chapter we do suggest options, however, that can be explored to minimize the effects of such asymmetrical power relations.

Our second case study by Black reveals the degree to which one of the most defining instances of what *could* have and *should* have been a very transparent, participative and well-considered foreign policy issue area, namely South Africa's controversial arms deal, was quite the opposite. He shows how—with the exception of a few actors in civil society—most opposition to the arms deal was not so much due to questioning the fundamentals—*why* do we need such a huge arms-build up (and expense!) in the face of massive material social needs—but rather whether the deal was equitably structured and its associated opportunities for corruption and official "cover-ups." Black draws attention to the allure of military prestige and the apparent need for the ANC government to have its sovereignty powerfully reinscribed as the ultimate explanation for Pretoria's military shopping spree.

The fourth question addressed by this book links up with the fact that Mr. Mbeki extends his declaratory commitment to democratizing policy making also to the broader African context. This raises the question of the potential of what du Toit calls "transnational democracy," that is, the scope for democratizing African institutions such as regional (the African Union) and sub-regional bodies (the Southern African Development Community—SADC—for instance). du Toit focuses on the SADC and concludes that this body is beset not only by the challenge of each and every member state becoming a functioning democracy—which is by no means guaranteed—but also by the challenge to create accountable, and transparent institutions within the organization.

A fifth and final question raised by the Mbeki commitment to democracy and to putting people first, and by the conclusions of the other chapters in this book, is *what are the options that citizens have in their desire to play a larger and more meaningful role in shaping policies beyond state borders?* Given that globalization in its current form perpetuates enormous global inequalities of wealth and power, it is difficult to see how anything approximating David Held's global democracy can be advanced. At the same time, however, such inequalities have often triggered moves toward liberalization. As much of the democratic transition literature reminds us, whether such liberalization actually leads to genuine democratization or its reversal depends upon a complex interplay of various conditions and strategic moves on the part of a variety of social forces. In concluding this book, we contend that a similar analogy can be drawn at the global or transnational level. Although it is premature to determine whether globalization is either deepening or restricting the potential for democratization, this process of contestation between the established world order and rival, counterhegemonic social forces can be broadly and very tentatively gauged according to four strategic shifts involving processes of co-optation, concession, reformism, and depoliticization. These areas of contestation nevertheless suggest that traditional, territorially based democratic institutions need to link-up with global movement-based efforts if space is to be created for the opening of a more participatory process of global governance.

Notes

1.   The ANC's discussion paper, entitled "Foreign Policy in a New Democratic South Africa" issued in October 1993, made much of the fact that in the ANC's conception "foreign policy belongs to South Africa's people" and that the future foreign policy of a postapartheid South Africa would be determined by the "belief that our foreign relations must mirror our deep commitment to the consolidation of a democratic South Africa." This document also echoed a theme that was given pride of place at a December 1991 ANC policy conference, namely that "the foreign policy of a democratic South Africa will be primarily shaped by the nature of its domestic policies and objectives directed at serving the needs and interests of our people." These commitments were taken up and expanded upon in Nelson Mandela's now famous article "South Africa's future foreign policy" which appeared in the November/December 1993 edition of the journal *Foreign Affairs*.

2.   See Nel, Taylor, and van der Westhuizen, 2001.

3.   Speech of the President of South Africa, Thabo Mbeki, on the occasion of the consideration of the budget vote of the presidency, National Assembly, 13 June 2000, www.anc.org.za/ancdocs/history/mbeki/2000/tm0613

4.   The one exception is reported in Nel (1999).

Chapter 1

International Causes and Consequences of South Africa's Democratization

Audie Klotz

South Africa's democratic transition heralds a new era for both internal affairs and foreign policy. Contributions to this volume explore the diverse dimensions of the connections between democratization and change in relations to the rest of the world. In contrast, this chapter reverses our sights to focus on the external dimensions of the 1994 transition and consequences for foreign policy. I emphasize that globalization is not a new phenomenon but rather the latest form in which international relations construct dimensions of the South African state.

This perspective, from the outside looking in, builds on the "second image reversed" tradition of international relations theorizing. Therefore, I first briefly explain the basic tenets of this approach, including recent modifications by "constructivist" theorists. My empirical story delineates four phases, highlighting ways in which international factors affected South Africa's domestic politics in the first place and then some of the consequences for foreign policy in each era.

The Social Construction of the State

Much ink has been spilled in the disputes between international relations and comparative politics experts on the explanatory primacy of external or internal factors for understanding the relationships among states. Security experts, not surprisingly, point to the degree of vulnerability of the state to attack from external enemies, while political economists stress the significance of a country's position in the world economy. Most famously, Kenneth Waltz (1959) proclaimed that such "third image" or system-level analyses should be our starting point for understanding international politics, rather than domestic ("second

13

image") or individual ("first image") approaches. Others, however, claim that we need to understand domestic politics (and perhaps leaders' personalities) to appreciate the variations in foreign policy; the chapters in this collection present a fine illustration of the strengths of second image analysis.

While diverse aspects of domestic politics certainly influence the foreign policy making project, too often this second image perspective (from the inside looking out) underestimates or ignores the extent to which international factors influence internal decision-making processes or domestic political structures. Particularly in the South African case, where decades of sanctions created relative isolation, analysts tend to underestimate the value of a third image perspective. A second-image-reversed approach, which focuses specifically on the ways in which the international system affects political institutions and coalitions (Gourevitch, 1978) offers a fruitful avenue for linking international and domestic determinants of foreign policy, allowing us to integrate the outside-looking-in and inside-looking-out viewpoints.

In outlining the key questions of the second-image-reversed approach, Gourevitch surveys a wide range of literatures in international and comparative politics, both contemporary and historical. He offers two dimensions of domestic structures affected by the international context of war and trade, regime type and political coalitions (1978:883), and then suggests four key questions to guide analysis (1978:906-7): (1) What is the country's position in the world economy? (2) Who benefits or loses from adoption of a particular policy? (3) Who defines policy alternatives? (4) How is the policy legitimated? The answers should, he claims, enable us to assess the range of responses to international pressures.

In one illustration, Gourevitch suggests that democracy appears most prevalent in early industrializers and those countries less vulnerable to physical attack. Since South Africa industrialized later but faced an ideological rather than physical sense of threat, clearly such general trends do not sufficiently explain its current democracy. Granted, Gourevitch proposes a general conceptual approach, not a specific theory of political change. So we need to make some modifications and elaborations in order to apply a second-image-reversed perspective to the specific question of democratization and foreign policy making in South Africa.

The central role of racism in South Africa's internal political development and foreign relations points to ideology as a critical factor to explore. Furthermore, democracy and democratization clearly are global trends; some aspects of South African experience are unique, but others are not. Such isomorphism cannot be explained solely with reference to internal political dynamics. It is precisely this pattern of variation within a general trend which second-image-reversed analysis is best able to explain. But while Gourevitch states that "ideas, along with war and trade, relate intimately to the critical functions any regime must perform," he then excludes this realm from his discussion "for reasons of space and mental economy" (1978: 883).

Our first modification, then, is to incorporate ideational factors (ideologies, norms, beliefs) into our second-image-reversed analysis. In the case of South

Africa's transition to democracy, that means exploring the role of international norms and institutions in the elimination of apartheid (Klotz 1995). This step also requires a theoretical elaboration, since traditional approaches to international relations (unlike studies of domestic politics) so often ignore or underplay the role of ideas in favor of material factors (military capabilities, wealth). Recent constructivist scholarship gives us tools for such elaboration (Finnemore, 1996; Wendt, 1999). Incorporating ideas into our understanding of the international system means taking social structures seriously; institutions matter.

Since Gourevitch's questions emerge out of his interest in foreign economic policy, he does not identify mechanisms for the transmission of ideas from the international realm to domestic politics. Adding such an ideational component leads Finnemore (1996) to propose that international organizations play a critical role in socializing states into dominant norms. States, in turn, often act according to a "logic of appropriateness" (in contrast to an instrumental "logic of consequences") when conforming to expectations set out by international norms. Socialization processes thus underpin our constructivist variant of second image reversed analysis.

For example, colonialism was dominant and accepted in the late nineteenth and early twentieth centuries. However, decolonization became the dominant value by the 1960s. One result of this shift away from colonialism has been the expansion of the international community both in terms of the number of states and their defining characteristics (Jackson, 1990). Evolving definitions of sovereignty at the global level have a significant impact on states' purposes and interests. In practice, sovereignty is a general principle, which defines states as actors, but the content of their identity (their reason for being or the interests they pursue) is defined by a set of more specific norms, which vary over time. Particularly in the post-Cold War era, membership in the international community of states increasingly includes broad notions of liberal individualism and human rights as well as a minimum level of social welfare.

South Africa contested these global normative standards for decades, leading it to be subjected to a broad range of international sanctions as part of a socialization process (Crawford and Klotz, 1999). Similar efforts to enforce an international human rights regime demonstrate a multiphased reaction of resistance and ultimate compliance (Risse, et al, 1999). Application of this model demonstrates how international and domestic pressures for political change converged in a negotiated transition to legitimate democratic rule in South Africa (Black 1999).

This socialization model also enables us to analyze more specifically the foreign policy dimension of South Africa's transition. Risse and Sikkink propose three distinct causal mechanisms: strategic adaptation, where states make tactical concessions; argumentation, where a regime and its critics engage in dialogue; and institutionalization, where new norms get incorporated in the laws and decision-making routines within governments (Risse and Sikkink, 1999:11-12; also Finnemore and Sikkink, 1998:895). These mechanisms thus link international norms to domestic institutions and coalitions, the aspects of domestic politics that

Gourevitch highlights in his second-image-reversed framework. Domestic institutions and coalitions, in turn, play a major role in foreign policy making.

Each of these mechanisms corresponds to an era in South African history. Until the end of World War II, South Africa figured prominently in international affairs. The emergence of a norm of racial equality marks the onset of a phase of strategic adaptation. The subsequent struggle over apartheid, leading to South Africa's status as a pariah state, illustrates the dynamics of tactical concessions. The peak of the sanctions period, culminating in a political system based on racial equality, demonstrates effective argumentation. Both the regime and its critics needed to engage in dialogue, with each modifying their goals and expectations, in order to achieve a mutually acceptable political transition. Contemporary debates over the implementation of international norms enshrined in the new constitution shed light on the still-contentious institutionalization phase, with implications for foreign policy making (as delineated in the other chapters in this volume).

Four Phases of Socialization

Analyses of South African domestic politics usually stress the peculiarities of the apartheid system. Nationalism, militarism, and isolation appeared to be natural outgrowths of Afrikaner rule. Many activists as well as scholars stress the importance of internal resistance in the eventual elimination of apartheid. Yet critical aspects of the transition to nonracial democracy resulted from international pressures. South Africa, like other states in the international system, never has been truly insulated, even when ruled by isolationists.

The clash between two fundamental international norms of the twentieth century, self-determination and racial equality, substantively influenced the historical evolution of South African domestic politics and foreign relations. During the interwar period, South Africa remained within the boundaries of international society, which legitimized (Afrikaner) ethnic nationalism and racial hierarchy. Self-determination legitimated Afrikaner nationalism and fueled demands for autonomy from the British Empire in the 1920s. In conflict with an increasingly global belief in individual rights, by the 1960s the Afrikaner government attempted to legitimize apartheid through the Bantustan system, claiming self-determination and decolonization. The contemporary international system, in contrast, reinforces norms of political and economic liberalism.

South Africa's progression from pillar to pariah, and now to professed reformer, demonstrates the phases of socialization processes operating in the international system. But before we look at the ways in which South Africa adapted to international pressures, we need to understand its original incorporation into the international system. Thus we add another stage to the socialization process, since Risse and Sikkink take for granted the sovereign status of the rights-abusing states in their study. Prevailing norms at the time of independence profoundly affect the nature of the institutions and coalitions, which establish a country's initial role in world affairs.

The newly emergent country of South Africa, like the other British Dominions, acquired an uneasy and ill-defined sovereignty in the early twentieth century (Hancock, 1937). While granting a substantial degree of local autonomy with the establishment of the Union in 1910, Britain still retained its command of foreign policy for its former colonies in the Commonwealth as a whole and expected the Dominions to provide troops for its wars. Indeed, the South Africa Act of 1909, which established the Union in the aftermath of the Boer wars, contained no provisions for foreign policy making institutions; only in June 1927 was the Department of External Affairs established (Pienaar, 1987; Geldenhuys, 1984). Thus sovereignty remained limited as long as South Africa lacked both juridical and de facto control over its foreign relations.

After WWI, South Africa became a founding member of the League of Nations. The League offered an alternative to the Commonwealth as a forum for defining Dominion autonomy from Britain, even though South Africa's High Commission in London remained its primary diplomatic mission (Pienaar, 1987:23-6). Indeed, many South African nationalists preferred participation in the European-dominated League as an alternative to British domination of the Commonwealth. South Africa further bolstered its independent status by acquiring a mandated territory (Namibia). A reluctant internationalism thus characterized South Africa's early international relations.

Anti-British sentiment, in South Africa more so than other Dominions, shaped this nascent internationalism, and foreign policy influenced internal politics as well. League support for a norm of self-determination in particular strengthened Afrikaner claims to independence from Britain. League internationalism also offered common ground for the domestic political alliance, which led to the Fusion government of 1934. Remaining outside this centrist coalition, however, a substantial faction of Afrikaner nationalists (precursors to the National Party) remained skeptical of participation in the League for fear that South Africa would be drawn into another European war. Growing concern about the ineffectiveness of the League, particularly in the 1930s, weakened the internationalists and strengthened the isolationists. In 1939, Hertzog resigned over the issue of neutrality (Pienaar, 1987:9-12, 175-77).

Interwar internationalism amongst Afrikaners was not solely a mechanism for counterbalancing British dominance and bolstering sovereign autonomy. In addition, the content of the League message established legitimacy for Afrikaner nationalist claims domestically. In particular, the League norm of self-determination included an emphasis on minority rights (Louis, 1984:201-13). Emerging in the 1920s, the Afrikaner movement modeled its nationalist claims of group identity and thus group rights on the more general pattern of interwar nationalist movements. For example, Afrikaners emphasized the authenticity of their language and territorial jurisdiction (Thompson, 1985; Thompson 1991).

While Afrikaners primarily emphasized their cultural differences from the British in South Africa, their views toward Africans played a secondary role in

defining group identity. Indeed, the "race problem" of the inter-war years referred to the Anglo-Afrikaner division, not discrimination against blacks. Again,
Afrikaner nationalism reflected prevailing international norms. Since racial hierarchy was generally accepted in the interwar period (despite Japanese objections), Afrikaners shared with most League members the assumption that
Africans were inferior and unprepared for self-government (Lauren, 1988; chapter 4). Thus Afrikaner nationalism could take race for granted because it went
unchallenged.

Only after WWII, when a strengthening norm of racial equality (to a large
degree a reaction to race-based genocide by Nazi Germany) challenged prevailing assumptions of white superiority did the racial dimension of Afrikaner nationalism emerge more explicitly. Institutionalized racial discrimination under
apartheid increasingly pushed South Africa outside the normative boundaries of
an evolving international community, which now proclaimed its belief in racial
equality. In the face of broad-ranging and increasingly stringent international
sanctions, the apartheid regime practiced strategic adaptation, seeking to circum-
vent its international critics without accepting the norm of racial equality.

That the global shift toward racial equality left the Afrikaners beyond the
normative bounds of international society is evident in the increasingly isolationist views among Afrikaners and their attempts to justify the apartheid
system. When South Africa quickly came under international condemnation
within the United Nations and other international organizations, the ruling National Party's foreign and domestic policy response defended Afrikaner national
self-determination and minority rights. While the international community
championed the new norms of liberal individualism, the Afrikaners defended
apartheid within the old framework of group rights by claiming that the South
African situation entailed special issues of cultural survival. At the same time,
African resistance strengthened with the post-war shift to decolonization. The
antiapartheid movement became global (Thomas, 1996), leading to more vocal
and widespread objections to white minority rule in southern Africa.

International condemnation influenced foreign policy choices, especially
with regard to memberships in international organizations. While international
criticism of apartheid increased, isolation replaced the previous reluctant internationalism of many Afrikaner nationalists. Since an isolationist faction among
Afrikaner nationalists originally founded the National Party, it used heightened
criticism as a vehicle for garnering consensus on Republican status in 1961,
instigating South Africa's subsequent withdrawal from the Commonwealth. Isolationism consolidated as the predominant perspective in foreign affairs for the
next three decades.

But a focus solely on explicit isolationism hides the domestic response to
international condemnation which demonstrates the extent to which South Africa still remained sensitive to international norms. The nature of apartheid policy,
based primarily on the Afrikaner fear of cultural survival, demonstrates the
extent to which the South African government sought to legitimate its policies
globally, in keeping with norms of decolonization.

Among the various components of apartheid segregation, the National Party government went to great—and expensive—lengths to create tribal "homelands" or "Bantustans" along the lines of (African) decolonization, rather than simply establishing an internal system of territorial segregation. In their attempts to create the trappings of sovereignty, the South African government created ten territories which, in its official pronouncements, represented nation-states among various cultural groups. While providing the juridical basis for ostensibly independent territories, including local parliaments, defense forces, and faux-borders, South Africa announced the decolonization of the homelands (Butler, et al., 1977; Southall, 1983; Ashforth, 1990).

In effect, the policy of creating independent homelands remained a mixed blessing for the advocates of apartheid. Satisfying neither external nor internal demands for African political representation, the homelands system also failed to control the process of urbanization (Greenberg, 1987). Furthermore, the homelands policy created an alternative base for antiapartheid opponents of various persuasions. While some homelands leaders supported the African National Congress, the most notable and persistent legacy of the Bantustan policy has been Buthelezi's Inkatha movement.

Three crucial group-actors thus emerge from the global shift from self-determination to individual rights in the postwar period: an isolationist Afrikaner government which became increasingly unable to legitimate its domestic policies in the new international normative context; a global (governmental and non-governmental) antiapartheid movement which campaigned for sanctions; and an internal Zulu nationalist movement which balanced precariously between demanding self-determination and the elimination of apartheid. Dialogue between them illustrates the argumentation phase of South Africa's socialization.

The notion of argumentation presumes that actors are willing to engage in dialogue. For countries like South Africa in the 1980s, in essence embroiled in civil war, we cannot presume a willingness to talk. International pressures fostered dialogue in (at least) three ways: enticing the government to the negotiation table, legitimating the African National Congress (ANC) as a critical participant in any settlement, and proffering normative focal points that structured the content of the negotiations.

Sanctions played a key role in bringing the National Party to the negotiating table. Most sanctions policies contained a list of demands for domestic reforms intended to foster negotiations. (Consensus over criteria indicating compliance was the result of often-vociferous international debates; the resulting five required reforms, however, became standard in almost all bilateral and multilateral sanctions policies.) These criteria included the repeal of the state of emergency and the legal pillars of racial segregation, the release of political prisoners, and the legalization of opposition parties including the ANC, as well as an explicit appeal to enter negotiations with those opponents. When the government initiated reforms in 1990, it followed step by step the measures outlined in these sanctions policies. Initial "talks about talks" built upon previously informal and secret discussions between the government and imprisoned anti-*apartheid* leaders. Going public in May 1991 enabled de Klerk to call for the end of international sanctions. Generally convinced of the sincerity of South African reforms, most sanctioners duly lifted restrictions (Klotz, 1995:156-8).

While the government now sat at the negotiating table, the question who else would join the discussions remained. Decades of political maneuvering among the opposition now came to the fore. Sanctions also influenced the relative strength of the various groups. For example, the ANC and (Pan Africanist Congress (PAC) benefited directly from United Nations (UN) and Organization of African Unity (OAU) resources while in exile. It would have been impossible to ignore Nelson Mandela after he became the symbol of the international antiapartheid movement. Yet Buthelezi, the most vocal black critic of sanctions, also benefited from international censure, as he brought Inkatha resources from international antisanctions constituencies. The South African government also secretly channeled support to Inkatha from a fund designed to undermine sanctions (*New York Times*, 22 July 1992), ultimately damaging Buthelezi's credibility when the relationship became public. Inkatha maintained strong enough support internally and internationally to be able to demand a place at the negotiating table.

That these deeply divided protagonists ultimately worked out a transition and new constitutional system surprised observers. International norms played a considerable role in demarcating the boundaries of a legitimate settlement (Black, 1999:100-105). International intermediaries, such as the Commonwealth Eminent Persons Group, actively fostered a culture of pluralism and tolerance while stressing the goal of creating a truly nonracial democracy. Even reluctant sanctioners indicated staunch opposition to any provision for a white minority veto, a primary demand of the National Party. At the same time, these outside forces did not demand major economic restructuring, a key expectation on the ANC side. The prospect of renewed sanctions hovered in the background as the negotiations continued, helping to keep the key players at the table and, ultimately, more willing to compromise than could otherwise be expected. That implicit threat reinforced international standards favoring political equality over economic rights, a trade-off that continues in the postapartheid era.

The negotiated and relatively peaceful nature of South Africa's transition itself had immediate consequences for foreign policy. Mandela attained unrivaled status as a global statesman, becoming mediator in diverse international controversies. The country also promptly rejoined most international organizations, signaling the end of its pariah status. The elimination of apartheid, moreover, fostered democratization globally. Perceived success of sanctions in this case bolstered the use of such measures against other regimes accused of violating human rights. Activist networks similar to the antiapartheid movement play an increasingly important role in diverse issues beyond human rights (Keck and Sikkink, 1998).

However, the long-term domestic consequences of South Africa's transition remain uncertain, as the other chapters in this volume detail. The fourth and final stage of socialization, institutionalization, depends on the extent to which international norms get embedded in legal provisions and political practice. Constitutional guarantees on questions such as equal rights for women will inevitably be sorted out through a process of challenge and high court decision. Bureaucratic changes in areas including foreign policy depend in part on the ability of the old administrators to retain their standard operating procedures. The deepest level of transition, the psyches of people educated in a society infused with racism, presumably will take longer to change. In the medium term, we can expect South Africa to play a role of moderate reformer in its foreign policy, as it seeks to balance the unresolved tensions that necessarily result from the negotiated nature of its transition.

Conclusion

South Africa's history illustrates the effects that international ties have on domestic politics and society. Second-image-reversed analysis shows that, rather than being insulated protagonists in the foreign policy making process, domestic parties and movements garner social and material resources from the international system. We cannot starkly separate domestic from international sources of foreign policy; states are constructed and reconfigured by their places in global affairs. Socialization is a multifaceted, ongoing process, which never reaches a final point of completion. South Africa will continue to affect and be affected by the forces of globalization.

Chapter 2

The Democratization of South African Foreign Policy: Critical Reflections on an Untouchable Subject

Ian Taylor

"What shall I tell them back in parliament?" Evita eventually asked. The unemployed people thought for a moment. Then, a mother of four, wearing a small green hat, spoke. "Tell them, Mevrou, that we fought for freedom. All we got was democracy." (Uys, 1999: 9)

According to official sources, South African foreign policy is already democratic and democracy underpins Pretoria's international relations. As one early briefing paper put it, South Africa's foreign policy is predicated upon a "belief that just and lasting solutions to the problems of human kind can only come through the promotion of democracy" (African National Congress, 1994: 2). The democratic nature of Pretoria's foreign policy is, it is claimed, derivative of the transition from apartheid. The Department of Foreign Affairs (DFA) for instance claims that 'South Africa's special position arising from our democratic transformation and the prestige and standing of our President' informs its foreign policy (Department of Foreign Affairs, 1997: 2).

The DFA's policy document, *Developing a Strategic Perspective on South African Foreign Policy*, indeed asserts that "our international relations must mirror our deep commitment to the consolidation of a democratic South Africa." These positions are consistent with Mandela's famous article on a postapartheid foreign policy for the country, where he claimed that "South Africa will....be at the forefront of global efforts to promote and foster democratic systems of government" (Mandela, 1993:88). Mbeki's presidency has made a variety of claims over the democratic input into policy making, with one document recently asserting that 'effective democracy means listening and then responding with appropriate action to what these people are saying' (Chikane, 2001:2). Mbeki has in fact sought to advance particular notions of democracy within Africa—raising critical questions as to Pretoria's motives (Taylor, 1999) as well as positing South Africa as a leading voice promoting particular political and economic goals on the broader continent as part of the much vaunted "African Renaissance" (Taylor and Williams, 2001; Taylor and Nel, 2002).

Though policymakers frequently invoke democracy in their rhetoric and imply the genuineness of this actuality, they rarely—if ever—problematize the nature of the democracy they are invoking. Thus Foreign Minister Dlamini-Zuma can confidently claim that

> The majority of Africans now live under systems of democratic governance, free to elect those to whom they entrust the responsibility of leadership and to determine their own future. A large number of African countries have in recent times conducted their successful democratic elections and others are preparing to do the same, thereby proving that democracy has put down deep and strong roots. (Department of Foreign Affairs, 2000)

Thabo Mbeki, in a speech at the University of Hong Kong in December 2001 similarly made ambitious claims, asserting that: "the number of democratically elected governments [in Africa] has been on the increase since the last decade of the last century, and accordingly many people on the continent have been empowered to assist in the entrenchment of the democratic processes and structures" (Mbeki, 2001). This is not the place to interrogate such claims in detail. What will be said is that the jury is very much still out deciding on the authenticity or otherwise of the commitment to democracy in Africa—even by the standards of the highly procedural and neoliberal form that it has taken during the democratization waves of the 1980s and 1990s. As Ottaway (1997:1) wrote, "it is far too early to talk of democracy in Africa. At best, these changes will prove to be the beginning of a long process eventually leading to democracy. . . . [T]he most difficult part of a democratic transformation—the move from an initial opening to a sustained process of liberalization and of consolidation of institutions—is still ahead for most countries." Nonetheless, there is a discourse, quite discernible within pronouncements from Pretoria that not only is South African foreign policy democratic, but that it also promotes democracy abroad.

Such accounts are heartening and suggest a distinct lack of controversy. After all, who can possibly be *against* democracy: as Rupert wryly asks, "democracy, peace; what's not to love?" (Rupert, 1998). Similarly, who can criticize Pretoria's commitment to democratizing its foreign policy? Yet, any discussion around the potential to democratize South African foreign policy cannot be separated from the wider socioeconomic order that such foreign policy is situated in (Vale and Taylor, 1999). This is so even if one were to (naively, to be sure) base one's analysis upon an understanding of South Africa's agency that is not firmly rooted in a profound recognition of the structural constraints that the new nation finds itself vis-à-vis global capital and the ongoing processes associated with the term "globalization" (Taylor and Vale, 2000).

Furthermore, if one wishes to avoid the reification of dominant discourses surrounding the democratization of foreign policy and refuses to take at face value commitments to "democracy" and "people-centered" policy inputs, a form of immanent critique of the content and promises of the type of democracy in place in South Africa is required. Otherwise, one is simply starting from a point of departure that is in itself, simplistic and highly problematic. Hence, just because the South African government claims to be democratic, or say, an African National Congress (ANC) *Discussion Document* claims that 'the democratic movement must resist the liberal concept of "less government"', does not mean that analysts should take such pronouncements at face value (African National Congress, 1996: 7). After all, "less government" is inherent within neoliberalism, the philosophical underpinnings behind the government's current macroeconomic framework which, as a self-imposed structural adjustment program, indeed pushes for "less government" as a logical part of its own project! (Williams and Taylor, 2000; Taylor, 2001)

This of course has led to profound tensions within the Tripartite Alliance among the African National Congress, the Congress of South African Trade Unions (COSATU) and the South African Communist Party (SACP). In late 2001 COSATU launched a general strike aimed at halting the government's privatization program. Both COSATU and the SACP are passionately opposed to the government's neoliberal macroeconomic policies. Whilst COSATU remains committed to building socialism, Thabo Mbeki stands by the Governments Growth, Employment, and Redistribution Program (GEAR) (Williams and Taylor, 2000). COSATU's General-Secretary, Zwelinzima Vavi, believes that the ANC leadership has "sold out" and that only capital, the emergent black bourgeoisie and the mostly white official opposition support GEAR—raising profound questions over the democratic mandate that GEAR enjoys. Indeed, the tensions within the Alliance highlight serious issues over taking the democratic practices of the current government at face value. This is not to say that the South African government "is not democratic," but rather that we should interrogate such issues thoughtfully and reflexively.

Indeed, conducting face-value appraisals of the democratic claims of South African foreign policy making would, I believe, correspond with Max Horkheimer's (one of the founder's of the Frankfurt School in social theory—Horkheimer, 1995) delineation between "traditional" and "critical" theory. Horkheimer argues that knowledge production cannot be separated from power relations and interests within society. Scientific activity should be conceived not only as part of the reproduction of the dominant order but also as part of its protection, despite the beliefs and the consciousness of the individual (Horkheimer 1995:189). "Traditional" theory seeks to obfuscate the real social function of science and hides the link between ideas and theoretical positions and their broader social environment. This acts to decontextualize ideas from their foundations within social processes. Refuting such a conceptualization of theory, Horkheimer asserts that "as a matter of fact the life of society is the result of all the work done in the various sectors of production. Even if therefore the division of labor in the capitalist system functions but poorly, its branches, *including science,* do not become for that reason self-sufficient and independent' (emphasis added).

In short, science is a social activity conducted by communities of researchers: it is socially constructed and is not isolated nor acting alongside society, but is undeniably *within* it. Theoretical constructions hence should be understood in the light of their specific historical context, the ideology that underpins these theories, and the forms of society that such theories promote, sustain or challenge (Lapid, 1989:250). Indeed, "theory is always for someone and for some purpose. All theories have a perspective. Perspectives derive from a position in time and space, specifically social and political time and space" (Cox, 1996:208). This is not to say that such a position leads ultimately to relativism. Jürgen Habermas argues that though knowledge is historically founded and interest bound, knowledge can emerge out of an intersubjective search for truth: truth claims are resolved through unfettered reasonable discussion culminating in consensus (Habermas, 1979:1-68). In his theory of discourse ethics, Habermas avoids the problem of relativism (inherent in post-modernism) and provides a non-metaphysical "base" on which a point of view may be reasonably situated.

Habermas examines the relationship between processes of constitution and justification via communicative competence, maintaining that all speech is directed toward the notion of a genuine discursively achieved consensus (which is rarely achieved). In short, communicative action outlines a rationality allowing universal norms. The analysis of consensus shows this notion to involve a normative dimension, which is formalized in the concept of what Habermas calls "an ideal speech situation," which he regards as implicit in the communicative act and which includes ethical and normative commitments. A consensus attained in this situation, a "rational consensus" is, according to Habermas, the decisive measure of whether a statement is true or not, or of the correctness of normative claims (Pusey, 1987:89). This allows for an emancipatory dimension which is closed by relativism's extremes.

Indeed, Habermas's critical theory has emancipation as its starting point. It is grounded in a normative base that is not arbitrary, but intrinsic in the structures of social activity and language. This can be used as a normative standard for a critique of dominant discourses that contribute to and formulate contemporary ideology. Such ideologies maintain their "legitimacy" only through coercion and would be invalidated if subjected to rational discourse—to ideal speech. This rational discourse presupposes that statements can be comprehensible, true, right, and sincere (Outhwaite, 1994).

One important process of any emancipatory project therefore entails the transcendence of existing systems of distorted communication so that the force of the better argument prevails (Habermas, 1990:66, 89). Hence, consensus on whether a statement is true and right can be achieved in an environment shorn of power and distortion (Outhwaite, 1994: 40). This process requires engaging in critical reflection and criticism and it is only through such reflection that domination, in its many forms, can be unmasked. This reflexivity avoids relativism. By doing so, such "foundations for making judgments between knowledge claims places [such analyses] as . . . direct descendant[s] of the Kantian enlightenment project . . . a great source of strength to those who want to link foundational knowledge to emancipation" (Smith, 1996: 28). It overcomes the relativism of post-modernism which, as Habermas points out, is unable or unwilling to account for its own normative foundations (Habermas, 1987:276).

In International Relations, Robert Cox has developed Horkheimer's theories to contrast "problem-solving" and "critical" theory. According to Cox, problem-solving theory

> takes the world as it finds it, with the prevailing social and power relationships and the institutions into which they are organized, as the given framework for action. . . . Since the general pattern of institutions and relationships is not called into question, particular problems can be considered in relations to the specialized areas of activity in which they arise. (Cox, 1996:88)

A problem-solving or traditional theory account of the democratization of Pretoria's foreign policy would proceed from a ready and uncritical acceptance of the terms "democracy" and "democratization," and then expand on how South Africa's foreign policy-making measures up against such definitions. This is surely common sense, such accounts would assert, for South Africa has elections, political parties, a free press *etc*. This is not to say that procedural democracy or constitutional checks on the ambitions of elites and the protection of citizens from arbitrary arrest can be simply written off as meaningless. Such considerations represent a considerable advance for the citizens of South Africa when viewed against the hsitory of apartheid's authoritarianism. But, we should be wary of overly concentrating on

> the notion of holding of free and fair elections rather than on the broader political, cultural and institutional transformation connected with a process of democratization. There is no doubt that holding free and fair elections is an important element in a transition to democracy. But as an isolated event the election should only be the tip of the democratic iceberg. If it is not closely connected with deeper-rooted changes it does not mean very much. (Sorensen, 2000:298)

While the powers of the President are prescribed by a Constitution and this does positively contribute to the democratic dispensation of the country, elections, the party system, even wonderfully progressive constitutions do not make democracy—they are simply procedural mechanisms. It is the socioeconomic system, state form, and the substantive content of state policies that "make" a democracy. Other countries within the region, such as Zambia, have gone through internationally-anointed "democratization" processes with profoundly unsatisfactory results that have exacerbated the insecurity of citizens, even while elections and appeals to good governance and democracy have marked their course (see Abrahamsen, 2000). This simple truism is, surprisingly highly contested, confused, or simply avoided in both the burgeoning literature on "democratization" and on South African foreign policy (Taylor, 2000)

For instance, in one of the more recent (and celebrated) accounts of "democratization" in Africa, the writers explicitly proclaim that the authors' "understanding of democracy refers to a set of political procedures [and] we dissociate it from rule for the people, which implies substantively, a distributive socio-economic order." (Bratton, and Van de Walle, 1997:12)

Samuel Huntington, in his equally celebrated work in the democratization canon, simply argues that "the central procedure of democracy is the selection of leaders through competitive elections by the people they govern" (1996: 6). Robert Dahl, in his book *Democracy and its Critics* (1989) and his later works seems to arrive at why a narrow definition of democracy—which he prefers to call "polyarchy"—is preferable. This describes a procedural system whereby an elite group rules and where popular involvement in decision-making is limited to periodic leadership choices organized by contending elites. The problem with Dahl's argument is that it does not logically follow through his own original contentions. Dahl asserts that there exist "criteria that a process for governing an association would have to meet in order to satisfy the requirement that all the members are equally entitled to participate in the association's *decisions about its policies*" (Dahl 1998:37. Emphasis added). Dahl lists five such criteria, namely effective participation; voting equality; enlightened understanding; control of the agenda; and inclusion of adults. "Each is necessary if the members....are to be politically equal in determining the policies of the association" (1998:38). In this formulation, Dahl boldly asserts that the demos has a right to an explicit say on discrete policies. This in itself indicates the need for mechanisms that permit the direct recording of the demos' dispositions vis-à-vis policies—and on a continuous basis. In organizational terms, this implies that there should be at least some form of direct gatherings of citizens for consideration and judgment, perhaps using today's technology via 'virtual' means *or* referendums in which the citizenry register their opinions on issues. Certainly, "control of the agenda" does suggest that the demos must have a real say over what are to be deemed the policy priorities (see also Chapter Three below).

Though Dahl powerfully suggests that large-scale democracy in the nation-state requires the institutions of polyarchy, this contradicts the logic of his own criteria for democracy. Dahl presupposes that the polyarchies actualize the supreme practicable fulfillment of his democratic criteria, but this has been arrived at by passing over a crucial part in his study, namely the contemplation of democratic governance that springs from Dahl's initial criteria. Hence institutional forms such as referenda and direct decision making are precluded. Instead, Dahl's polyarchy becomes indirect, with political elites in the paramount decision-making roles and controlling the policy agenda, even though in his initial criteria Dahl envisaged the demos having a direct say over discrete policies. Contradicting his earlier statements on what constitutes democracy, the criterion of "control of the agenda" becomes satisfied by the existence of "elected representatives" and procedural institutionalized democratic governance (1998:92).

Yet, such minimalist and procedural definitions completely fail to interrogate questions relating to substantive issues connected to democracy and certainly avoid analyzing the pattern of relationships and institutions that have been historically constructed. Investigations into equity, the distribution of resources, and equal access to life chances are simply swept under the carpet. This liberal preoccupation with form over content vis-à-vis democracy is not entirely by accident and responsible scholarship should seek to analyze why this is so.

In the context of a globalizing international political economy and the seeming upsurge in "democratization studies," how and why a particular view of democracy has achieved hegemony (in the Gramscian sense, cf. Gramsci, 1971), and in whose interests this is, and is not, is essential (see Moore, 1996). Only by subjecting this dominant paradigm to immanent critique can we then properly proceed to discuss the related topic, that is, the democratization of South African foreign policy. Certainly, if the subject of our research is the democratization of foreign policy, then the task of this book should be to ask "democratization for whom"? Posing the problem in this way enables critical attention to be directed to the democratization of state structures of decision-making (rather than to public policy arguments which would avoid such interrogations). In this sense, this chapter takes one step back from the usual point of departure when tackling the subject of the democratization of South Africa's foreign policy, whilst at the same time questioning those positions that take an unreflective stance toward the subject and who naturalize South Africa's democratic order as unproblematic. This is necessary as, sadly, much of the writing on South Africa's foreign policy remains uncritical with scant regard for reflexivity or theory building (Taylor, 2000).

The Power of Immanent Critique

Approaching the democratization of foreign policy debate by means of an immanent critique of dominant discourses of democracy provides us with certain advantages. For instance, such an approach would not attempt the construction of new foundations for democracy. Obviously, critics might well respond with "what's your alternative?" but in doing so they miss the point of the power of immanent critique. As Adorno remarks, "if philosophy were to stoop to a practice which Hegel already mocked, if it were to accommodate its kind reader by explaining what the thought should make him [sic] think, it would be joining the march of regression without being able to keep up the pace" (1995:32).

Instead, immanent critique simply attempts to critically reinterpret dominant discourses on the understanding that *all* norms are historically contingent and contested phenomena that are revisable as circumstances change. The method of immanent critique constitutes the core of critical theory and it is what brings together various social theorists such as Marx, Engels, Gramsci, Marcuse, Hork-heimer, Lukacs, and Habermas (see Antonio, 1983).

The role of immanent critique is to attempt to examine how hegemonic norms can be made more consistent and pertinent to the historical milieu which the theorist finds herself in and consequently less restrictive in their practice. Immanent critique follows the Hegelian logic of dialectics which argues that truth is arrived at through the process of critique and positive change lies in the process of contesting established givens. In his work *Critique of Hegel's "Philosophy of Right"* Marx argued that Hegel's understanding and exposition of social reality was fairly close in its depiction of nascent capitalist society, when its speculative trappings were taken away (Marx, 1970). But, Hegel believed that the State was the highest social organization and he attributed a substantive a priori rationality to its institutions. As Hegel enjoyed the patronage of the Prussian state and his work was thought to be a true picture of reality, Hegel's political philosophy *defined* social reality for those in power and rationalized their power. Logically, such ideas regarding the ordering of society legitimized those in power *and* curtailed alternative choices.

The same might be said of both policymakers and academicians within South Africa. Much of the analysis on South Africa's foreign policy has been unreflective of the choices available to the government and also accepts at face value a standpoint—often the "realities" of the global order—in which South Africa is presumed to have minimal agency. Stremlau's assertion that "the twin processes of globalization and liberalization have become irreversible realities" is a case in point (*Mail and Guardian*, November 13, 1998). This is then marshaled to push for greater 'policy fit' with the United States. Demands that "first and foremost, South Africa. . . . must present itself as a stable and reliable partner in diplomacy and business" and that its "foreign policy should in most circumstances be non-confrontational and non-ideological" reflects not good analysis, but the demands of international capital (Mills, 1996:5).

Any emancipatory project must thus first understand the dominant ideas within any one given timeframe and subject them to rigorous critique, not taking the subject at its word, but rather as it actually is. Such critiques reveal the potentialities in any given social reality and seek to demonstrate how such potentialities may be realized. Immanent critique allows the contradictions between a particular discourse and its actual on-the-ground social practices to be exposed. "The emphasis on the contradictions, rather than correspondence, between concrete social formations and their ideologies is the basis of Marx's immanent critique" (Antonio, 1981:334). Holding up ideational claims to its social reality, Horkheimer asserted that immanent critique "confronts the existent, in its historical context, with the claim of its conceptual principles, in order to criticize the relation between the two and thus transcend them." (Horkheimer, 1974:182)

Hegemonic norms are held accountable to their own precepts, by describing 'what a social totality holds itself to be, and then confronting it with what it is in fact becoming' (Shroyer, 1973:31). If found wanting, the totality is critically appraised for inherent potentials which can then be used as a means by which theory and praxis may be brought closer together. This method 'is a means of detecting the societal contradictions which offer the most determinate possibilities for emancipatory social change' (Antonio, 1981:332). As Antonio goes on to say, "immanent critique attacks social reality from its own standpoint, but at the same time criticizes the standpoint from the perspective of its historical context." (Antonio, 1981:38)

"Democratization" in a Globalizing Epoch

Discussions regarding the democratic nature of postapartheid South Africa's foreign policy hinge on critically interrogating what is ascribed to the term "democracy," and calling such ideas accountable to their own discourse. The term democracy itself is an "essentially contested concept," that is, a concept with different and competing definitions existing side by side, so that the term itself is problematic in that each definition provides different interpretations of "reality."

Interrogating *what* form of democracy is being advanced goes to the heart of any debate on the alleged democratic character of Pretoria's contemporary international relations. In a study on Canadian foreign policy and democracy, Mark Neufeld argued that

> the differences between democratic and non-democratic foreign policies may be less significant than might appear at first glance. The real question in evaluating the significance of democracy as a source for and objective of [a state's] foreign policy is "what kind of democracy is being instituted?" (Neufeld, 1998:17)

In interrogating the democratization of South Africa's foreign policy, this paper follows Neufeld's concerns over the form and content of Pretoria's "democratic foreign policy" and subjects such commitments to immanent critique.

As in all states, South Africa's leaders have had to (re-)negotiate their position in an increasingly globalized world where a project based on liberalization and privatization—"neoliberalism"—has achieved hegemonic status (Nel, Taylor, and van der Westhuizen, 2001; Taylor, 2001). Yet, this project contributes to profound dislocating effects, undermining its chances of becoming truly hegemonic across all classes: a consensual element is required alongside coercion (see Robinson, 1996a). This consensual component in the neoliberal project is liberal democracy, otherwise labeled 'polyarchy' by Robert Dahl (1971). In their influential studies of democratization in the developing world, Diamond, Linz and Lipset suggest that there are three key ingredients to "democracy," namely

1. "Meaningful and extensive competition among individuals and organizational groups (especially political parties) for all effective positions of government power through regular, free and fair elections."

2. "A highly inclusive level of political participation in the selection of leaders and policies such that no major (adult) social group is prevented from exercising the rights of citizenship."

3. "A level of civil and political liberties—freedom of thought and expression, freedom of the press, freedom of assembly and demonstrations, freedom to form and join organizations....—sufficient to ensure the integrity of political competition and participation." (Diamond, Linz and Lipset, 1988)

This description of democracy resonates with a Schumpeterian conceptualization, wherein democracy is regarded as "that institutional arrangement for arriving at political decision in which individuals acquire the power to decide by means of a competitive struggle for the people's vote" (Schumpeter, 1952:269). This approach, which reduces political participation to simply voting in periodic elections, appears to have become the dominant view. Certainly, this particular definition of democracy—polyarchy—has gained hegemony among academics and policymakers and is probably the "most commonly used by American social scientists" (Schmitter and Karl, 1996:61). Given the overall domination by the American academy, such a hegemonic definition is problematic.

Polyarchical understandings of democracy place a particular emphasis on the process of formal democracy and invariably disregard the social and economic outcomes of the political system under review (for a critical look at how this has played out in southern Africa, see Good, 1997a; and Taylor, 1999). This stems from a separation of the political from the economic, ignoring the actuality that "the so-called economic realm is inseparable from its political and ideological effects" (Burawoy, 1985: 63). Indeed, Diamond, Linz, and Lipset admit that their studies "use the term democracy....to signify a political system, separate and apart from the economic and social system....Indeed, a distinctive aspect of our approach is to insist that issues of so-called economic and social democracy be separated from the question of governmental structure" (Diamond, Linz, and Lipset, 1989:xvi). This refreshingly honest admittance by such prominent academics that economic and/or social justice is of no concern vis-à-vis democracy is, unfortunately, usually left unspoken by the majority of those political scientists working within the democracy industry.

Yet the theoretical, historical, and indeed practical justification for separating politics from economics and in particular separating social concerns from the democratic system is unclear and marks but one democratic tradition—and one that is relatively modern and inextricably bound up with the American experience. In this understanding I am influenced by Ellen Meiskins Wood's work on democracy, which points out the powerful influence conservative—indeed, reactionary—interests had in framing the republican Constitution in the United States. This redefinition of democracy "gave the modern world its definition of democracy, a definition in which the dilution of popular power is an essential ingredient" (Meiskins Wood, 1995).

Such an alienation of power underpins the democratic order within the United States and has had a profound influence on our common sense notions of what constitutes "democracy." As Smith points out, "factors such as the prevalence of economic inequality within every liberal democratic state are considered conceptually and analytically irrelevant. Within this discourse, alternatives to the reigning conceptual framework are made either invisible or illegitimate—the dominant conceptions are 'naturalized'" (Smith, 2000:5).

Meiksins Wood argues that the dominant definition of democracy sprang from a deep-seated suspicion by the political and economic elites of the people:

> The founders of the United States Constitution were faced not only with a democratic culture but with fairly well-developed democratic institutions, and they were at least as much concerned to contain as to entrench the democratic habits which had destabilized themselves in colonial and revolutionary America not only in "civil society" but even in the political sphere, from town meetings to representative assemblies. (Meiksins Wood, 1995:223)

This suspicion of the people justifies a political order that necessarily insulates power and decision making from the masses. It necessarily leads to an elite ordering of society whose hierarchy prevents decisions being overly influenced by the citizenry. This elitism grants powers to the "experts" who are "in the know" and those who are deemed ignorant of such matters are actively prevented from any meaningful participation or input. Walter Lippmann, in an influential intervention on democracy indeed claimed that

> The common interests very largely elude the public opinion entirely, and can be managed only by a specialized class whose personal interests reach beyond the locality. the public must be put in its place so that we may live free of the trampling and the roar of a bewildered herd whose function is to be interested spectators of action, not participants. (Rossiter and Lare, 1982:253)

At the same time, there is a conscious separation of political systems from their economic and social concerns. This is readily apparent in the discussions relating to democracy in Africa and the rest of the South, particularly where polyarchy has gone hand in hand with neoliberal restructuring and liberalization. Writers such as Diamond have filled the role of organic intellectuals, arguing that "a balanced [democratic] culture—in which people care about politics but not too much" is needed in the South, "restraining the partisan battle [by] deflating the state and invigorating the private economy" (Diamond, 1993:106). His assertion that the "continuation and deepening of economic liberalization is an important element in the construction of a viable democratic order in Africa," clearly demonstrates the particular political and economic project Diamond and his cohorts within the democratization industry are attempting to advance (Diamond, 1988:27).

Owing to the hegemony enjoyed by the polyarchic definition of democracy, policymakers as well as academics enthusiastically refer to democratization "waves" in Africa and the transitions from authoritarian rule to supposed democratic orders in unproblematic terms. In fact, it is quite remarkable that writers on African democratization processes can so glibly expound on the "democratic" nature of many African states. Meanwhile, the gross social inequalities, so apparent to any visitor who spends five minutes in countries such as Zambia or Malawi, are ignored as the fallacy of electoralism runs its course. In these cases, it does not take too much effort for the claims to democracy within such states to be shown, by an immanent critique, to be hollow, whatever the measurers of African democracy may say.

As a definition of an essentially contested concept, the polyarchic definition of "democracy" competes with the concept of popular democracy. Popular democracy has its roots in the Athenian tradition and has been sustained by both Rousseau and later Marxian conceptualizations. It promotes a distribution of power and responsibility throughout society via mass participation in decision-making processes (see Saul, 1997). This is achieved through various representative forms of government, a healthy civil society, and the usage of elections. The aim of such forms of democracy is to construct a political order aiming toward social and economic justice and equality. For real democracy to flourish, social and economic structures that inhibit the full participation of every citizen need to be challenged and overcome. Contrasting strongly with polyarchy and the procedural limitation of democratic practice, popular democracy is inextricably associated with *both* the processes and the outcomes of what democracy is.

Indeed, polyachical definitions restrict themselves to the procedural realm. This means that there is no intrinsic contradiction between a "democracy," with all its free elections, free press, free debate, and a social order marked by inequity and elite control. Certainly, a polyarchical democracy can quite happily affect a democratic appearance without any real democratic content or, crucially, consequence (Robinson, 1996b:625).

The separation of the political from the economic is crucial for this definition. As Meiksins Wood (1995:235) asserts:

> The very condition that makes it possible to define democracy as we do in modern liberal capitalist societies is the separation and enclosure of the economic sphere and its invulnerability to democratic power. Protecting that invulnerability has even become an essential criterion of democracy. This definition allows us to invoke democracy *against* the empowerment of the people in the economic sphere. It even makes it possible to invoke democracy in defense of a *curtailment* of democratic rights in other parts of 'civil society' or even in the political domain, if that is what is needed to protect property and the market against democratic power. (Emphasis in the original)

One sees this logic working itself out within the currently dominant neoliberal theory underpinning most contemporary political orders (including South Africa's). The neoliberal theorist, Milton Friedman, indeed asserted that as the pursuit of profit is the essence of democracy, any government that inhibited the market's operations was per definition undemocratic, even if such antimarket policies were supported by the people (see Friedman, 1963). It does not require a major leap of imagination to see such a distorted understanding of what democracy is or isn't being used to justify, for example, the coup d'etat by Pinochet against Allende.

In contrast, popular democracy sees democracy as a vehicle to advance progressive change and struggle against social imbalances. By replacing the Athenian definition of democracy with polyarchy, profound issues related to the control of the material riches of a given society, who should benefit from these, whose interests are prioritized, how society is organized and how participation and solidarity are promoted, are delegitimized and deemed external to the democratic process. They become the musings of "radicals" or whimsical academics: something to be listened to politely, but certainly not seriously entertained nor actively discussed. Instead of such utopian pie-in-the-sky what becomes central—what is "real"—are circular debates and banal expositions on political contests amongst elites *via* elections. Even when the electorate disdain from taking part in such processes and the participation rate in elections plummets, the polyarchical system is not at fault: it is people's "apathy" that accounts for such lack of interest!

Yet the workings of the polyarchical model encourage apathy and a decline in a tangible democratic culture. The result of polyarchy is to soothe the social and political pressures that are created by an elite-based neoliberal order and create a state of "low intensity democracy" (Gills, Rocamora and Wilson, 1993) and low-intensity citizenship (O'Donnel, 1993:1361). Going hand in hand with the liberal prescriptions of separating politics from economics, polyarchy dissipates the energies of those marginalized by the ongoing order into parliamentary procedures that in themselves are acted out by political fractions whose power and prestige are dependant on an elitist model. In short, polyarchy expresses "not the fulfillment of democratic aspirations, but their deflection, containment, and limitation" (Good, 1997b: 253) and negates a scenario "in which the free development of each is the condition for the free development of all." (Marx and Engels, 1973: 127)

Popular democracy points us inextricably toward the conclusion that political orders too are contested and open to interrogation. The fact that polyarchy is promoted as common sense and unquestionable and that political scientists of the Huntington ilk invoke polyarchy as a defense against the people's 'excessive demands' indicates that not only advancing polyarchy consciously (á la Diamond, Linz, and Lipset) but naturalizing it through our uncritical acceptance of it as "normal" and unquestionable, is intensely political. Such invocation of simply reporting "the facts" and of neutrally "measuring" democracy do not stand up to investigation and in fact serve to reify the continuation of unjust social orders. They in fact help continue the insulation of political elites from the social and economic implications of their decisions.

This implies both shortcomings on the democratic transition in South Africa and makes it possible to understand the limitations on the "democratization ' of the South African government's foreign policy. Certainly,. the promotion of democracy and claims to being democratic are hugely powerful in ideological terms. Resonating with the aspirations of most humans for representation and consultation, claiming to advance democracy can instantly garner mass support: "practical politicians and political theorists agree in stressing the democratic element in the institutions they defend and the theories they advocate" (McKeon and Riockan, 1951). After all, "politics is a communicatively constituted activity. Words are its coins, and speech its medium" (Ball and Pocock, 1990:1). Hence the contestation over the meaning and usage of words or concepts is inextricably bound up within the broader struggle for power, both political and economic.

Concluding Remarks

The term "democracy" is (perhaps as a consequence of its popularity) used both by policy-makers and by policy analysts as part of this struggle for power and legitimization. Yet interrogations of what is meant when the term "democracy" is used are surprisingly rare and precise definitions are avoided. In fact, what South African policymakers refer to when they use the term democracy is polyarchy. This basic fact, overlooked by most discussants when investigating the democratization of Pretoria's foreign policy, is hugely important. Certainly, it contributes to the ongoing milieu where there is considerable tension and frustration in the lack of popular input into the country's foreign relations, with only a few "experts" (often of dubious political or economic persuasion!) seeming to have any type of influence.

Yet the responsibility of governing a society cannot be left to the "experts," nor can democracy be built and struggled over an unchanged or unchallenged economic and social terrain such as South Africa's, with its massive inequalities and gross differences in life chances for most of its peoples. South Africa's peoples will remain frustrated with democracy as long as it is an elite-driven process and as long as social and economic policies remain in the hands of those who, by the very nature of the system, are insulated from the effects of the policies pursued. Sipho Seepe captures this when he asserts that:

> While the new ruling elite liberally pays homage to notions such as "people-centered" government, evidence abounds that it fails to appreciate that democracy is not what governments do, but that it is fundamentally what people do to make their governments accomplish things for the common good. Democracy is not a grant from government to the people. In a democracy people must have a right to discuss national affairs and be able to communicate their ideas freely (*Weekly Mail and Guardian*, November 30, 2001).

As input from non-office holders is vital for a vibrant democracy to take root and for policy-making to be participatory and involved, "nothing could be more foreign to the spirit of the Commune than to supersede universal suffrage by hierarchy investiture" (Marx, 1973:221). By its very nature, polyarchy subverts the democracy of the Commune—and other forms of popular governance—and indeed locates "democracy" within an elite-managed system of rank. This is frequently cast as the only "realistic" form of democracy in modern political (capitalist) systems, in contrast to the supposed anarchy of alternative notions of democracy. But, popular or direct democracy does not imply uncontrolled or incessant popular voting and decision making on all matters with some sort of anarchical-like discarding of the state and its institutions. According to Budge, in mediated democracies of the direct sort, political parties, parliaments, and elections would remain. The major difference is that the demos votes directly on major policy issues in a range of binding referendums (see Budge, 1996). If this was to exist, direct democracy would imply a substantial deepening and broadening of the democratic input by citizens, with a variety of secondary institutions serving to advance and nurture an ensemble of indirect institutions in order to facilitate the operation of the referendums and direct decision making. Informed citizenry is an essential aspect of direct democracy—not least if we are to talk of the democratization of foreign policy. Direct democracy would then demand a range of secondary institutions essential to the working of its primary instruments.

In the foreign policy context this would mean much greater openness to debate and discussion over the country's foreign policy direction. It would mean that input by the demos is not restricted to well-funded organic intellectuals but would require a broadening of inclusion so that the voices of others are included. The very nature of the foreign policy establishment would need to be re-thought. Opinion would be sought and much of the secrecy behind which diplomats operate would be lifted. This does not mean that all and sundry information would be thrown open to the public's gaze—direct democracy does not imply an abandonment of notions of national security! But, it would require an interrogation of what and why is material withheld from the public's gaze and how does this impact on informed opinion by the demos? Countries such as Sweden have profoundly open access to the workings of officialdom. If Stockholm, why not Pretoria?

By subjecting "democracy" as instituted in South Africa to immanent critique, the topic of the democratization of Pretoria's foreign policy can be embarked upon from a more coherent and reflexive position. This approach takes note of the limitations within the particular democratic project that the postapartheid compromise has adopted and within which it must operate. Only by subjecting the claims to democracy by Pretoria to a form of immanent critique and critically engaging with the issue at hand can justice be done to what is a most pressing and urgent *problematique* in the study of South Africa's international relations: the democratization of foreign policy.

Chapter 3

Democracy, Participation, and Foreign Policy Making in South Africa

Philip Nel, Jo-Ansie van Wyk, and Kristen Johnsen

Our analysis starts with the assessment of South African democracy made by President Thabo Mbeki during his address on 8 January 2002 to celebrate the ninetieth anniversary of the founding of the African National Congress (ANC) in 1912. Using the vision of a non-racial, non-sexist democratic South Africa as spelled out in the Freedom Charter adopted by the Congress Movement in 1955, Mbeki set out what he regards as the main achievements of the South African government, and the main challenges that still had to be overcome in the pursuit of this vision. Under the heading of the Freedom Charter's slogan "The People shall govern," he had this to say:

> One of our tasks during the next decade will be to defend and further entrench this important gain of our people. Building on what we have already achieved, we must work to activate the masses of the people more directly to participate in our system of governance. We must translate into reality our vision of people-driven processes of change as well as the fundamental principle that the people are their own liberators. (Mbeki, 2002)

Although this statement was clearly intended as a declaration of intent, it can also be read as an implicit acknowledgement that participation by the people in "our system of governance" is not what it should be. The first section of this chapter, "Participation Denied," reviews the extent to which this implicit acknowledgement holds true, specifically as far as the making of foreign policy is concerned. This raises the question, of course, why it is so important for us that the people should be more directly involved in the governance of foreign policy, and should be "their own liberators" (as Mr. Mbeki puts it) also in this arena?

Part of the answer is of course suggested by Mbeki's words themselves: If a government commits itself to a larger degree of public participation in policy making and implementation, then it is surely germane to ask how much of this declaratory position is realized in practice. However, we must also make room for the possibility that the declarations of the government in this regard are based on a set of assumptions that cannot stand up to critical investigation: maybe it is not correct to assume that public participation is a requisite or *desideratum* for foreign policy making. Put differently: why is public participation in foreign policy to be desired?

In a second section to the chapter, "Participation Challenged," we suggest some answers to this question, by looking at the arguments of those who argue that it is for the better if the public is kept out of foreign policy making. We then proceed to develop a positive conceptual and normative argument in favor of public participation in foreign policy making.

What does "public participation" mean, and what are the practical steps that can and should be put in place to make it a reality, also on the terrain of foreign policy making and implementation? As David Braybrooke reminds us, "to demand to participate is . . . to demand to play a recognized role in a joint human activity"(Braybrooke, 1975:58) In the context of a national system of governance *public participation* would thus imply that the citizens of a polity play a recognized role (or recognized roles) in the formulation and implementation of authoritative decisions. Public participation entails that citizens are acknowledged and respected as being not only subjects but also *agents* of public policy. Parry, Moyser and Day describes participation as:

> taking part in the process of formulation, passage and implementation of public choices. It is concerned with citizen action that is aimed at influencing decisions, which are, in most cases, taken, by public representatives and officials. This may be action, which seeks to shape the attitudes of decision-makers to matters yet to be decided, or it may be action in protest at the outcome of some decision. (Parry, Moyser, and Day, 1992:16)

In view of the development of the literature on participatory democracy and deliberative democracy in particular, this definition of public participation is clearly inadequate if we want to give expression to Mr. Mbeki's wish that the people must become their own liberators. For us, and in line with what has been said in the introductory chapter and in Chapter Two, participation by the public would not be fully *democratic* if the purpose were simply to influence the decisions of officials and representatives. Therefore, in the final section of this chapter, "Participation Redefined," we focus on the limitations of the concept of public participation, and how these can be overcome by the notion of *democratic participation*, that is, a process through which citizens can collectively and deliberatively decide on the goals, values, and means of policies that transcend the borders of their state.

Participation Denied

Indeed, much remains to be done in South Africa in terms of achieving higher levels of participation by citizens in the governance of our democracy. A recent assessment of experiments in democratic participation (Heller, 2001) is quite critical of the inability of the ANC and its ruling allies to translate the participatory gains made during the liberation struggle into what can be called "empowered participatory governance." Heller attributes this failure to a combination of factors, including the government's desire to co-opt civil society into its ruling bloc, the "political affinities between technocratic domination and neoliberal reform" that have recently come to characterize the post-*apartheid* government, and the ANC's belief "that the key to transformation lies in the instrumentalities of the state" (Heller, 2001:156-157). While in general subscribing to Heller's pertinent assessment, we believe that there are also other features that, in addition, have contributed to undermining the general popular-democratic potential of the postapartheid regime. A fuller account of the low level of empowered citizen participation in South Africa would need to include at least an assessment of the form that "democracy" has taken in the post-apartheid South African state.

The Nature of Democracy in South Africa

The type of democracy that was established by the multiparty negotiations that inaugurated the regime change in South Africa, and which was eventually codified in an interim constitution of 1993 and then in the final constitution of 1996, is best described as an evolving mixture of *competitive elitist democracy* (with heavy emphasis on constitutionalism) and *clientelistic corporatism*. The term "competitive elitist democracy" is used by David Held in his discussion of the realist and technocratic vision of democracy as conceived of by Weber and Schumpeter (Held, 1996:157-98). In terms of this political vision, the regime best suited to fulfill the demands of political stability, restrict the potential excesses of semi-permanent political majorities and their leaders, and to generate the administrative means to deal with a host of developmental problems, is one with the following features: (a) parliamentary government with strong executive; (b) competition between rival political elites and parties; (c) domination of parliament by party politics; (d) centrality of political leadership; (e) an independent and well-trained administration; and (f) constitutional limits on political decision making (Held, 1996:197) These features define South African politics to a large extent, with the possible exclusion of (e). However, it can be argued that the Mbeki presidency's technocratic vision of speeding-up delivery and improving the quality of services to the public, is an attempt to achieve at least part of (e). Nevertheless, it is quite clear that a government who has used a policy of affirmative action (which could be defended on moral grounds) to stock the upper ranks of the executive branch with inexperienced political clients has seriously jeopardized the independence of the bureaucracy in South Africa.

The Constitution, and the accompanying Bill of Rights, and the wide oversight responsibility of the Constitutional Court, are perhaps more pronounced in South Africa than what the idealtype of the competitive elitist democracy model would prescribe. The saliency of constitutional mechanisms in South Africa, is largely the result of the political deal that was struck between the negotiating teams of the opposing sides in the early 1990s. Unable or unwilling to demand group rights, the dominant group of pre-1994 establishment negotiators opted for the constitutional protection of individual rights as the next best thing. Those from the liberation movements endorsed individual rights for a host of reasons: some believed it to provide the best means to prevent anything similar to apartheid ever happening in South Africa again, while others saw it as cheap bargain, and one that could be changed in any case given the likelihood of a two-thirds majority in future.

Whatever the motivations of the various parties involved in the negotiations, the eventual deal that was struck largely excluded the public, beyond participation in competitive elections, from political decision making. This is, of course, exactly the type of effect that the proponents of the competitive elitist democracy model have in mind. Skeptical of the possibilities of organizing any form of direct democracy in modern, large, industrial and industrializing societies, and mistrustful of the emotional fickleness of a generally ill-informed public in any case, these proponents see the right to take part equally in competitive elections for elite representatives as a sufficient guarantee of political freedom and equality. By opting for this model of democracy, the drafters of the constitutional and institutional future of South Africa condemned the public to a very restrictive political role.

The proportional electoral model introduced in 1994 exacerbated these restrictions. Moving away from the single-member constituency model of the previous regime, the interim and the final postapartheid constitution opted for a system of proportional representation using closed ordered party lists.[1] This guaranteed representation for smaller parties in Parliament, but also introduced a huge gap between voters and those who are supposed to represent them. Consistent with the logic of the elitist model, this proportional list system also placed an inordinate degree of power in the hands of party leadership, which in the case of the ruling alliance means President Mbeki himself.

The gap between voters and members of Parliament is one of the reasons why Parliament in South Africa is judged not to live up to its full potential. In a comprehensive survey in 2000, The Southern Africa Democracy Barometer found that only a third of South Africans trusted Parliament "to do what is right most of the time," much lower than comparable figures for Namibia and Botswana. The same survey found that South Africans tend to be more skeptical than citizens of Namibia, Botswana, Malawi, and Lesotho about the responsiveness of state institutions to public opinion (Mattes, Davids, and Africa, 2000:37).

The firm establishment of constitutional rule in postapartheid South Africa, and the exemplary and fearless execution by the Constitutional Court of their duties, are milestones in the evolution of democracy in South Africa. However, there is a sense in which strong constitutionalism can lead to a narrowing of the political space, and by extension thus further restrict the issues on which public opinion is one of the factors that may influence the outcome of decisions. This is a moot point (see Kymlicka and Norman, 1992; Saward, 1994, Elster, 1988), but the introduction of positive rights in a Bill of Rights (such as economic rights, for instance) does tend to remove discussions of the government's positive obligations from the public to the legal sphere, and thus has the potential to undermine the majoritarian principle which is a core principle of public participation in democracies. Something like this may be happening in South Africa.

Commentators have noted that the postapartheid regime also display some features of *corporatism*, that is an arrangement in which the state grants exclusive opportunities for organized interests such as trade unions and organized business to take part in bargaining with the state on specific functional issues, thus in effect guaranteeing a bargaining monopoly. Under ANC rule, an arrangement very close to such a bargaining monopoly has been institutionalized in the National Economic Development and Labor Council (NEDLAC), comprising the state, business, labor, and "the community." The introduction of corporatism can be seen partly as an attempt to pre-empt a possible campaign of mass discontent about the inability of government to fulfill the populist agenda on which it came to power in 1994 (van der Westhuizen, 1998:443). Habib sees the resort to corporatism as a deliberate attempt to choose an alternative to repression:

> A repressive response would have provoked a mass counter-reaction that could have threatened the viability of the transition [to democracy] itself. At the least, the mass reaction which such a response would have provoked would have generated political instability and threatened the much-heralded investment that the GNU was so eager to attract. Corporatism thus seemed the most feasible response for state elites intent on neutralizing a potential opposition while simultaneously retaining a sense of political stability. (Habib, 1997:71)

As is common in corporatist arrangements, the effect of the specific form this has taken in South Africa has been "a decline in relevance of parliament and party politics for the formulation and development of public policy," as well as an "erosion of political influence of rank-and-file members of political and economic organizations" (Held, 1996:229). Corporatism in South Africa is as much a creation of the initial post-1994 Government of national Unity (GNU) as it is an inheritance of the growing policy influence of organized business under National Party rule, and of attempts by the apartheid government "to curtail the Congress of South African Trade Unions" evident success at mobilizing mass popular support, with the aid of the United Democratic Front (UDF) in the mid-1980s (van der Westhuizen, 1998:443). Although NEDLAC officially makes provision for "community representation," in practice there has been a growing rift between non-governmental organizations (NGOs) and other civil society forces on the one hand, and the state apparatus on the other.[2]

As was pointed out in the introductory chapter to this book, the Mbeki presidency has chosen to present itself as an institution that "puts people first," using the slogan *Batho pele* as its motto. We believe that the impact on low levels of citizen participation by the factors mentioned above, is exacerbated by a very specific understanding of what it means to "put people first." In his expressed commitment in this regard, Mr. Mbeki fails to clearly distinguish between two senses of the word in which a government can be said "to place people first." It can, on the one hand, mean that the relevant government is gearing its policies toward addressing what the government perceives to be the needs of the people. This is the meaning that prevails in policy initiatives such as those taken by the Mbeki presidency and the Cabinet that is aimed at better delivery of services and amenities to the majority of people in South Africa. These initiatives are very necessary and may prove to be fruitful in their own right. But it should be obvious that such governing "in the interests of the people" reflects only one meaning of the phrase: 'putting people first'. Let us call this a *guardianship* understanding of democracy, perhaps best captured in the phrase "government *for* the people."

A second meaning, on the other hand, would be invoked when we place emphasis on direct public participation in the act of governing, that is, in deciding what the most pressing needs of society is, what should be done about them, and how. "Putting people first" then has the meaning of giving priority to the opinions and wishes of the people, and setting in motion mechanisms to capture these opinions and wishes, and to take them seriously. We call this a *participatory* understanding of democracy (government *by* the people). This is the understanding of democracy that Mbeki has in mind, we hope, when he calls on the ANC to "work to activate the masses more directly to participate in our system of governance," and when he invokes "the fundamental principle that the people are their own liberators." However, it seems as if it is not this understanding of democracy, but the notion of guardianship, that informs practice in current South Africa.

Public Participation and Foreign Policy

In the introductory chapter it was noted that the ANC already in the early 1990s committed itself to a style of foreign policy making that would be people centered. The ANC's pre-election Discussion Paper, entitled "Foreign Policy in a New Democratic South Africa," issued in October 1993, made much of the fact that in the ANC's conception "foreign policy belongs to South Africa's people," and that the future foreign policy of a postapartheid South Africa will be determined by the "belief that our foreign relations must mirror our deep commitment to the consolidation of a democratic South Africa." This document also echoed a theme that was given pride of place at a December 1991 ANC policy conference, namely that "the foreign policy of a democratic South Africa will be primarily shaped by the nature of its domestic policies and objectives directed at serving the needs and interests of our people." These commitments were taken up and expanded upon in Nelson Mandela's now famous article "South Africa's future foreign policy" which appeared in the November/December 1993 edition of the journal *Foreign Affairs*. Mandela added that at that stage there were "preliminary negotiations" underway concerning a process in which all the political parties who have an interest in foreign relations could find common ground on important policy questions (Mandela, 1993:87). Nothing much ever came of these preliminary negotiations and although the opposing parties during the all-party Convention for a Democratic South Africa (CODESA) negotiations from 1991 to 1993 did seem to find one another on a number of foreign policy issues, a broad participatory and compromise-seeking institution for foreign policy was never created in CODESA and the eventual Transitional Executive Council. Such compromise-seeking institutions were created in a number of other policy areas.

Once in power after the founding election of April 1994, the Government of National Unity (GNU) took a number of steps to live up to its promises to democratize the making of foreign policy in South Africa. One step was aimed at turning the Portfolio Committee in Parliament responsible for Foreign Affairs (Portfolio Committee on Foreign Affairs—PCFA) into the core institution where broad public participation in foreign policy making could be focused. The ANC in particular placed much hope in this Portfolio Committee as a place where the representatives of the people could interact with the Department of Foreign Affairs, and where non-governmental organizations and other representatives of civil society could be given opportunities to have their say.[3] And indeed this portfolio committee under the dynamic leadership of its first Chair, Raymond Suttner, played a key role in promoting public debates on a whole range of foreign policy issues, notably on the promotion of human rights and the challenges faced by South Africa in negotiating a free trade agreement with the European Union.

In 1994 there were some discussions within the ruling party concerning the establishment of a Foreign Relations Council, a permanent body drawing on a wide range of expertise from society that could act as both a sounding board for, and as a font of expert input into the policy process. By 1995 this idea was watered down to make provision only for a Foreign Affairs Advisory Council, still with broad representation from society, but with a limited advisory mandate only.[4] However, so far nothing of this kind has been established.

In 1996 the Department of Foreign Affairs launched the *South African Foreign Policy Discussion Document* and solicited responses widely among academics and NGOs. Putting into practice the commitment made in this document to the democratization of foreign policy making in the country (Department of Foreign Affairs, 1996:15), a workshop was hosted by the Department of Foreign Affairs to discuss South Africa's foreign policy with stakeholders in civil society. As one observer noted, though, "the response has been more a trickle than a flood, no surprise at a time when South Africa has more priorities than potential solutions on truly pressing problems" (*The Star*, September 12, 1996). This discussion document was followed by the release of draft documents on a "Framework for cooperation with countries of the Southern African Region" and the "National External Security Strategy." At the time the South African Institute of International Affairs (SAIIA), the oldest foreign policy think tank in South Africa (established in 1934), made a substantial submission on the discussion document (SAIIA 1996). On the policy process, SAIIA's emphasized that although the President and Cabinet takes responsibility for the execution of South Africa's foreign policy, this must be subjected to the scrutiny of Parliament as representative of the people of South Africa. SAIIA also reiterated the importance of encouraging civil society such as the media, academics, interest groups, professional associations and concerned citizens to become involved in this process (SAIIA 1996:4). Today, even such moderate pleas for the democratization of South Africa's foreign policy are no longer heard.

The years 1995-1996 were the heady days of a "heroic era" (Nel, Taylor, and van der Westhuizen, 2001) in South Africa's foreign policy in which the government attempted very hard to put into practice the ANC's commitment to a foreign policy that is based on democratic principles, in its formulation and execution, but also in the values that it wanted to promote abroad. As the country gradually gravitated toward more of a "routine-based" foreign policy in the period 1997-1998, less was heard about broadening participation in the policy process. In fact, a gradual erosion of the achievements of the previous era took place to the extent that a Department of Foreign Affairs and the Cabinet were increasingly sidelining the once dynamic Parliamentary portfolio committee. This prompted the Deputy Minister of Foreign Affairs, Aziz Pahad, in March 1998 to lament the fact that "there is still not a system whereby major foreign policy issues are taken to Parliament, even to give information only." (Pahad, 1998:21)

The appointment of Mr. Jackie Selebi, South Africa's Representative to the United Nations Human Rights Commission, as Director General of Foreign Affairs in 1998, led to an attempt by the DFA to redefine its operational focus, and streamline its internal process and increase the accountability of the Department to the taxpayer. This thoroughgoing transformation was accompanied by a series of consultative conferences and workshops in which the DFA involved a wide variety of civil society and media actors. Strikingly, however, these consultative workshops and conferences dealt almost exclusively with transformation matters in the DFA, and not so much with the substance of South Africa's foreign policy. Participants from academia, the media, and the NGO sector nevertheless reveled in the official recognition of their inputs into foreign policy making.[5]

By 2000, such attempts to give expression to the ANC's desire to turn the people of South Africa into "their own liberators" as far as foreign policy is concerned, came to an end. In place of a process of foreign policy making that was at least partly driven by the desire to encourage and institutionalize public participation, a centralized system of foreign policy making, ostensibly for the sake of greater foreign policy coordination, has come into being. Based on a assessment that policy making and delivery of services by the state machinery had become fragmented, ineffective, and expensive, Mbeki embarked on a major overhaul of the policy-making and implementation machinery of the state. With respect to foreign policy, the brunt of this overhaul has been to locate policy making squarely within the president's office, where a Policy Coordination and Advisory Service (PCAS) has been created in which one of its five chief Directorates is responsible for International Relations, Peace, and Security. Each of these five chief directorates mirror two sets of decision making 'clusters': in the Cabinet. In the case of foreign affairs, a sectoral Cabinet Committee on International Relations, Peace, and Security brings ministers and their staff together and "allow for intensive and focused debates on difficult policy choices and the resolution of these issues by the relevant ministers before issues are taken to the full cabinet" (Chikane, 2001:17). There is also a cluster of Director Generals whose line functions bear upon International Relations, Peace, and Security, and this cluster's task is to see to it that the implementation of cabinet decisions takes place in a coordinated fashion.[6] Whether this was the intention or not, the net effect of this exercise in greater coordination has been to centralize inputs into the foreign policy process, and to make it even less accessible for the public at large. Despite expressed wishes to the contrary, the ANC-led government has not succeeded in breaking down the traditional apathy of South Africans about foreign policy issues, nor have opposition parties done enough to give these issues the prominence that they deserve during election campaigns and during parliamentary debates (*see* Masiza, 1999).

What exactly is the level of public participation in foreign policy making today? The constitution and the rules and procedures of the transformed Parliament in principle provide access to and opportunities for public participation in decision making and policy implementation. Compared to the situation prior to 1994, the number of independent civil society groups monitoring Parliament has increased dramatically. A total of 27 groups are registered at Parliament for this purpose. Some of these include the Black Sash, the Environmental Monitoring Group, the International Institute for Democracy and Electoral Assistance (IDEA), the National Democratic Institute for International Affairs (NDI), the Parliamentary Monitoring Group (PMG), Chamber of Mines of South Africa, COSATU, the Open Society Foundation for South Africa, the Parliamentary Information and Monitoring Service (PIMS), organized agriculture (AgriSA), and the South African Chamber of Business (SACOB) (Parliament, 2001).

Despite the abundance of such parliamentary monitoring groups, and despite Parliament's repeated attempts to involve the public in the law making process,[7] South Africa has no culture of public debate about foreign policy issues, and when such debate does occur, only a small group of people participate—mostly members of the portfolio committee, a number of academics, and some NGOs. A number of foreign policy research institutes, or think tanks, operate in South Africa such as the South African Institute of International Affairs (SAIIA), the African Center for the Constructive Resolution of Conflicts

(ACCORD), the Institute for Global Dialogue (IGD), the Center for Policy Studies (CPS), and the Institute for Security Studies (ISS).[8]

A rare survey on South African public opinion on foreign policy issues concluded, among others, that

- only a small percentage of the public is interested and informed about foreign policy issues
- domestic social concerns override global concerns for respondents
- government needs to explain more, educate better, and consult wider on foreign policy issues (Nel and van Nieuwkerk, 1997:1-15).

Despite wide-ranging changes since 1994, Parliament as an institution for public participation is poorly equipped to compete effectively with the Presidency when it comes to directing South Africa's foreign policy. A number of interrelated factors explain this: (a) Parliament is more orientated toward domestic than foreign affairs. All 490 members of the National Assembly and the National Council of Provinces are up for re-election every four years. Interest and attention to foreign policy issues by Members of Parliament (MP) tend to be short-lived. (b) Power and political responsibility within Parliament is fragmented. A number of portfolio committees have broadly defined foreign affairs jurisdictions. These include the portfolio committees on Defense, Trade and Industry, Agriculture, Intelligence, Water Affairs and Forestry and Health. In addition to these overlapping jurisdictions, a large number of MPs serve on more than one portfolio committee, which contributes, to the fact that an MP cannot really specialize in the issue the committee has to deal with. (c) Parliament's weakness in foreign affairs issues is further derived from the Union Building's greater command of technical expertise and its ability to control the flow of information. Preparation for portfolio committee meetings requires sound research. In the *Who's who* survey of 1997, 52.8% of MPs responding regarded daily newspapers as very reliant sources of information. This indicates the non-availability of research staff for MPs as well as the little information obtained from government departments (Kotzé 1997:19). A related issue is the lack of foreign affairs expertise among members of the portfolio committee on foreign affairs. Parliament has tried to overcome this lack of expertise entrenched by a client-patron relationship between the Portfolio Committee on Foreign Affairs (PCFA) and the DFA. However, Parliament remains very dependent on DFA for briefings to the PCFA on aspects of South Africa's foreign policy. MPs were kept informed of international events via the information service provided by the parliamentary office of the DFA. In most cases these briefings occur ex post facto, or serve to merely inform Parliament about intended policy initiatives.

Ironically, then, public participation in foreign policy making in South Africa has declined since 1996 despite the ANC's original commitment to institutionalise it among others through a vibrant parliamentary committee system. Today, the citizenry of South Africa is largely excluded from decision making on public policy issues "beyond the borders of their state." This contributes to their disempowerment in the face of seemingly inevitable and anonymous forces of globalisation, and adds to their alienation from and apathy towards foreign policy.

Participation Challenged

The argument that has been developed in this chapter so far, is based on the assumption that public participation in foreign policy making is a desideratum. But can this assumption stand up to critical investigation? It is the purpose of this section to see if that is the case.

That the practices of *direct* democracy (defined as a regime form that allows for extensive public participation in the decisions of government) and that of sound and prudent foreign relations are not compatible, is an illustrious and well-pedigreed belief. The arguments in favor of this conclusion take different forms. Miroslav Nincic has helped us to systematize these, by pointing out the difference between arguments that emphasize, on the one hand, that foreign policy can be "disrupted from below," once we allow the presumably ignorant and fickle public to have too great an influence on the course of diplomacy, and, on the other hand, that leaders in pluralist democracies can "derail foreign policy from above" if they let their foreign policy decisions be guided by what they believe will enhance their popularity amongst the public (Nincic, 1992a:5).

Ironically, original warrants for the arguments made by the proponents of the "disruption from below" point of view are found not so much in the work of principled opponents of democracy, but in the work of authors who otherwise would be strong defenders of accountable democracy. Take John Locke as an example. Despite Locke's otherwise strong commitment to accountable government, he believed that prudence calls for leaving matters of foreign policy to those entrusted with the responsibilities for foreign policy:

> What is to be done in reference to foreigners, depending much upon their actions, and variations of designs and interests, must be left in great part to the prudence of those who have this power committed to them, to be managed to the best of their skills for the advantage of the commonwealth. (Locke, 1690/1947:195-196)

Similarly, one of the strongest arguments against giving the public too large a say in foreign policy matters comes from a famous admirer of democracy, at least of the American republican kind. In his *Democracy in America,* (1835 /1966, Vol I: 279-284), de Tocqueville famously challenged the assumption that decisive public influence is good for foreign policy making, by pointing out how disastrous it would have been if President George Washington heeded the American public's enthusiasm for the French revolution and declared war on

England. According to de Tocqueville, Washington correctly interpreted America's best interests to lie in a course of action that would keep the USA out of European "entanglements," despite the wishes of the majority of American citizens—a course of action that history eventually proved to be prudent. This, and other considerations, leads de Tocqueville to eventually question the Enlightenment assumption that the foreign policies of democracies (that is, regimes that are responsive to the wishes of its citizens) are decidedly and always preferable to those of nondemocracies. Instead, de Tocqueville argues

> For my part, I have no hesitation in saying that in the control of society's foreign affairs democratic governments do appear decidedly inferior to others. Experience, mores, and education almost always do give a democracy that sort of practical everyday wisdom and understanding of the petty business of life which we call common sense. Common sense is enough for society's current needs, and in a nation whose education has been completed, democratic liberty applied to the state's internal affairs brings blessings greater than the ills resulting from a democratic government's mistakes. But that is not always true of relations between nation and nation. (De Toqueville, 1835/1966: 281-282)

In the twentieth century leading Realists have turned this cautious and qualified doubt raised by de Tocqueville against the Enlightenment assumption that people's democracy is always better into an article of principle as far as foreign policy/diplomacy is concerned. For Hans Morgenthau, for instance, the point is not only that democracies may sometimes be at a disadvantage compared to autocracies when it comes to foreign policy making, but also that public participation is inherently harmful:

> The kind of thinking required for the successful conduct of foreign policy must at times be diametrically opposed to the kind of considerations by which the masses and their representatives are likely to be moved The peculiar qualities of the statesman's mind are not always likely to find a favorable response in the popular mind. The statesman must think in terms of the national interest, conceived as power among the powers. The popular mind, unaware of the fine distinctions of the statesman's thinking, reasons more often than not in the simple moralistic and legalistic terms of absolute good and absolute evil. The statesman must take the long view, proceeding slowly and by detours, paying with small losses for great advantage; he must be able to temporize, to compromise, to bide his time. The popular mind wants quick results; it will sacrifice tomorrow's real benefit for today's apparent advantage. (Morgenthau, 1973:147)

From this general statement of principle, Morgenthau deduces his three "basic requirements" for a government to be able to deal prudently with public opinion. Firstly, the government must accept that conflict between the requirements of good foreign policy and public opinion is inevitable and unbridgeable. The implication is that this conflict must be managed, but can never be overcome by means of concessions to public opinion. Second, government should see itself as the leader of public opinion, not its slave, and should realize that public opinion is dynamic and that it can be "created and recreated" by informed and responsible leadership. Thirdly, government must have a clear idea of what is desirable and what is essential in its foreign policy, and while it may be willing to compromise with public opinion on the first, it must resist doing so on the second.

While Morgenthau puts his faith, as did Locke, in the prudence and responsibility of those leaders who have been given the duty to deal with foreign policy issues, some commentators warn that these leaders may be forced to sacrifice prudence for "grand-standing" and short-term electoral gain by the pressures of a competitive pluralist democracy in which public opinion takes on determining proportions. This fear that foreign policy will be derailed "from above" by professional politicians who are compelled to secure their political survival by pleasing a fickle public, leads George Kennan, amongst others, to argue that it is best to leave matters of foreign policy in the hands of professional diplomats whose bureaucratic tenure insulates them from the vicissitudes of public opinion (Kennan, 1950). As Nincic points out, in this he differs from someone like Henry Kissinger who is more steeped in the Weberian tradition and therefore places much store in visionary and charismatic political leadership which, to paraphrase Morgenthau, "leads" public opinion, rather than simply responds to it.

The "disruption from below" and the "derailment from above" arguments have been subjected to trenchant empirical and conceptual criticism (see Harriott, 1993; Nincic, 1992a; 1992b). Adding to this, one should at least ask of the likes of Locke and de Tocqueville why the obvious domestic benefits of direct democracy cannot be extended to foreign policy making in principle? De Tocqueville, in particular, is quite eloquent about these benefits when he says that "democracy favors the growth of the state's internal resources; it extends comfort and develops public spirit, strengthens respect for law in the various classes of society" (p.282). Are these attributes not important when it comes to a state's foreign policy as well? The fact that George Washington was well advised not to heed the clamor of his citizens to come to the aid of revolutionary France against the British, does not necessarily translate into a principle for all time. Especially in our age with its growing global normative convergence, questions of democratic legitimacy in the making and implementation of foreign policy are becoming increasingly salient.

Also, a blanket dismissal of public participation in foreign policy making does not take into consideration two sets of findings that have recently gained increasing importance: findings related to the credibility of international commitments, and the two-level game approach.

Despite differences among scholars about how to interpret "the democratic peace" findings that democracies seldom make war against one another,[9] most of the empirical work that has been done in this burgeoning field shows that domestic institutions and foreign policy interaction are crucially linked. Although this literature is agnostic about the effect on foreign policy outcomes produced by higher or lower levels of public participation in foreign policy making, there is an argument to be made that foreign commitments made on the basis of extensive public participation, either directly or indirectly via legislatures, are more credible from the viewpoint of international cooperation than those that are not (see Martin, 2000). Furthermore, conceiving of "prudence" in foreign policy making by not allowing for the benefits that a "statesman" (to use Morgenthau's word) can derive from systematic and institutionalized interaction between him and the public, seems to be a very narrow conception. One of the important points about the recent "two-level game literature" is that negotiators can use the dynamics of the domestic games that they increasingly have to engage in, as tactical and strategic tools in the negotiation game that they engage in their foreign policies. Naturally, his/her foreign counterpart can also use the degree of exposure to a domestic game strategically and tactically against a negotiator. To acknowledge this, however, is not the same as to argue that short-term oriented, fickle public opinion presents a drawback, in principle, on effective foreign policy making (see Moravcsik 1993; Putnam 1993).

Both the arguments on "disruption from below" and "derailment from above" are based on the assumption that the public is ignorant of the complexities involved in foreign policy issues, and that the public's responses and attitudes are therefore chaotic, volatile, and untrustworthy. Now, it is not at all self-evident that there is or should be a direct correlation between being informed and having stable and/or prudent views about foreign policy issues. Conceptually, it can be argued that although a prudent decision on a matter does assume that the agent of the decision has some knowledge of what is at stake, the conditions that have to be met in order for an opinion or decision to be categorized as "prudent" clearly extend beyond "being informed" about all the detail of an issue. To describe someone as prudent primarily means that such a person is able to reason cogently and clearly, has a balanced outlook on matters, and has a notion of what is fair and appropriate. This extended list of attributes implies, and coincides with our experience, that informed experts are not always capable of making prudent decisions. Conversely, we all know individuals who may have only limited knowledge of a topic, but who nevertheless have the uncanny capacity to make reasoned, balanced, and fair assessments of what is at stake. That does not imply that being informed (at least to some extent) is not also one of the necessary condition for sound judgment, but it clearly is not a sufficient condition.

Thus, principled skepticism against public participation in foreign policy making based on the assumption that the public is poorly informed, is conceptually a non sequitur. Recent reassessments of the extensive data on American public opinion and foreign policy also challenge the assumed correlation between being informed and being able to make a prudent judgment. These reassessments also challenge the notions that public opinion on foreign policy is fickle, chaotic, and imprudent. They focus exclusively on public opinion in the United States, and the findings can therefore not be said to apply ipso facto to other contexts. However, because there is no reason to believe that the US public is in any way more informed about foreign policy issues than the citizens of other democracies, nor that the US public has some in-built superior ability to deal prudently with foreign policy issues, we cannot dismiss the potential relevance of the US experience for the South African context. So, let us briefly review some of these recent reassessments.

Scepticism concerning the untrustworthiness of public opinion on foreign policy issues was based on what has been called the "Almond-Lippmann consensus" (Holsti, 1992) initiated by Walter Lippman (1925). Almond's work on the weak public interest in foreign affairs and the general public's unstructured and inconsistent attitudes toward foreign policy issues became very influential and dominated the perspective on public opinion and foreign policy in the 1950s and 1960s (Rosenau 1961; Converse 1964). Caspary (1970) criticized Almond's work on methodological grounds and found that the views of ordinary Americans on foreign policy issues were much less volatile and incoherent than assumed previously. Caspary's work was groundbreaking in that it altered the view of general opinion on foreign policy issues: their views were held to be more consistent and coherent than previously, and they were seen to be more informed and engaged than was believed in the 1950s and 1960s (Page and Shapiro, 1988; 1992; Wittkopf 1990; Hinckley 1998; Holsti 1992).

Focusing on the question of the patterned nature of public opinion, Wittkopf (1986) proposed that the standard internationalist/isolationalist dichotomy was not adequate to illustrate patterns of opinion on foreign policy issues among the American general public. He devised a more nuanced definition of internationalism, adding the descriptors "cooperative" and "militant" to create a grid of four categories that would better capture the range of foreign policy attitudes. Those who support militant internationalism but oppose cooperative internationalism he labeled "hardliners." Those who support cooperative internationalism but oppose militant internationalism are known as "accommodationists." Those in support of both militant and cooperative internationalism are "internationalists," while those that oppose both types of internationalism are 'isolationists' (Wittkopf 1986, p. 428; Wittkopf 1990; Holsti 1992). Holsti applied Wittkopf's four expanded categories to a comparison between American opinion leaders and ordinary citizens. He found a correlation between opinion leaders' and citizens' distribution among the four categories, concluding that citizens' attitudes and opinion leaders' attitudes are relatively coherent (Holsti 1996). Although Wittkopf and Chittick, et al. (Chittick, Billingsley & Travis 1995) disagree as to how many dimensions adequately reflect foreign policy attitudes, they do concur that the dimensions are horizontal, which means that an individual's opinions correspond to each other and thus reveal a patterned consistency over time.

Primary among revisionists espousing the American public's ability to respond reasonably to foreign policy issues is Bruce Jentleson. His concept of the "pretty prudent public" refers to the 'stronger disposition of the American public to support the use of military force to *restrain* rather than *remake* governments" (Jentleson 1992:53. Emphasis added). Important to Jentleson's argument is the periodization of the post post-Vietnam era: it is identified as the 1980s including the Gulf War of 1990-1991 and is differentiated from the 1970s post-Vietnam era and the consensus of the Cold War era of the 1950s and 1960s. Jentleson identified a pattern in this "post post-Vietnam" public opinion: a pattern that represented the general public's foreign policy attitudes. He found that public opinion regarding the use of military force varies based on the "principal policy objective" underlying the decision to use force and identifies the two prime motivations for the use of force: *foreign policy restraint* and *internal political change.*

His research was based on eight examples of the use of limited military force in the 1980s and the Gulf War of 1990-1991. Jentleson identifies a "halo-effect" that surrounds successes that also increases public support, but found that in general, fluctuations in public support for military aggression are explained by the "principal policy objective" (PPO). Differences in the PPOs where force is used to compel "foreign policy restraint," or where it is used to achieve "internal political change" account for changes in public support. Jentleson finds that the American public has been much more supportive of the use of military force when the PPO was to encourage changes in foreign policy and not changes in the internal political structure of target states. Jentleson concludes that the distinction between PPOs in formulation of attitudes toward the use of military force allows for a more rational decision making framework than do military or economic interests alone. The formula also "overrides Vietnam-taught risk aversion" (Jentleson 1992:71) in that that war experience was one of the primary reasons for the general public's aversion to the use of military force. Furthermore, his findings put some faith in the general public's ability to come to their own conclusions, independent from political machinations. The "pretty prudent public" distinction suggests that public opinion does not sway with the breeze, nor is it overly susceptible to elite manipulation. The public's attitudes toward the use of force are governed by pragmatism and reasoning and reinforces the revisionist view that the public is not simply reactionary. Rather, they are rational and capable of reasoned deliberation despite often being ill-informed (Jentleson and Britton, 1998).

Whether we accept the validity of these empirical findings in all respects or not, and regardless of whether we regard them as being transferable to a South African context or not, it is at least clear that we have cause to believe that there is more to public opinion than was assumed by the likes of Almond, Lippmann, Morgenthau, and Kennan. Yet, even if we were to assume that the public is ill informed, and that their views as a result are unstructured and fickle, then this would count more as an indictment against the way in which public participation is structured in contemporary democracies, than an argument against public participation per se. As the literature on deliberative democracy (reviewed below) suggests, an ill-informed public is a function of a specific mode of public participation in public life. There are alternative modes of democratic participation that have to be considered as well. As Harriott notes:

> The realist position concerning the alleged ignorance of citizens in a democracy begs significant questions concerning the public's intelligence and competences.

For it seems a real and not merely a *notional* possibility that deficiencies in democratic institutions might be remodeled in such a way as to allow for more reasoned public input. There is nothing in principle that says that we cannot go from what we have now in our liberal democracies to a better normative ideal. (Harriott, 1993:221)

What is this "better normative ideal?" In the next section of this chapter, we suggest one possibility by means of a critique of the established notion of what public participation in a democracy implies. As a prelude to this, we have to point out that Morgenthau's principled opposition to public participation in foreign policy making (because of the presumed incapacity of the public to value the national interest) is based on the notion that the national interest is something that exists independently of the social discursive contexts within which people speak about such things as national goals and priorities. Empirical research has shown that leaders often differ among themselves about what the national interests of their state may be, and the recent social-constructivist turn has opened our eyes to the essentially constructed and therefore disputed nature of what used to be regarded as fundamental givens in the international system— anarchy and sovereignty, for instance (see Checkel, 1998; Finnemore, 1996; Wendt, 1992 and 1994). Once we accept the discursive and socially constructed nature of "state interests," the space opens for an inquiry into the conditions under which such social-discursive construction *should* take place. This is the focus of the next section.

Participation Redefined

Democracy is widely believed to be the regime that makes best provision of all regime forms for public participation by institutionalizing rule *by*, *for*, and *of* the people. Michael Saward quite rightly warns us, however, that "defining democracy is a political act" (1994:7), and so we have to be aware of the various ideological positions that parade in the guise of "democratic theory." In particular we have to recognize that not all proponents of democracy would necessarily see public participation as a key indicator of democracy. Parry and Moyser make a useful distinction in this regard between, on the one hand, "realist" theories of democracy that emphasize representation, responsible leadership, and elite responsiveness as the key elements of democracy, and on the other hand, theories that see direct participation as the sine qua non of democratic practices (Parry and Moyser, 1994:44-46).

The first set of theories point out that the degree of direct democracy that was exercised by citizens in the relatively small assemblies of ancient Athens is no longer possible in large, complex societies. Power of the people in Athens meant that citizens "exercised control over policy by direct acts of will in the assembly. In addition, the citizens had the opportunity to be chosen, by lot, to carry out the executive tasks of government." (Parry and Moyser, 1994:44)

Instead of directly participating in the deliberation about and voting between policy options, citizens of modern, large democracies articulate their interests /preferences mostly by indirect means, such as by voting regularly in nonarbitrary pluralist elections for representatives who then engage on their behalf in a process of competitive public bargaining to determine how and to what extent the interests/preferences of the majority will prevail. According to such theories, well represented in the work of Schumpeter (1952), Sartori (1987) and Nordlinger (1981), democracy is the result of a competitive process of leadership selection, and to the extent that every citizen can, in principle, become a leader, political equality is guaranteed. Of course, the mere competition between potential leaders is not the end of the democratic process, because competitors have to appeal to the public to decide who wins. In this way, politicians and policies in a democracy have to be responsible and accountable leaders, responsive to the will of the people, exercised for the most part by those members of the public who care to show up at the polling booths. Thus, to the extent that this "realist school" of thinking about democracy does recognize public participation as a feature of democracy, they reduce it to only one manifestation, namely voting.

A second set of theories emphasize, on the other hand, that democracy in its original sense of "rule by the people" is hardly conceivable without a whole range of participatory activities through which citizens not only vote for the sake of appointing and monitoring representatives, but through which they become *political* citizens in the full sense of the word. Parry and Moyser (together with Day) are prime examples of this approach (see their 1992), as are Verba and Nie (1972; see also Verba *et al.*, 1978), Dahl (1956; 1998), Barber (1984), Bachrach (1975), and Pateman (1970), to name but a few. There are marked differences among these authors and although we do not have the space to go into details here, we should highlight at least two strands of thinking within this group of theories.

The first strand of thinking is exemplified by the work of Robert Dahl and is determined by liberal notions of interest aggregation and regards participation as the means through which citizens' "drives, needs, and wants assume political saliency when transformed into demands, that is, articulated preferences" (Keim, 1975:4). According to Keim, liberals assume that articulated preferences (or demands) are the "only satisfactory indicators of men's [sic] interests," which has led them to assume that when all demands have been voiced then all interests have received an adequate public hearing. "The representation of interests," according to Keim's summary of this position, "is thus the function of participation....and democratic politics is a process in which....all active and legitimate groups (i.e., all articulated preferences) receive a hearing at some crucial stage in the process of decision making." (Keim, 1975:4-5)

Despite its limitations (see below) this conception of participation opens up democratic space for a wide variety of citizen activities beyond elections, such as

- voting in referenda;
- contacting members of Parliament, civil servants, councilors, civic authorities, or the media, and voicing demands;

- taking part in public policy hearings or conferences organized by Parliament;
- demanding to address or petitioning Parliamentary study groups (and similar groups on other levels of government);
- attending public meetings;
- the organizing and signing of petitions;
- taking part in protest marches or political strikes or boycotts;
- partaking in opinion polls;
- becoming involved as a client in the implementation of social policies;
- establishing or joining policy oriented nongovernmental organizations and/or social movements or pressure groups;
- joining consumers' councils for publicly owned enterprises;
- joining, when the opportunity offers itself, to act on official advisory committees.[10]

Even on the basis of fairly limiting assumptions, then, the scope for public participation in modern democracies is quite wide. The above list can also serve as a first and approximate barometer for the sake of conducting a participation review as part of a larger democracy audit (see Beetham, 1994). However, it should also be clear that a conception of democracy that regards the above without qualification as the essence of public participation has a few weaknesses. For one, it is evident from even a cursory overview of the list of participatory options that the initiative to make use of these options rests exclusively with the citizens, and that in the absence of effective incentives to make use of them, one should not be surprised to find that very few citizens do (*see* Parry and Moyser, 1994:47). Complaints that the public have become complacent and largely apathetic in most established democracies are justified, but the real source of this is not so much the absence of a civic consciousness among citizens (although this surely also plays a part), but the lack of incentives and enabling mechanisms to facilitate larger degrees of participation. It is ironical that a system of participation that is based on the assumption that people are rational maximizers of their interests fails to provide the necessary incentives and compensatory mechanisms to induce people to take part in existing opportunities of participation.

There is a second problem related to the fact that self-initiative is such a dominant feature of the mode of participation being discussed here. The above list of participation opportunities says nothing about the real-world problem that not all citizens are in a position to explore these opportunities. Inequalities in personal resources do have an impact on levels of participation as adumbrated in the list above (see Verba, et al., 1978; Parry and Moyser, 1994), and so does membership of gender and societal groups. Without measures to compensate for underrepresentation of groups that may have historically been excluded from participation, and to compensate for large inequalities in terms of personal resources to participate, the ideal of democracy as a regime where all articulated preferences (demands) are heard will not be realized.

In contrast to the problems of lack of incentives, inequality and restricted access (problems which can be said to refer to the implementation of this particular conception of participation), a third set of problems has to do with the basic assumptions of the conception that sees the purpose of public participation as the representation of articulated preferences (or demands). Peter Bachrach highlights the core of the problem when he points out that there is a conceptual distinction to be made between preferences and interests (Bachrach, 1975). This distinction is similar to the one made by critical authors between the perceived and the "real" interests or needs of people, between "false and true consciousness" if we are to use terminology that has now gone largely out of fashion. One does not have to assume that anyone else than the individual or the group in question have privileged access to these "real interests" to accept the point that what people in a particular political process advance as their preferences may be based on an incomplete or skewed understanding of the conditions under which they find themselves. Any adequate conception of public participation in a democracy must therefore make provision not only for mechanisms for the registering of preferences, but also for allowing people to investigate and question their own preferences and that of others, and in the process to discover what their real interests are. Public participation implies not the registering of pre-existing "given" preferences (which liberals assume are simply carried over from the social/economic sphere to the political), but a process of self-discovery. Political participation for Bachrach "plays a dual role: it not only catalyzes opinion but also creates it." (Bachrach, 1975:43)

In summary, then, the challenge is to conceive of modes of participation that would provide citizens with the necessary incentives to participate, would empower them to do so, and would provide the space within which they can discover what their real interests are. The proponents of what has become known as "participatory, deliberative democracy" believe that these three requirements can be met if the loci of decision making is radically *decentralized* and brought closer to the citizens, and if *deliberation* becomes the mode of interest articulation and mediation. Following Peter Bachrach, we prefer to call this mode "democratic participation" so that we can distinguish it from "public participation" as conceived of by Dahl and others . Bachrach defines *democratic participation* as:

> [A] process in which persons formulate, discuss, and decide public issues that are important to them and directly affect their lives. It is a process that is more or less continuous, conducted on a face-to-face basis in which participants have roughly an equal say in all stages, from formulation of issues to the determination of policies. (Bachrach, 1975:41)

To achieve democratic participation, as we conceive of it, it is important to "diffuse power sufficiently throughout society to inculcate among people of all walks of life a justifiable feeling that they have the power to participate in decisions which affect themselves" (Bachrach, 1967:92). Such decentralization is relatively easy to achieve when issues of local public policy are at stake, and it is worth our while to remember than many "national issues" can indeed be recast into local public policy questions, if competencies and powers of government are decentralized enough. On issues that cannot be translated and localized in this way, a system of regular referenda, involving all those who would be affected, can be instituted (Held, 1996: 320-325). Held also calls for the creation of electronic and analogue channels for "voter feedback," whereby elected politicians and officials can be more regularly informed about the responses of voters to policy initiatives, and the establishment of "voter juries," that is, carefully selected representative panels of citizens who are addressed by different groups of experts, and are then given the brief to systematically consider the strengths and weaknesses of controversial policies and to come up with reasoned conclusions on what the policy priorities are and how they should be addressed. Akin to such initiatives are the deliberative polls that were held on an experimental basis in Britain in 1994 and 1995, and then replicated by means of a National Issues Convention (NIC) in the United States in January 1996 that brought together a nationally representative sample of citizens to deliberate on national issues ahead of the 1996 presidential campaign (Fishkin, 1997). The opinion of citizens expressed in such a reasoned and deliberative process would be of much greater value as inputs in policy making than would be the results of opinion polls that actually just measure at-the-moment attitudes. Also important is that this decentralization of power enhances one of the core principles of democratic theory, namely "self-rule" (Keim, 1975:9) or "democratic autonomy" (Held, 1996:322). This in itself serves as a strong incentive for citizens to make use of the opportunities for public participation offered by such innovative mechanisms.

Those mechanisms just mentioned that are based on deliberation imply a new mode of interest articulation that provides the opportunity not only for face-to-face interaction (Bachrach), but also for interest mediation between competing interests that goes beyond bargaining and voting (neither of which provides the opportunity for discovery of real interests). Following the lead of Jürgen Habermas's notion of deliberative praxis as the core element of a regime that purports to place power in the hands of the people, and Hannah Arendt's rescue of the public, civic sphere from "social suffocation," authors such as Bohman (1996; see also Bohman and Rehg, 1999), Mansbridge (1980), and Cohen and Rogers (1983) have identified public deliberation as a mode of inter-action and mediation that entails "that citizens and their representatives engage in a dialogue about public problems and solutions under conditions that are conducive to reasoned reflection and refined public judgment; a mutual willingness to understand the values, perspectives and interests of others; and the possibility of reframing their interests and perspectives in light of a joint search for common interests and mutually acceptable solutions."[11] Apart from the bonus that deliberation holds in terms of enabling citizens to reasonably discover their real interests, such mechanisms for participation also induces a stronger orientation toward the common good and civic responsibility than would a system of participation that relies solely on preference articulation for the sake of advancing demands. Most of all, it facilitates an unprecedented level of political self-realization, that is, a conscious appropriation by the individual of what it means to be a citizen.[12]

In the most recent work on democratic participation as defined here, the attention has been turned to real-life experiments in what Fung and Wright calls "empowered participatory governance" (Fung and Wright, 2001). These experiments include (apart from those introduced by Fishkin and discussed above) neighborhood governance councils in inner-city Chicago; the Wisconsin Regional Training Partnership which involves government, large firm management, and organized labor in providing career opportunities in the rust-belt of the United States; the participatory budget processes of Porto Alegre, Brazil which involves citizens directly in setting the city's budget; and the so-called Panchyat reforms in West Bengal and Kerala that have given substantive administrative and fiscal power to Indian villagers. While the verdict is still very much out on these and other attempts to institutionalize democratic participation,[13] there is no reason to believe that its principles cannot be applied to the issue areas of foreign policy. Foreign policy, as traditionally defined, is perhaps less amenable to the decentralization and localization of decision making employed in the examples above, but there is no reason why local communities cannot institute fora for deliberating on the effects of global trends on these communities and how they can come up with appropriate responses. In fact, the intense interaction between the local and the global that has accompanied globalization makes such deliberative councils indispensable.[14] Also, to the extent that foreign relations has become part of the activities of local councils (whether in dealing with labor migration in border areas, or in establishing investment and/or cultural exchanges with localities elsewhere in the world), locally based innovations in empowered participatory governance have a clear foreign policy dimension. On a more national scale, deliberative polls as practiced by James Fishkin can also be extended to foreign policy issues. For instance: traveling deliberative hearings in which the government initiates a draft 'white paper' on foreign and trade policies which is then presented for deliberative polling in selected centers by a carefully selected cross section of the population, is an option that has to be further investigated. Other mechanisms of democratic participation in policy making across national borders are discussed in the final chapter to this book.

Debates continue about the merits and shortcomings of deliberative democracy[15] and it is not our task to mediate between the opposing views. Much more important for our purposes is to point out that none of the proponents of deliberative democratic participation proposes that the mechanisms briefly reviewed above should or could replace older, more established mechanisms of public participation. Although there are indeed real tensions between modes of public participation that take their cue from interest aggregation in the "marketplace," and mechanisms of democratic participation that has the "forum" as its model,[16] in this chapter we were interested in exploring the different meanings that "participation" has acquired in the literature. We also wanted to come up with some initial checklist of the different mechanisms for public/

democratic participation that have been identified in the process of giving meaning to these terms. This list of participatory mechanisms provides an approximate standard in terms of which existing practices in South Africa can be judged in order to determine whether Mr. Mbeki indeed has a point when he suggests that South Africans are not participating sufficiently in our system of governance so that they can be truly called "their own liberators."

Notes

1.   Two hundred Members of the National Assembly are elected on the basis of national lists, while another two hundred members are elected in terms of regional (provincial) party lists. For a discussion of the detail, and the benefits and shortcomings of these electoral arrangements, see Faure and Venter, 2000.

2.   The resentment of the NGO community toward what they perceive as the exclusionist tactics of the government is evident in "A Statement from the South African NGO Forum for the World Summit on Sustainable Development, Johannesburg 2002," at www.johannesburgsummit.org/web_pages/prepcom_one_statement_by_sangos.pdf

3.   For an explicit endorsement of the participatory role of the Portfolio Committee, see 'Reply by the Deputy Minister of Foreign Affairs, Mr. Aziz Pahad, during the Debate in the National Assembly, 18 May 1995," in Department of Foreign Affairs, 1995: 25.

4.   See Department of Foreign Affairs, 1995:25.

5.   See "The fire-starter at foreign affairs," *Mail and Guardian*, March 5, 1999.

6.   See le Pere and van Nieuwkerk, (2002:256-257) for a discussion of the finer details of this new system of integrated policy making.

7.   See Deegan (2002) for a review and discussion of such attempts.

8.   See Chapter 4 in this volume.

9.   For a review of the literature, see Elman, 1999.

10.   This list is partly based on Birch, 1993:81, and Parry and Moyser, 1994:47.

11.   Taken from 'Deliberative Democracy', CPN Tools, www.cpn.org/cpn/sections/tools/models/deliberative_democracy.html

12.   See especially the volume *Deliberative Democracy* edited by Jon Elster (1998)

13.   But see the special edition of *Politics and Society* (vol 29, no 1, March 2001) which contains a set of case studies on these and other experiments.

14.   See Scholte (2000:261-282) for detailed suggestions in this regard.

15.   See Elster (1998).

16.   See Elster (1999) for an extensive treatment of the differences between the "market" and the "forum" when it comes to political practice.

Chapter 4

Civil Society and Foreign Policy

Garth le Pere and Brendan Vickers

The processes and institutions inaugurated by political liberalization, constitutional change, and competitive electoral politics have all been salutary for sustainable democratic rule in South Africa. During the apartheid years, but especially in the last two decades, the proliferation of a rich and heterogeneous tapestry of autonomous organizations and social networks has been regarded as a dynamic catalyst in the advent of democracy in 1994 and since then, as a crucial bulwark for the maintenance of democratic governance. Civil society is viewed as the critical agency for creating public accountability and participatory government. Indeed, "prospects for the consolidation of democracy in South Africa depend on the ability of its citizens to uphold principles of democratic behavior" (James and Caigure, 1996:64). In democratic South Africa, the solidarities of civil society and its separation from the state imply a tension. Civil society is simultaneously arrayed against the state and engaged with the state in setting the boundaries of public power while guarding its own prerogatives. While civil society intrinsically resists state encroachment, the various interests within civil society also seek to influence the state in the exercise of public policy and the allocation of valued resources. This engagement may be either cordial or antagonistic but it does reflect a common recognition of state sovereignty and legitimacy. In the words of Lewis (1992:36), "state and civil society are engaged in a dialogue at arm's length." In a normative sense, civil society thus presupposes a viable political community, in which participants recognize certain consensual boundaries of common destiny and shared interests.[1]

From the vantage point of democratic theory, the delineation of boundaries between state and civil society creates a context for the emergence of a public sphere or civic space, in which state and nonstate actors seek to influence the forms and content of the polity.[2] Civil society organizations and their repre-

63

sentatives thus play strategic roles in negotiating, articulating and fostering their interests vis-à-vis the state and they are equally crucial in sustaining democratic rules and procedures.

An area which has not received much scholarly attention is the role of civil society in the crafting, shaping and influencing the conduct of South Africa's foreign relations. Since South Africa's democratic transition in 1994 there were great expectations—given the African National Congress' (ANC) avowed commitment to "democratizing" foreign policy—that civil society and its subspecies, nongovernmental organizations (NGOs), would enjoy a robust and active engagement in the process of charting South Africa's place and (re)entry in world affairs. This was perhaps consistent with the sanguine spirit of the post-Cold War era whose anticipated dividend yield would encourage the emergence of global civil society, empower trans-national social movements and raise the profile of non-state actors in processes of democratic reforms. In one reading, this was largely a consequence of the dissolution of "the absolutes of the Westphalian system—territorially fixed states where everything of value lies within some state's borders; a single secular authority governing each territory and representing it outside its borders; and no authority above states' (Mathews 1997:50). Thus NGOs in South Africa—essentially those with research, advocacy, or activist functions and mandates—hoped for synergistic links with the new foreign policy mandarins and practitioners who would consolidate an interactive ethos and evolve a formal framework for debate and discussion. However, a general sentiment is emerging that these hopes have been misplaced. If anything, the relevant state institutions and concerned bureaucracies have proven themselves "off-limits," unresponsive and recalcitrant, perhaps victims of their own inertia and apathy. Foreign policy oriented NGOs have viewed as effete and perfunctory whatever efforts have originated in government departments to engage them. And NGOs do produce useful "social capital" which could inspire creative policy making and assist problem solving capacities in government.

The problems encountered by civil society actors in making their voices heard in foreign policy making processes raise interesting empirical questions for this enquiry but the dilemma of influence and independence points to the question of how truth speaks to power. In the view of Smith (1991:xviii)

> Truth speaks to power in many different tones of voice. The philosopher and cloistered intellectual, free of ambition to serve a leader directly, can speak with an authority that does not need to bend the truth to justify pressing political ends. . . . The political adviser and expert, however, if they aspire to be of use, must speak to power in a political and bureaucratic context; and they must always speak a useful truth. Their claim to speak the truth must always be viewed in the light of their relationship with power.

This chapter examines the evolution and pertinent conceptual underpinnings of civil society in South Africa, but more importantly, it takes up the challenge of representing the views of a sample of NGOs active in the area of foreign policy and depicts their attempts to speak truth to power.[3] The findings reveal a range of tensions, ambiguities, and an abiding sense of frustration at the NGO interface with policy.

Aspects of the South African Civil Society Debate

In South Africa there is a great deal of rhetorical convergence around the idea of democracy on the part of a variety of ideologically opposed political actors but little substantive consensus about its content and implications. The changed political terrain since 1994 is forcing greater attention to the modalities of democracy and democratization, as society and the state restructure themselves. It is within this context that the present debate about the role of civil society has to be located. It is part of the process of spelling out what democracy is all about in the changed sociopolitical milieu since the elections of April 1994. This concerns relations between the reconstituted South African state and society and between the state and the "people." The debate about civil society is primarily linked to the politics of reconstruction, about non-state organizations of newly empowered citizens being able to call the new state into account, about ensuring the principle of political pluralism, and about securing grassroots participation in development planning and implementation, all of which were systematically denied by successive apartheid regimes. In the longer term, however, the civil society debate also encompasses the expectation that some form of social democracy underpinned by a vigorous welfare state could be established in South Africa.

The attention to the notion of civil society as part of the democracy debate has different impulses emerging from within and outside the country. The first impulse is based on the history and experience of resistance to oppression in South Africa and the desire to carry the lessons of struggle against apartheid authoritarianism into the era of building a different kind of state and society. The second impulse has its origins in the attempt to understand the collapse of a number of "socialist" regimes in Eastern and Central Europe and the implications of this failure for any future socialist project in South Africa. The third impulse emanates from the decline of weak predatory states and the autocratic rule in Africa, the legacy of failure of state-managed development initiatives, and the emergence of prodemocracy movements with their general demand for social and political democratization.

The more explicit use of the notion of civil society as part of the debate about how democracy is to be constructed in South Africa has gained momentum after the unbanning of organizations representing the broad liberation movement in February 1990. But there has been a solid tradition of organizing within the different areas of civil society, based on a clear demarcation between the apartheid state and the people. Trade unions, civic organizations, professional associations, youth and women's groups, educational, religious, and sporting organizations all formed a rich tapestry of resistance against an autocratic state. In the view of Friedman, "exclusion from the franchise and the banning of national movements forced [these organizations] to seek a power base in civil society" (Friedman 1991:8).

Within the politics of apartheid resistance, civil society activity has been inextricably interwoven with the attempt to dislodge state power and not simply to move it in a more accountable or less repressive direction. The concerns of civil society and political society largely overlapped in a common struggle against apartheid. It is only within the present context of the new order that a classical Hegelian[4] separation of state and society has occurred between organizations and movements that have appropriated state power and those that continue to represent the interests of civil society constituents.

Despite its frequent usage and its acquiring the status of a radical cliché that functions as a metaphor for all and any kind of state-restricting, democratizing procedures, the notion of civil society remains controversial and contested among different ideological persuasions.[5] There are "democrats" who view civil society as the only hope for making democracy real and manifest, given the disastrous statism of Eastern European and African politics. But there are also other 'democrats' who see it as a weakening of political will and radical vision, a replacement of revolutionary goals by a bourgeois democratic diversion or compromise. Thus Friedman (1991:5) asks rhetorically whether "yesterday's populists and socialists [are] today's liberals and libertarians." There are spokespersons of big business who welcome the call for the strengthening of civil society, in anticipation of maximum state withdrawal from the economic sphere. And there are those on the left who see civil society as the incarnation of the syndicalist project crystallized and underpinned by a vibrant and strong trade union movement (Marais 1998:226-30).

Clearly there are a variety of interests and strategic considerations which lie behind this stark divergence of opinion on the meaning and role of civil society in South Africa. Part of the conundrum is soberly explained by Marais (1998:205): "many of the assumptions and affinities inherited from the anti-apartheid struggle have translated poorly into the new context. Disaffection with statist routes of transformation has coupled with the perception of the state 'withered away' by globalization, yielding hugely amplified assessments of the scale and role of civil society."

Allowing the Voices to Speak: NGO Views on Foreign Policy

Eight years have elapsed since the formal and constitutional inauguration of democracy in South Africa, allowing perhaps for more or less coherent perspectives to emerge on how NGOs have fared in their engagement with foreign policy processes. The euphoria about the "vanguard" role of civil society in South Africa's transition has given way to a "postliberation depression" and has exposed a range of pathologies ranging from "internal dysfunctions, funding crises, political incoherence and overall strategic disorientation" (Marais 1998:206). A reflective period of assessing the role, place and identity of civil society was therefore necessary with the changing political and social terrain. Of particular importance was how civil society would reposition itself with regard to promoting values, norms, and processes of liberty, democratization, reconstruction and development.

In the area of foreign policy, the ANC espoused a set of aspirational principles whose central pillars—human rights and democracy promotion—invited NGO participation and monitoring.[6] How have NGOs as an important constituent element of civil society responded to the challenges of democratizing foreign policy and what have been their concerns?

The Appropriate Role for NGOs in Influencing Policy

In terms of South Africa's transitional experience, NGOs have a constructive and responsible role to play in influencing policy. This is especially so in transiting from the old order with fixed ideas of governance to the new order where the policy environment is extremely fluid and amenable to influence. The change from one form of government to another occasions the opportunity to develop new policy documents and draft new legislation consistent with the values and norms of the new regime. This provides a window of opportunity for NGOs to be an integral part of transition processes. A new government—especially one inexperienced in the art of national policy making—does not and cannot have all the necessary expertise, skills and capacity on the myriad and complex issues for which it must formulate and tailor new public policy instruments. If the government is able to pursue an effective foreign policy, then it must be informed by as wide an array of opinion, information, and expertise as is available. There is an institutional civil society network—NGOs, independent policy research institutes, think tanks, and universities—that disposes of considerable levels of expertise, information and resources which could enhance the government's own capacity in formulating foreign policy (Kornegay 2000). Furthermore, NGOs can play a very important and constructive role in independent critical reflection on government policy and act as a constructive sounding board in policy development (Cassim 2000). Maloka (2000) says, "We recognize that government has the imperative to make decisions and implement them, but we think that we can play a role in being a social reference capacity for government to check its own policies in terms of the direction that society accepts."

The role and efficacy of NGOs in influencing policy before and after the transition have changed quite considerably and dramatically. Before the transition NGOs were very active in the antiapartheid struggle. Civil society articulated its role in terms of opposition and resistance to apartheid oppression but it also assisted with developing and promoting an alternate vision of the future, largely maintaining an ideological symbiosis in the country with liberation movements in exile (van Nieuwkerk 2000, Paulecutt 2000). The heady and intoxicating days of the transition period represented a "golden era" for NGOs and the policy/analytical community. In the context of the transition, there were no ready-made panaceas, the country needed new ideas, and there was a broad national consensus on what constituted the essential elements of domestic and foreign policy. Foreign policy had to keep abreast of and pace with harsh and bitter domestic realities and legacies of the past. But the new government did not have the experience or abilities to deliver policy in a manner they had promised prior to the election (Mills 2000).

Since many of the incumbents of the new government had their political incarnations in NGO activist backgrounds, they approached specialist NGOs— such as the Institute for Security Studies (ISS) and the African Center for the Constructive Resolution of Disputes (ACCORD)—as well as academics to develop draft policy positions. In fact, NGOs and academics crafted many position papers that ultimately became government policy. Many independent policy research institutes and think tanks came into existence during this period, including the Institute for Global Dialogue (IGD) which was specifically established to assist with research and analysis on foreign policy issues. Research-oriented NGOs and academic institutions informed these policy processes intellectually, had a hand in shaping the form and content of debates, and enjoyed inordinate power in the policy making process. In the view of Cilliers: "We can look at every sector of South African society, including the areas that we engage in [security], where government has been so weak and has been so mistrustful of its own people and particularly of the old guard that government almost laid itself bare to policy influence on anything from land reform to security issues" (Cilliers 2000). However, NGOs have played too dominant and irresponsible a role in the transitional period. Policy was often developed without the necessary oversight by and accountability to Parliament and the cabinet (see Chapter Three). The result has been policy frameworks that are perhaps too advanced or inappropriate and not always consistent with the ability of government to deliver. NGOs often make the fatuous claim that they represent a constituency, and sometimes they do, but very often they do not. This leads to an inflated projection of their contributions to policy exercises. Thus the challenge in a transitional society such as South Africa is at times to clearly define the boundaries and terms of NGO involvement in policy. According to Cilliers (2000), 'NGOs and government have to be responsible in their engagement so that government policy is not made by NGOs'. Where there is ambiguity about who is responsible for developing policy, there is always a problem of ownership and implementation.

At the conclusion of the Mandela era and the advent of the Mbeki era in 1999, the period of policy development (in the form of White Papers) also came to an end. The new administration concentrated its collective energies on policy implementation and service delivery to key constituencies. The window to shape policy outcomes during the transition started closing very rapidly. As the government now builds its own institutional capacity and develops greater confidence in its own officialdom, there is a gradual diminution in the scope of intellectuals, academics and NGOs outside the state to influence or shape the contours of policy and a deliberate attempt is being made to now situate policy making inside the apparatus of government. The role of NGOs "has become much more circumscribed, limited and by invitation only. Voices in civil society have been slowly marginalized so that current challenges in our foreign policy, such as arms sales, will be decided not by outside influences, the media or business but internally by the state and those decisions will be informed by the interests of the state" (van Nieuwkerk 2000). In foreign policy matters, van Nieuwkerk strongly contends that any future policy will be influenced by the thinking and vested interests of: the ANC as the ruling party, Parliament, and the government department concerned [the Department of Foreign Affairs (DFA) in the case of foreign policy; the Department of Trade and Industry (DTI) on trade policy; and the Department of Defence (DoD) on security and defence issues]. For example, NGOs and academic analysts have found it difficult to play an influential role in shaping policy around the South Africa-Southern African Development Community (SADC) trade relationship and the renegotiation of the Lome Convention in comparison to the richly textured contribution they made in the course of South Africa's free trade agreement negotiations with the European Union. The IGD tried through two workshops to facilitate the development of negotiating frameworks but the government had by then decided that its strategic direction, conceptual approaches and the process would be managed by a triad consisting of mandated players in the department of trade and industry, the ANC and Parliament (van Nieuwkerk 2000). Mills (2000) further remarked, "from the perspective of SAIIA, we certainly have been involved over the last 18 months in some very interesting debates with government, but these have been far less public in nature than they were perhaps in the first five years of the Mandela presidency."

The Openness of and Access to Government Institutions and Departments

Since the transition, government institutions and departments have been remarkably open and receptive to intellectual contributions from NGOs. There is a real need in government for ideas on foreign policy. NGOs after all work in the marketplace of ideas. When NGOs have approached people like Deputy Minister Aziz Pahad to discuss cooperation, he will usually name the issues and areas where the DFA would appreciate contributions and has often mentioned the fact that publications from the ISS, the South African Institute of International Affairs (SAIIA), and the Institute for Global Dialogue (IGD) are widely read and very highly regarded (Schoeman, 2000). There is, however, a marked difference between NGOs making intellectual inputs into the policy process and NGOs as part of the final policy decision. While NGOs aspire to be participants—if only marginally—in foreign policy making processes, it is the government that ultimately makes and decides policy. Hence in the opinion of Mills (2000): "through their activities NGOs may create a groundswell of opinion and debate which is ultimately fed through political principals and becomes policy....NGOs have a role in helping to create and facilitate debate that may have an influencing effect upon policy formulation and ultimately on policy."

In the case of the ISS, it interacts at the official level more than any other research-oriented NGO. There is a consistent flow of senior government officials with whom it interacts both in South Africa and the region. Because of its expertise in security matters, the ISS was actively involved in the defense review process (in its previous incarnation as the Institute for Defense Policy), the White Paper on Defense, the White Paper on Peace Missions, and even the White Paper on Safety and Security. The ISS furthermore drafted the new Organized Crime Bill and more controversially, the Firearms Bill for government. And all this was done free of charge. For Cilliers it is important that NGOs should not become sub-contractors to government since this can compromise their independence. Independence—a degree of detachment both from government and from immediate partisan political debate—should be one of the cardinal virtues of NGOs (Cilliers 2000). Mills (2000) believes that government is important but it is not the sole reason for SAIIA's existence. SAIIA's constituency includes business, government and academia. The Institute's role is "to raise the level of debate and through that to find solutions and not to act as an unelected executive in that process" (Mills 2000). Since by definition NGOs are independent and are not bound by party or ideological affinities, they can be more candid and critical in presenting their views in policy debates (Govindjee and Spiegelberg 2000).

There is a critical tension between independence and closeness to government. NGOs and their associated analysts are caught in the dilemma of wanting to play a "watchdog" role and at the same time, wanting to be close to government so as to benefit from "inside information" for developing sound analysis and useful reports. According to Landsberg (2000), "if you want to be close, you are going to have to learn to respect secrecy. Your first inclination should not be to try and divulge this information in public; I think there's a tendency to want to do that." These tensions are complicated and exacerbated by a number of fundamental weaknesses in the foreign policy think-tank community because of competition for access to government, personality clashes, an extreme lack of cooperation among think tanks and most tragically, by deep racial divisions. Landsberg (2000) adds: "There must be a balance between cooperation and competition. We shouldn't all say the same thing and we shouldn't all come from the same perspective. We should have different views; after all we live in an era of globalization and there are lots of illogical tensions and debates." The NGO world in South Africa is not homogenous, but reflects various interest groups. Some NGOs recruit or lobby different positions on different issues (Maloka, 2000).

The receptivity of government to NGOs is very much a function of what the government considers to be the appropriate role and use of civil society. If the

DTI, for example, thinks that the Trade and Industry Policy Secretariat (TIPS) can constructively assist with making more informed decisions about whether the government should enter into a free trade agreement with the EU, they display an eager willingness to engage TIPS's trade policy expertise. However, if DTI plans to move in a certain direction and NGOs generate research which is antithetical to such decisions, then receptiveness obviously declines. Influence is essentially based on how government feels it can best use NGOs to assist its own strategic thinking.

NGOs which have a broad philosophical orientation closely aligned with that of the government and compatible with the interests of transformation will enjoy greater scope to engage in government policy processes. The cynical corollary to this is that there is limited space for NGOs located on the opposite end of the government's ideological spectrum (Cassim 2000). This is where tensions arise. Much of TIPS's research output, for example, is tailored to meet the needs of DTI. The problem with this kind of research is that it is very much personality driven. The role of personalities or individuals in key positions of power is a critical and decisive factor in the whole process of NGO access and influence. If there is a director-general or a deputy director-general who is receptive to research and independent critical reflection and who is not insecure or anxious about criticism, the relationship can be mutually very productive. If such a key personality is not in place, the partnership could collapse. Given the demands of the transition, there is an imperative for NGOs to collaborate with government where they can assist or engage constructively in issues but there is also a premium on maintaining their independence from government.

Although the Freedom of Expression Institute (FXI) was promised by DFA that it would be invited to meetings where it could make interventions on behalf of civil society, they were never notified of such meetings. This could have proven to be a useful way of establishing contact and acquiring relevant information from the DFA. In Paulecutt's view, "I think even though we have quite a progressive approach to foreign affairs, the secrecy that surrounds diplomacy is a hampering factor." FXI is much more activist and human rights-oriented than other international relations research institutes such as SAIIA and the IGD. FXI and Paulecutt herself were heavily involved in the Nigeria Democracy Support Group (Paulecutt 2000).

The Ceasefire Campaign made inputs into the 1996 foreign policy workshop and the defense review process. It convened a workshop in August 1996 to develop a response to the DFA's *Foreign Policy Discussion Document.* The participating organizations and individuals were concerned with promoting peace, economic equity, environmental justice, and human rights as key components of South Africa's emerging foreign policy. The extent to which the final document from this exercise, *Rethinking Foreign Policy,* was taken seriously by DFA was certainly not reflected in its subsequent thinking and emphases. Ceasefire and other civil society organs were invited to defense review consultations, but no program space was allocated to any NGO. The agenda was predetermined and speakers from government and the military filled the entire program. Civil society participation was relegated to being a part of the audience and at times NGOs were infelicitously addressed as "members of the defense community"! Guni Govindjee says: "we were there as the audience to witness the proceedings and we had the feeling in the end that, on the one hand, we did appreciate being involved on this level. On the other hand, we sometimes felt that we were misused because government afterwards tried to justify all the decisions by saying that they came about through major consultation with civil society." On one particular occasion during the defense review process, Ceasefire had to remind and correct minister Ronnie Kasrils that "consultation" did not amount to "consensus building" (Govindjee and Spiegelberg 2000).

The peace support policy development exercise was a very positive process and took very seriously the contributions made by civil society actors. The commitment of key personnel in the DFA and DoD to involve civil society and to democratize the policy making process largely contributed to the success of the venture. Ronnie Kasrils and Kader Asmal are counted among those with whom civil society has a good relationship and rapport. However, since the 1999 election there has been no contact between Ceasefire and DoD. In the words of Heike Spiegelberg: "it was made very clear to us that we are not a priority, that they don't know us....And then we gave up our efforts. And it's a big change from what it was before."

Alongside the global civil society campaign to secure a ban on the use and further manufacture of landmines, there was a campaign among local NGOs to persuade the South African government to adopt a position on the banning and the campaign proved very successful in moving the government to adopt the NGO's preferred position. These efforts were part of a global confluence of civil society pressures leading to the final adoption of the treaty to ban landmines in Ottawa in February 1997. What was interesting was the government's disingenuousness in taking all the credit as the sole South African player in the Ottawa process. There was no mention of civil society's robust contribution and effort in securing the ban. Even the parliamentary portfolio committee on foreign affairs was marginalized in the process. The committee had decided in favor of implementing a ban on the production, use, and transfer of all types of antipersonnel mines at the 1996 Review Conference of the UN Convention on Conventional Weapons. However, in Geneva that position was over-ruled by the DFA which supported the retention of "smart mines" (*Mail & Guardian,* 26 April-2 May 1996).

South Africa's decision to support an indefinite extension of the Nuclear Non-Proliferation Treaty (NPT) at the 1995 Review and Extension Conference contradicted an earlier agreement developed by South African legal experts which allowed for a rolling extension, "which was said to meet some of the objections of the developing countries while simultaneously satisfying the weapons states that the non-proliferation regime could not be extended." Yet as David Fig from the Group for Environmental Monitoring argued, "all of this was decided over our heads by the Ministry of Foreign Affairs, which never sought to make the debate public in South Africa" (cited in van der Westhuizen 1998: 446).

There is general agreement that it is extremely difficult to arrive at a precise empirical measure of the impact that NGOs have on policy formulation. One reason for this, according to Kornegay, is that there is not enough of a proactive outreach from government to NGOs to assess whether research and information provided by NGOs make a discernible difference in foreign policy processes (Kornegay 2000). Landsberg and Mills believe that the civil society constituency often aspires to and indeed, sometimes presumptuously demands participation in such processes. South African NGOs are very concerned with how much impact they have on the process of policy formulation and there is extreme competition for access to government. Thus, says Landsberg (2000): "It will be great if we can have influence on policy making processes but that's different from demanding a stake in the process." It should not be civil society's business to want to have impact and influence; these should evolve naturally in a dynamic process of interaction.

Landsberg (2000) believes that government does take seriously quick policy analyses and opinion pieces that are introduced in the public domain and print media. A free and democratic press is extremely important for Schoeman so that the necessary and critical debates over foreign policy can take place and that one knows that there are channels though which inputs can be made and that these will be considered. It is important not only to look for positive impact. There can also be negative impact, as when NGOs offer policy pronouncements which contradict those of government and so incur its wrath. The impact of NGOs on policy is diverse and should not be restricted to the foreign policy making process. Their impact is also reflected for example, by those academics, researchers and executives of policy research institutes who regularly teach at the Foreign Service Institute or the Defence College. In this regard, NGOs are highly regarded. Then more importantly, different individuals have different levels of access to the minister, the deputy minister, the director-general, or spokespersons for the minister. Academics are regularly called on to draft speeches for DFA personnel. SAIIA has been approached from time to time to act as facilitator in "closed meetings" between the DFA and NGOs and business. The government sees a definite role for NGOs in investigating the possibility of civil society dialogue in the Democratic Republic of Congo and Angola. The areas of attempted influence can be tracked by surveying NGO publications and the content of their newsletters. These are the mechanisms used by NGOs to advance or lobby for certain positions or provide policy prescriptions (Schoeman 2000, van Nieuwkerk 2000).

The Importance of Democratizing Foreign Policy Making

There is a vigorous debate about the practice and theory of democratizing foreign policy. Democratizing foreign policy means allowing a plurality of civil society voices open access to communicating with concerned officials in government responsible for policy implementation. A process of communication between government and civil society would include formulation of foreign policy, assisting with the development of available options, and shaping the nature of the discourse. In other words, democratizing foreign policy involves enhancing a process of participation and transparency in decision making. This would entail an active engagement between DFA and the relevant network of NGOs, think tanks, research institutes and universities (Kornegay 2000, Maloka 2000, Mills 2000). Or as Landsberg (2000) puts it: "There is nothing wrong in a democracy with having sound relations between the 'two worlds' of foreign affairs: the scholarly world and the practitioner's world." Government also needs to share information with civil society and explain its foreign policy decisions (Maloka 2000). But as Govindjee (2000) cautions: "The outcome of our experience is that if government embarks on a public consultation process, then they have to take those who they invite seriously and not just use them as an audience or as some authority to rubberstamp its arguments."

The debate over democratizing foreign policy is split between two opposing views. One argument stems from the ANC as the governing party. It holds that to democratize foreign policy is a non sequitur because the government has been democratically elected by an overwhelming majority of citizens and therefore has the right to ultimately make policy choices free from any societal pressures. The constitution sets out clearly that policy making is the responsibility of government and its departments. According to this view, there is nothing to democratize, and "it is an argument that every democratically elected government in the world will use, from the industrialized North to the developing South" (van Nieuwkerk 2000). By their very nature, democracies consist of a noisy cacophony of voices and a mercurial shifting of positions. How successfully these are integrated as social forces depend on the maturity of the society and whether a healthy, vibrant, and strong civil society exists. Although the governing party is entitled to develop its own positions on foreign policy according to its own guidelines, principles, values, and norms, it would be useful for government to recognize other interests in civil society, whether it be NGOs, trade unions, business, or the media. These different views enrich debates which otherwise would be sterile and strengthen ultimate positions which would otherwise be uninformed. Thus "democratizing foreign policy can help government refine its policy, make it more sophisticated, and build in more elements that bring together more interests." (van Nieuwkerk 2000)

Given South Africa's history, there is a definite need to democratize foreign policy. During the apartheid era, there was almost no public input into policy making. In the current democratic order, the public needs to be educated and understand that it is not just sufficient to elect a government but necessary to actively participate in the democratic process. To date very little has been done to promote this public education function. The opportunity to discuss and debate the uncharted yet fertile areas of foreign policy is important. The public space and civic realm is much wider in the new South Africa but it is not totally open or sufficiently accessible to citizens. South Africa has to move to a system that reconciles foreign policy with the real wishes of the majority of the population

(Cilliers 2000). These are often very different from those of the elites who typically engage in such discussions. When it is claimed that foreign policy is elite driven, it is not only the foreign policy of the state that is elite driven but also the highly specialized field of international relations (Cilliers 2000, Landsberg 2000).

Foreign policy and national interests should be debated much more vigorously. The sad fact is that in practice there is no debate on these issues. Government increasingly does not appear to be consulting about its foreign policy objectives and certainly is not explaining them to the country. This has a lot to do with the personality of the president and minister of foreign affairs. Cilliers ascribes this to "the old guard who are still terrified of saying anything and the new guard who basically lost interest after Mbeki's accession. The official opposition have a role to play but because of [inter-party] animosities, their role is unconstructive." Because of South Africa's history, foreign policy issues are very politicized and polarized. Criticism of South Africa's policy toward Zimbabwe, for example, places an analyst or academic in a particular political if not a hostile camp (Cilliers 2000).

It is perhaps important to distinguish between NGO "input" and "participation" in foreign policy making. The incumbent government is very open and receptive to inputs. There are numerous examples where the government has considered formal and informal suggestions by NGOs. It was recently revealed that an IGD publication by Dot Keet is compulsory reading in DTI[7] (Schoeman 2000). In his meetings with SAIIA, ISS, and IGD, Aziz Pahad has frequently spoken about NGO and government cooperation on specific issues and concerns. This is the advantage of a democratized foreign policy process, that is, tapping into the considerable analytical expertise that NGOs tend to develop. It bears repeating that NGOs do not make policy and "participation" presupposes much closer cooperation than merely making "inputs." Under the present government, there is ample room for making inputs but whether these are taken into account is another matter. In the actual making of foreign policy, the government certainly maintains its distance from NGOs and academics (Schoeman 2000).

The government's receptiveness to NGO contributions is perhaps "a function of the balance of political forces which would allow voices in civil society or the non-state sector to either be heard or be marginalized." If a NGO's relationship with those in power is weak, tenuous, or marginal, NGO input will not be taken seriously. A strong and symbiotic relationship and appropriately organized interventions, by contrast, will enjoy the necessary attention. The South African Council of Business (SACOB), for example, represents powerful business interests. The strength and composition of SACOB's constituency will ensure that its voice will be heard and heeded by government. In this vein, "the powerful will listen to you if you have a constituency." (van Nieuwkerk 2000)

Cassim, however, warns that "a democratic process is important but if you're going to have civil society that needs to be educated constantly about these issues, it could in an odd kind of way [decelerate] an important process."

One of the overriding reasons why NEDLAC has become so cumbersome and stagnant is because it reduces democracy to a logical absurdity, thereby being caught in an endless cycle of consultations without arriving at firm decisions, offending as these might sometimes be to its corporate members. For Cassim (2000) the more critical issue is "empowering NGOs to make a noise and to monitor constantly what government is doing. That's more a priority than actual democracy."

Consistent with this sentiment, the ISS sees itself as "moving away from broader policy development and implementation to more policy monitoring and capacity building" (Cilliers 2000)

Constraints and Opportunities Posed by Globalization and other External Dynamics

Globalization has meant that critical areas of foreign policy have become internationalized. In view of the declining Westphalian system of state sovereignty and state autonomy, governments can no longer be the sole arbiters of national decisions on international issues whether they are related to trade, macroeconomic policy, the environment, or arms sales. The government by virtue of South Africa's reintegration in global affairs, is pursuing a strategy of cooperative multilateralism. The worldwide expansion of productive and service activities, the growth of international trade, the diminishing importance of national frontiers, and the intensive exchange of information and knowledge throughout the world imposes a responsibility on governments to act globally and an obligation to participate much more seriously in institutions and processes of global governance whether through the United Nations, the World Bank, the International Monetary Fund, or the World Trade Organization. This provides new opportunities and spaces for well-organized and transnationally connected NGOs to oppose or influence the government's strategic direction. For example, during the Seattle WTO ministerial conference, broad social movements and citizens' groups (intellectually guided by NGOs and activist academics) challenged the WTO negotiating agenda before governments and managed to successfully oppose the inclusion of certain sensitive issues. Globalization and its discontents—essentially its marginalizing and atomizing effects—have become part of the new NGO agenda.

The Ceasefire Campaign is active in several transnational networks: CARMS (Campaign Against Arms Trade) in Britain; COAT (Coalition Against Arms Trade) in Canada, DFD (Demilitarization for Democracy) in the United States, as well as smaller groups against small arms proliferation. The Trade and Industry Policy Secretariat (TIPS) has numerous links with experts from the WTO and World Bank, and has even had better direct access to global institutions and key think tanks than government. This has given TIPS the leverage to influence government's thinking on multilateral trade issues and this has better equipped government to try and change the "rules of the game" in international trade. As Cassim (2000) puts it, "we can use the WTO disciplines which the government takes very seriously to pressure it to think about changing certain domestic policies." The ISS tends to work more with intergovernmental organizations than civil society. It is closely involved with projects for the Organization of African Unity (OAU), SADC to a lesser extent, but also actively participates in United Nations research activity in security and peacekeeping. In the Organization of African Unity (OAU) the ISS was responsible for its agenda on small arms proliferation and organized an all-Africa ministerial meeting in November, 2000 which defined the African position on small arms ahead of the Geneva 2001 Global Conference on Small Arms (Cilliers 2000).

However, while there are opportunities, the economic dimensions of globalization make it difficult for NGOs to have much of an impact. Global economic issues have become so complex and intricately interwoven that NGOs need to develop specialist niches to register any impact on government. Economic globalization is mainly driven by rules-based international regimes. In the long-term, it becomes very difficult to influence the institutional custodians of the global economy once the rules are internationally accepted and broadly implemented by governments.

Because it is so subject to the vagaries of globalization and external factors, the South African government needs to avail itself of the expertise that resides in the NGO community. It is paradoxically the exclusionary and fragmenting effects of globalization that offer greater scope for collaboration and cooperation between state and civil society. This is one manner in which government can ensure that it has sufficient information to make informed decisions about managing the range of imperatives and challenges that come with globalization. It would be extremely dangerous to ignore this resource and simply rely on government capacity to negotiate formidable obstacles associated with South Africa's integration in world affairs (Kornegay 2000).

Conclusion

The expectation that civil society can contribute to democratizing foreign policy is twofold and quite reminiscent of the distinction which Isaiah Berlin made about negative and positive liberty.[8] Two dimensions, echoing as well Gramscian impulses, exist within the context of South Africa. For Gramsci (1971:135-40), civil society is a site of tension, the terrain on which state hegemony is both realized and challenged. For our purposes, the negative function of civil society thus pertains to its watchdog role as a check against the claims of the government to monopolize decision making in foreign policy. In this sense, it is an instrument of popular accountability. The positive dimension of civil society pertains to it fostering and promoting solidarity and an associational ethos that leads citizens to a better understanding of the objectives of government's foreign policy. In this sense, civil society actors and citizens alike enjoy enlarged frameworks for self-directed participation at different levels of policy. This type of activity is more compatible with democracy and is anchored in activist advocacy as well as reflective critiques.

What this enquiry demonstrates is that civil society has lost considerable ground in its watchdog function and in its ability to influence the contours of policy. Attempts by the DFA, as the primary locus of policy formulation and implementation, to engage civil society have (perhaps more so during the Mbeki presidency) proved effete and perfunctory. A certain wariness appears to have set in among concerned nonstate actors about their ability to monitor government performance in terms of an accountable and transparent normative and ethical construct. This has resulted in a growing chasm and void between state and nonstate actors. While difficult to substantiate, there is a view that this growing distance has been exacerbated by a trend to increasingly centralize decision making in the office of the president, especially on critical foreign policy matters (see Chapter Three). Thus while not conclusive from this investigation, there are emerging tendencies among nonstate actors to concentrate their energies and resources in the positive aspects referred to above. By promoting research, analysis, public debate, and other interventions, they are beginning to develop critical perspectives on policy and its conduct.

Ultimately however the connection between civil society and democratization of foreign policy in South Africa can only be an ambivalent one given the problems of inchoate interests, centrifugal tendencies, institutional friction, limited access, and influence. Prescriptively, there is a need for NGOs and other civil society actors involved in foreign policy research and advocacy to transcend narrow interests and parochial agendas in order to develop an intellectual and knowledge-driven consensus about norms of collaboration and resource sharing. This will demand a readiness by a few to move away from their primus inter pares and empire-building mentality which so militates against constructive cooperation among civil society actors active in the foreign policy arena.

South Africa as a transitional society is bound to experience a range of tensions in governance. These are becoming ever more evident in the crucible of redefining state-society relations in the postapartheid era. Sadly, civil society in South Africa appears to be increasingly marginalized by government, with dire consequences for the country's democratization and the consolidation thereof.

We would do well therefore not to "forget how violent and disruptive democratization can be, how long it takes to construct a foundational free society before a democratic constitution can be raised upon it" (Barber, 1996:277). The turbulence of post-Cold War international relations presents great opportunities and challenges to civil society in a transitional context like South Africa. It cannot afford to fail what after all is a historic mission of evolving a new type of civic architecture and democratic citizenship out of the detritus of apartheid.

Notes

1. See Bendix (1977:22-30).
2. See, for example, Huntington (1968).
3. Broadly speaking, the NGOs sampled and individuals interviewed for this paper have the following capacities in the area of foreign policy:

- Analytical, advisory, and consultative services;
- Concern with ideas and concepts which underlie policy and questioning the "conventional wisdom" which shapes policy;
- Collection and classification of information relevant to policy;
- Longer term perspective which examines trends and causal linkages rather than immediate events;
- Lobbying and activist involvement around discrete policy issues; and
- Commitment to educate a wider audience through publications, seminars and workshops.

These functions roughly conform to those set out by Wallace (1994:142-43).

4. Hegel discussed the idea of civil society as a distinct private realm of commerce, class interest, religion and other individual and group prerogatives, distinguished from and juxtaposed to the universal and encompassing power of the state. See Keane (1988:50).

5. Among its varied meanings, civil society can include, according to Hutchful (1995-96:56-57), "any or all of the following criteria: location (between the state and the citizen), functions (serving and defending the interests of private memberships), institutions and politics (opposition to and collaboration with the state). According to how these criteria are deployed, the definitions are relatively apolitical (emphasizing the growth of horizontal solidarities, the growing solidity of civil associations and their autonomy and self-distancing from the state) or relatively activist (emphasizing the conflictual relations with the state and the emergence of a social sphere protected from state intrusion)."

6. Of the seven principles which ought to guide South Africa's foreign policy, those relevant in this context are

- A belief in and preoccupation with human rights which extends beyond the political, embracing economic, social and environmental dimensions;
- A belief that just and lasting solutions to the problems of humankind can only come through the promotion of democracy world-wide; and
- A belief that South Africa's foreign relations must mirror a deep commitment to the consolidation of its democracy.

See African National Congress (ANC), 1994, *Foreign Policy Perspectives in a Democratic South Africa.*

7. The publication referred to is Keet (2000).
8. See Berlin (1969).

Chapter 5

Women and the Making of South Africa's Foreign Policy

Maxi Schoeman and Yolande Sadie

Although women traditionally occupied a marginal position within the realm of foreign policy and international relations, South Africa's transition to democracy created an opportunity for more inclusive approaches to women and a more gender-aware policy environment. The heavy emphasis placed in the country's constitution on gender equality finds expression in legislation and the institutionalization of processes aimed at addressing gender issues while at the same time, the 'issue of gender' has become, for all intents and purposes, "acceptable" and part of what postapartheid claims to be about.

The same can be said in a broader context. Reviewing the 1980s and 1990s, Halliday (1998:839) remarks as far as teaching and research on gender and international relations are concerned that '[i]n all three categories—International Relations, the social sciences in general, the political world—much has changed for the better over the past decade'. Perhaps one of the main indications of this 'change for the better' is the fact that it is no longer necessary to justify a focus on women in academic writing, and that it has become a regular feature within the international donor community to insist on a gender component in all development aid programs. The focus on the justification of inclusion has shifted to ways and means of realizing the objectives of making women more 'visible' and of empowering them through strategies of inclusion in decision making processes and through projects that take their concerns into account.

The above does not mean, though that the issue of gender inequality has been solved, or that women have been emancipated. Halliday (1998:840-46) points to a number of trends that have a negative influence on attempts at addressing the status, position, and role of women:

- The manipulation of the "gender agenda" for political purposes and the underfunding of institutions, processes, and projects dealing with women's concerns. This is a point returned to in the body of this chapter.
- The growing numbers of poor women in the face of economic globalization and the reign of (ultra) liberal economic ideas and practices. In Southern Africa, for example, the gender-related development index for the region declined by 0.87 between 1995 and 1998 (SADC 2000:77).
- The gendered dimension of civil and intraethnic war, particularly as far as the use of violence, and specifically of rape, has become common. In South Africa violence against women and children may not take place within the context of civil war, yet the incidence of these crimes are excessively high and a source of great concern.

Halliday (1998:846) concludes his overview by remarking that because gender inequality remains "a global phenomenon, universally present and transnationally reproduced," it should be 'a central concern of the contemporary social sciences'.

This chapter is in part a response to Halliday's "call for action" as it engages with the lived concerns of women in a changing world. It also explores the extent to which South Africa's foreign policy making reflects the characteristics of democratization as set out by the editors in the introduction, although we adjust these somewhat to focus more particularly on women's participation as foreign policy officials:

- a sustainable increase in opportunities for participation in decision making and policy implementation and
- systematic attempts to use foreign policy to improve the situation of the marginalized and most vulnerable segments of society.

The chapter provides an overview of the strategies and policies of South Africa's Department of Foreign Affairs (DFA) with a view to assess the extent to which the status and position of women are being addressed in the policies and activities of the department. An exploration of the democratization of South Africa's foreign policy cannot be complete without paying attention to the way in which women, whether as objects or agents, feature in the work of the government department most directly involved with the multitude of issues and domains that link South Africa with its external environment.

Section one contains a discussion of the concepts *gender* and *woman/ women* within the context of international political economy, explaining our preference for the category *woman*, though *gender* is also utilized. It furthermore deals briefly with two very different arguments about the inclusion of women in the foreign policy process, both as decisionmakers and as referents of such policies. Section two deals with women's position in the DFA since 1994, covering not only their locus within the various tiers of the department, but also providing some information on perceptions of their status within the department and with differences between men and women regarding foreign policy issues and management.[1] The discussion is based on a number of randomly selected exploratory interviews conducted with women in the DFA during 1998 and 2002. The fact that the interviews span a period of four years enabled the authors to assess the extent of change within the department over time. Nevertheless, conclusions must be regarded as being tentative, though this preliminary research does give an indication of the nature and existence of a diversity of views that relate to the maximizer-minimizer debate (see section 1). In the conclusion we measure the activities and achievements of the DFA against the characteristics of democratization as set out above and in the introduction to this book.

Concepts, Markets, and Debates

Over the past two decades feminism and the various feminist schools of thought, theorizing and scholarship moved from the category of *woman* to that of *gender*. This seemed a logical move—gender encompasses both sexes and would therefore allow for comparison, and furthermore it deals with the roles and functions "allocated" to female and male within different societies as social constructs. It therefore allows for the possibility of discrimination against and oppression of women to be transcended: if something is socially constructed, it can be changed. Furthermore, *gender* is viewed as being the "intellectually competent position" (Zalewski, 1998:849) and a more inclusive concept than the category *woman*. However, what remains the object of study, though not exclusively so, but nevertheless overwhelmingly, is the category *woman* and most references to *gender*, particularly when it comes to policy issues, are to women.

As far as studies of the position, status, and role of women in the developing world are concerned, it is women, and not necessarily gender (i.e., something that can be changed) that receive attention, despite constant reference to *gender* in policies and programs (e.g., *gender* machinery; *gender* mainstreaming). Moser's path-breaking work (1993) on gender and development to some extent "reified" gendered structures within developing societies, aiming at empowering the incumbents and recommending strategies to improve their positions *within* the category *gender*. The aim is therefore the emancipation of women—to overcome their subordination in order to fulfill their various roles and functions in a way commensurate with dignity and quality of life. It is for this reason that we use the category *woman* and mostly refer to *women* in this study. By this we do not artificially create a "collective identity" that assumes that "all women [are] the same and [are] oppressed in the same way" (see Prugl and Meyer, 1999:6).

In our analysis in subsequent sections in this chapter we are clear about the "category/categories" of women that are the objects of our discussion, focusing primarily on black women for the simple reason that they have historically been the most oppressed and excluded people in the country and that they, particularly rural African women, are among the poorest of the poor within South African society.

South African economic performance and indicators in the post-1994 era seem to point to the fact that markets are seriously failing large sections of the population. Despite high praise internationally for the government's economic policies (in essence a shift toward large-scale liberalization in line with the so-called Washington consensus), the country fails to attract a steady supply of direct foreign investment, experiencing speculation by currency traders that (among other reasons) resulted in a 33 percent drop in its currency between January and early December 2001 (see *The Economist*, 15 December 2001). Furthermore, what growth there is, is largely "jobless" and socioeconomic indices are deteriorating. So, for instance, the South African economy grew on average 2.1 percent between 1995 and 1998, but formal sector wage employment dropped by almost 2 percent during this time, as did gross domestic investment and savings and life expectancy (see SADC, 2000:100-105). The South African government's approach to these problems, particularly in view of discrepancies between gender groups, is to "mainstream gender", in other words to attempt to make the market more accessible to women and to provide them with more opportunities of economic activities, as will be shown in a later section. The question is of course whether in the face of the failure of markets to address poverty and other social ills, such policies do in fact benefit women and contribute to an improvement in their quality of life.

Two fundamentally divergent arguments are put forward by feminists for the inclusion of women in the foreign policy process. One argument holds that women as citizens have a right to participate on an equal footing with men in decisions affecting their future, women, do, after all, make up one half of the world's population. Whether women, once included, will differ from men in their policy positions is irrelevant (McGlen and Sarkees, 1993:5-6 and Miller, 1991:71). The other argument asserts that women hold different views of the international arena. Women would therefore exert a unique influence in foreign affairs if they were included in foreign policymaking. It is suggested that women hold a different conceptualization of power and adhere to a different system of morality (Phillips 1991:4). Stimpson (as cited in Snitow 1989:41) has labeled the two sides of this debate, the "minimizers" and "maximizers". According to Stimpson, the "minimizers are the feminists who undermine the category 'women' to minimize the meaning of sex difference" The minimizers' position, reflected, for instance, in the work of Radcliffe Richards (1990), is that the inclusion of women in the foreign policy arena is just a matter of basic human and democratic rights. Liberal values should therefore be applied more consistently to women. Hence, women are simply added to conventional accounts in order to improve accuracy by exposing and rectifying traditional male biases. In this argument, a male-as-norm point of view is assumed, and women are therefore just "added."

The maximizers, says Stimpson (cited in Snitow, 1989:41), "want to keep the category [woman] (or feel they can't do otherwise), but they want to change its meaning, to reclaim and further elaborate the social being woman, and to empower her." This position is reflected by those who are presently labeled moral feminists or women's value feminists (Snitow, 1989:48). One of the foundation works in this regard has been the work of Gilligan (1982)[2] who argues that women's psychosocialization results in an ethic of care or an ethic of responsibility, while men are socialized to adopt an ethic of justice or one of rights. Women's moral judgments will take others into account, while those of men will rely on universal standards of equality or fairness without concern for the individuals involved.

Empathy, intuition, compassion, relationality, and commitment (the willingness to make connections) are important epistemological values in the feminist ethics of care. Ruddick (1990:229-54) therefore argues that taking the ethics of care into foreign affairs may alter the direction of international relations. Due to women's roles as mothers and caregivers, for example, it will make them more cooperative and peaceful peacemakers. Scholars such as Tronto (1990 and 1995) and Sevenhuijsen (1998) have radicalized the 'ethics of care' notion into a universal sociopolitical practice. The controversy between the minimizers and maximizers is important to the subject matter of this chapter, as the inclusion of women in the foreign policy process has the potential to impact on foreign policy issues. Both viewpoints, though, support the argument that women should be included in the foreign policy process and in decision making at more than a token level.

Women and Women's Issues in the Department of Foreign Affairs post-1994

The extent to which women are (directly) part of the foreign policy environment in South Africa can be measured in at least four ways: the employment profile of the department, with special reference to the distribution of female officials (level and rank), mechanisms for ensuring the advancement of women and gender issues, foreign policy issue areas, and the perceptions of women within DFA with regard to their position and status. We pay brief attention to each of these aspects, though the separation is to some degree artificial.

The employment profile of DFA

Compared with the situation during the apartheid era (see Sadie, 1999), the employment profile of DFA has changed dramatically since 1995, with almost half the employees in the department being women. Employment practices at DFA are based on the *White Paper on the Transformation of the Public Service* (1995), (WPTPS), the *White Paper on Affirmative Action in the Public Service* (1998), and the *Employment Equity Bill*. As a baseline objective, the WPTPS required departments to endeavor to have 30 percent women as new recruits to middle and senior management echelons by 1999 (Casoo, 1 June 1998; RSA

Government Gazette No. 16838:55). However, it has not yet been possible to achieve this objective and gender imbalances still exist, particularly at senior management levels. In 2000 the (then) director-general of DFA commented that DFA was lagging behind most other government departments in this respect (Pityana, 2001:147). On the other hand, by 1999 African women dominated senior management positions (57 percent) against white women (39 percent) (see Table 5.1) indicating that as far as race is concerned, the department was making good progress in changing its demographic profile.[3]

Table 5.1: Employment profile—Gender distribution, June 1999

	Total	Male	Female
Senior Management*	147	124 (84 percent)	23 (16 percent)
Foreign Service officers**	503	340 (68 percent)	163 (32 percent)
Foreign missions (all levels)	493	289 (59 percent)	204 (41 percent)

Source: DFA, 1 October 1999.
* Senior management (Pretoria head office and foreign missions)—Director General, Deputy Director General, Chief Directors, Directors.
** Includes al ranks from Assistant Foreign Service Officer to Deputy Director (head office and foreign missions).

One way of increasing the number of women in middle and senior management positions is through training. The DFA has a Foreign Service Institute (FSI), established in 1994, that deals with, among other issues, the training of cadets in order to prepare them for external postings. The course can accommodate 25 people and certain requirements need to be fulfilled for admission, such as one-year experience on a desk and a 50 percent pass rate in both an international English language test and an evaluation by the human resources division on aspects such as management skills, interpersonal skills, and initiative. Although not a formal requirement, candidates with at least a bachelor's degree would also stand a better chance to be accepted, though a matriculation certificate is viewed as a minimum entry level requirement. Since 1994 a consistent trend has been that fewer women than men apply for admission to the course (Casoo, 1 June 1998), though prior to 2000 no special effort was made to encourage more women to apply. In 2001 the director-general relaxed the requirements in an effort to attract more women applicants. This was only marginally successful and the fact that the matriculation requirement was waved allowed trainees into the course who found it very difficult to keep up with the group (Ngcobo, 28 February 2002). In 2002 requirements were again strictly applied and only 15 out of 100 applicants complied. Eventually 21 trainees were admitted, eight of whom were female (Ngcobo, 28 February 2002).

There seems to be at least three reasons for the failure of the FSI in attracting female applicants. The first is probably a reflection of the fact that the majority of female employees in the department is still to be found in its lower echelons. A second reason is that there is such a small pool of highly educated senior (particularly black) women available to draw recruits from. According to Ngcobo (28 February 2002), there are heavy demands placed on these women exactly because of their small number and few of them can afford the time for attending months-long training courses. The third reason is to be found in the status of the FSI. The institute has experienced a high staff turnover ever since its inception and it is difficult therefore to ensure continuity and quality. In the minds of most people, working for DFA entails being a diplomat and few officials are willing to move into training. Ngcobo (28 February 2002) emphasized the fact that she had initially not wanted the position in the institute because "nobody wants to work here" and "women don't want to come to FSI." Furthermore, she commented that the general perception of FSI was that "standards were going down," that the FSI was isolated, that little importance was attached to it, and that because a moratorium on the appointment of top managers, it was difficult to attract strong leadership to the FSI. The fact that women are regularly appointed in positions at FSI (though not exclusively so) shows that "women are still sent to unimportant divisions."[4] These sentiments to some extent confirm those of the official who served in Ngcobo's position during the 1998 interview who, though enjoying the work at FSI, made it clear that she was first and foremost a diplomat and would therefore again apply for a foreign posting (Graham, 1 June 1998).

As far as women's issues in the training curriculum was concerned, both in 1998 (Graham, 1 June 1998) and in 2002 (Ngcobo, 28 February 2002), no specific courses were presented. Presenters are required to incorporate these issues in their courses and though an attempt is made to be gendersensitive in the selection of presenters, this is not always successful, as there are very few women academics and researchers involved in the field of international relations and foreign policy. At most therefore, one can conclude that attempts are made to recruit women into diplomatic training in the department (although there is no indication that this is given serious attention in terms of a long-term strategy), along the lines of the minimizers' position. Yet, there is no evidence of a maximizers' position which holds that the inclusion of more women and attention to women's issues could change the way in which the department functions. In fact, as was the case in 1998, women still wanted to be viewed as being equal to and not different from men—the "male as measure"-norm still exists.

Mechanisms for the Advancement of Women and Gender Concerns

Since 1994, the DFA has not only been involved in a number of issues related to women, but also committed itself to the promotion of gender issues. Examples of such involvement include the following:

- The allocation of money to promote women's rights: This involves identifying and getting information on human rights and women's rights instruments and working toward the promotion and protection of women's rights, both internationally and nationally (Ministry of Welfare and Population Development 1996:17). The money was used, amongst others, to send delegations to events abroad and in the region, focusing on women's issues (CEDA, undated: 8-1,2)
- The contribution of humanitarian aid, and the prioritization of the needs of women and children: Examples include assistance to Tanzanian flood victims in 1997 (Mazibuko, 1998), and humanitarian aid to women and children in Angola's most conflict-affected communities (Debatte van die Nasionale Vergadering 1996: Col.3357). Other "aid" projects that the DFA has funded include skills training for sustainable employment creation in Mozambique, Angola, Lesotho, and Swaziland (SA Communication Service 1996: 185) and to disabled women in Lesotho (Ajam, 1997:114).
- When South Africa was elected chair of the Southern African Development Community (SADC) in 1997 for a period of three years, the minister of foreign affairs at the time, Alfred Nzo, identified the meaningful integration of gender issues in the activities of SADC as one of the three areas that would receive priority (Debatte van die Algemene Vergadering 1997: Col 1946). It was during South Africa's tenure as chair of SADC that the organization's Council of Ministers approved the establishment of a policy framework that would allow for the mainstreaming of gender in all the activities of the organization. This framework consists of a Standing Committee of Ministers responsible for gender affairs, gender focal points at sectoral level, an Advisory Committee consisting of one government and one NGO representative from each member country, and a gender unit in the SADC secretariat (SADC, 1999).
- In the DFA's budget vote in May 1998, the minister of foreign affairs said that South Africa's assumption of the chair of the Non-Aligned Movement (NAM) in September would provide South Africa with the opportunity to strengthen, among others, the empowerment and development of women (Foreign Affairs Budget Vote press release 1998).

South Africa's National Machinery for Advancing Gender Equality[5] consists of a 'package' of structures. With regard to government departments, in particular, the primary goal of the National Machinery is to ensure that a gender perspective is integrated into all departmental work. In May 1996, cabinet approved the establishment of gender focal points in all government departments. In the DFA, eight gender representatives (males and females) from various branches were appointed to keep watch over gender issues (Mazibuko, 18 June 1998).

As to the working conditions and environment of female officials in the department, there was wide consultation within the department, after which a policy document on sexual harassment (DFA Reference SS9/21/P, 10 March 1997) was drafted that was subsequently endorsed by the departmental bargaining council (Casoo, 1 October 1999). The department also appointed a gender officer in October 1999, at director level attached to the director-general's office (1 October 1999). The gender officer's functions included

- ensuring that the department implements the National Gender Policy;
- reviewing all policy and planning accordingly; and
- co-coordinating the gender training and education of all staff.

The status of the gender representative (i.e., director) and the authority conferred upon the position, suggested, at the time of the appointment, that the Department was committed to the promotion of a gender perspective within the Department and its work. However, by early 2002, during follow-up interviews, it transpired that the gender officer had been removed and that the gender office was no longer operational. It was indicated though that this was only a temporary situation that was receiving attention within the department. One interviewee who insisted on remaining anonymous claimed that the gender officer "didn't do anything and was therefore moved to another section."[6] Ngcobo (28 February 2002) suggested that the reason for the apparent lack of concern about and interest in a gender focal point within the department could be ascribed to the fact that "gender issues are not taken seriously. . . . There are other things to fight for."

Foreign Policy Issue Areas

The fact that South Africa has a woman as its minister of foreign affairs is often taken to be proof of the "importance" of women to the present government and that it is serious in promoting women's equality and participation at all levels of decision making. However, history has shown that women in important and powerful positions do not necessarily act differently from men. The examples of the "famous few" (Pettman, 2001:583)—"strong leaders [such as Indira Gandhi, Golda Meir and Margaret Thatcher] who showed no hesitation to use force in international relations"—would suggest to some that women in power "behave like men." Such a viewpoint does not leave room for a maximizer's position— that women in decision making positions would act "differently" from men, being more peaceful, cooperative, etc., (see section one). Rather, it seems to confirm a belief that contemporary politics is masculinist, privileging values very different from those of care, responsibility, and peacemaking.

Yet, particularly with a view to South Africa's foreign policy, one can point to the fact that the country has, with the exception of its military intervention in Lesotho in 1998, consistently followed a policy of negotiation, mediation and the peaceful resolution of conflicts, as can be witnessed in its stance toward the conflict in the Great Lakes region and the civil war in Angola, and, though a completely different case, in Zimbabwe. It is doubtful, however, whether this approach to foreign policy can be ascribed to the fact that South Africa has a woman as minister of foreign affairs, as it reflects a central tenet of the country's foreign policy objectives as spelled out on numerous occasions since 1994.

DFI established a fully-fledged Women's Human Rights subdirectorate within the multilateral branch of the DFA. This subdirectorate focuses on human rights, particularly women's rights. The desk concentrates on external gender issues and advises multilateral missions on how to handle international conventions and agreements concerning women.[7] For example, inputs that have been made between 1997 and 1998 to multilateral organizations (through the missions), include the following

- violence against women;
- women and armed conflict;
- the girl child soldier;
- the resolution on *The Human Rights of Women*; and
- *Mainstreaming a Gender Perspective in Policies and Programmes of the United Nations* (Grobbelaar, 1 June 1998).

The Earth Summit to be held in South Africa in September 2002 has also to some extent brought the issue of women to the fore again. All position papers in preparation for the Summit, arranged into different issue areas, needed to take account of gender as a crosscutting issue. With DFA playing a leading role in the organization of the summit, it was to be expected (and was confirmed by a number of officials interviewed) that gender issues will once again receive serious attention, even if only in the run-up to the event.

Although the department's attention to gender issues and women's concerns seems commendable on paper, the reality is somewhat different. According to a written communication from an official from the department (Conradie, 14 February 2002), there is only one official responsible for women's human rights. She is responsible for organizations such as the UNCHR, the Third Committee of the U.N. General Assembly, ECOSOC, the Commission on the Status of Women, the African Commission on Human and People's Rights, CEDAW, and a whole range of international instruments aimed at promoting women's human rights. The huge brief of this official is not necessarily an indication of neglect of women's issues, but can also, at least partly, be ascribed to the fact that DFA is struggling to make ends meet. In his budget vote address to Parliament in

1999, former minister of foreign affairs, the late Mr. Nzo, pointed out that between 1997 and 1999 the department's budget had declined by 18 percent, though demands on the department were increasing and the bulk of its expenditure was in foreign currency (1999:225). It is not only women's issues and gender relations that are 'neglected'; budgetary constraints apply to the whole spectrum of the country's formal external relations.

Perceptions of Women within DFA Regarding Their Status and Role

Despite the entrenchment of gender equality in the country's Constitution, legal commitments made by the government to ensure gender equality, and the introduction of various measures to advance women's representation and ensure future gender-sensitive policies, women, by 1998, seemed to experience the DFA still as being very much an "old boys' club" (Mazibuko, 18 June 1998). Although it was acknowledged that the conduct/behavior of men had changed (due to legal requirements) in respect of issues such as the appointment of women in the diplomatic service and equal treatment (in a very general sense), the women who were interviewed in 1998 expressed a very strong view that stereotypical attitudes toward women had not changed. Remarks in this regard ranged from "mentally, men are still paternalistic" to "women cannot rise above the image of a secretary." Stereotypical views of women, however, can have serious implications for the type of issues "suitable" for women to handle in the foreign service. It has been suggested that, in some foreign missions, women are assigned to handle the sociocultural relations involving "youth choirs, art exhibitions and orphanages," in a manner of speaking. Some women regard such expectations as "subtle discrimination." Interviews conducted in 2002 largely confirmed the sentiments expressed by women during the 1998 interviews.

This stereotyping of women's gender roles may also be exacerbated by assigning the 'soft' issues in politics and management, such as poverty and other humanitarian issues, rather than "hard" issues like conflict and nuclear arms issues to women, as women are perceived to be 'better equipped' than men to handle these soft issues. The experience of Ngcobo (28 February 2002) in the FSI, referred to in an earlier subsection, still seems to prevail: women are appointed to what is perceived to be "less important" positions and to take care of "soft issues," including training. Care should be taken, however, not to confuse this stereotyping of gender roles in the workplace with the maximizer's view of the existence of a "women's perspective." Maximizers do not "claim" certain policy issues as the domain of women; rather, they emphasize women's *different* perspective, which can be incorporated in a broad range of policy issues.

Research on the presence or absence of a gender gap in attitudes regarding foreign policy issues has yielded mixed results. Some studies have revealed that gender is among the weakest correlates of foreign policy beliefs (Holsti and Rosenau 1981) and Wittkopf (1981), while others contradict these findings (see for example, Fite et al. 1990). In addition, research that focuses primarily on attitudes toward the use of force as an instrument of foreign policy has generally found a significant gender gap (Jensen 1987), while statistically significant differences between men and women on policy attitudes regarding, for example, solidarity with oppressed people in developing countries, have also been found (Togeby, 1994).

Although specific attitudes toward general foreign policy issues were not tested in the interviews, the question of a possible gender gap in foreign policy issues was addressed. Women emphatically denied the existence of any difference between them and their male colleagues on policy issues. Although it was admitted that many foreign issues have acquired gender-specific components, such as human rights and war and peace, they emphasized that their perspectives on such issues were not different from those of men. This could very well be the case if it is taken into consideration that their exposure to foreign issues tends to be similar due to, for example, the same professional working environment and training. However, the women's adamant insistence that there is no difference between them and their male colleagues over foreign policy issues seems to suggest instead that they, perhaps due to their subordinate position in the DFA under apartheid (which some of the women who were interviewed experienced) and in South African society in general, are so intent on providing proof of their equality with men, that they would not even contemplate the suggestion or acknowledge the fact that they may indeed hold different views on certain issues.

The liberal feminists' commitment to a recognition of the rights of women and equality with men therefore seems to be popular and influential. As Andrea Nye (1988:5) postulates, it is often the first form of feminism that women encounter: "When a woman in the United States or Western Europe first identifies herself as a feminist, it is often as a liberal feminist, asserting her claim to the equal rights and freedoms guaranteed to each individual in democratic society." This certainly seems to be the attitude among those women interviewed—particularly since women's rights have not been acknowledged in South Africa until fairly recently. Whelehan (1995:42) adds that such liberal feminists may rarely define themselves as feminists, although they support and fight for women's equality in the workplace and in law. Furthermore, the notion also exists that pressure to conform to male norms seems to be the greatest in situations where the proportion of women is small—which is indeed the case in the higher echelons of the department, as has been pointed out.

The women who were interviewed expressed the view that women should be more involved in issues such as peacekeeping, human rights, and conflict resolution, but the reasons for wanting greater input are not clear: is it because of the "special" contribution they can make, or are these types of issues just more associated with women's traditional, stereotyped, gendered roles? On the other hand, these issues clearly impact either directly or indirectly on the lives of women (who constitute more than half of the world's population). It can therefore be argued that it is entirely fitting that women participate in decisions that affect them. In addition, these issues are currently high on the agenda of many states and international organizations and women's exclusion would perpetuate male dominance in international relations. This quest, moreover, complies with section five of the *Beijing Platform of Action* which requires governments to strengthen and increase women's role in policy formulation around peacekeeping matters. These issues have also been emphasized as important components of South Africa's foreign policy. In his budget vote in Parliament on 7 May 1998, the minister of foreign affairs reiterated the view that the prevention of conflict and the promotion of peace, as well as the promotion of human rights, among others, are basic principles in South Africa's foreign policy relations.

Furthermore, women in the DFA do not seem to feel that being female has limited their ability to influence foreign policy issues. In many instances (according to those interviewed), their inputs on various policy issues have been incorporated in recommendations. Their only complaint was their limited representation or sometimes exclusion from many areas of foreign policy, foreign delegations, and regional summits. An example was the fact that only one woman from the DFA participated in the interdepartmental working sessions on drafting a White Paper on South Africa's role in peacekeeping. As mentioned earlier, this is also one of the most important areas in which, according to the maximizers, women can make a "special" contribution.

A striking difference that was found between responses from women interviewed in 1998 and those interviewed in 2002 relates to a type of generation gap that has become apparent. The initial intake of women into DFA after 1994 consisted in large measure of those who had been active in the liberation struggle. They joined a small group of white female officials who had suffered discrimination during the apartheid era. Together, these women were intent on changing the culture of the department and to improve the position of women. They were also committed to women's issues and women's rights in particular, exhibiting a strong concern with the idea of change, improvement, and service. However, this has changed with the changing profile of new women entering the Foreign Service. There seemed to be a general consensus that, as one interviewee expressed it, "women in power are not interested in women's issues and women" (Ngcobo, 28 February 2002), but that they were first and foremost career oriented and concerned with their own progress and position within the department,[8] not hesitating to "compete with each other in stead of helping each other."

This trend of women becoming more career oriented and ambitious, rather than exhibiting a concern with the idea of "service" and a commitment to the ideals and principles of the woman's movement and the liberation struggle, would seem to point at most to a version of the minimizers' position: women are equal to men, deserve to be treated like them and *are*, in fact, like men. This attitude can be explained by the fact that a younger generation of women has been educated in a different way, that they do not share the experience and ideals of an older generation who participated in the antiapartheid struggle, and that for them careers in the foreign service is largely just that—careers in a field that they are interested in. In a broader sense, though, one can also make a different kind of sense of this finding: it accords with the prevailing global hegemony of hypercapitalism and its fierce individualism. This is what Gill (1995:67) refers to as a "crass consumerist materialism, which lies at the heart of the neo-liberal discourse."

Conclusion

Excluded from the foreign policy process for generations, women in South Africa have begun to make slow progress in entering the domain of international relations since 1994. Democratization in South Africa and the subsequent embodiment in the Constitution of a firm commitment to ensure equality between women and men, as well as the measures taken to achieve gender equality in the public service, paved the way for greater participation by women in the foreign policy-making process, particularly in the DFA.

An interesting and rather contradictory picture of DFA emerges from this study. On the one hand, and in line with the approach of the Mbeki presidency, there is an increase in opportunities for women to participate in decision making and implementation. To this end the ideal has become a principle enshrined in the Constitution and other legislation. On the other hand, the DFA does not seem to succeed in building the capacity of its female officials in order to turn opportunity into reality. The lack of attention and status of the FSI inhibits the potential of this institution to mainstream gender. Furthermore, an overall lack in capacity in terms of a shortage of staff and other resources precludes the mainstreaming of gender or of serious attention being paid to use foreign policy to improve the situation of women in instances where such ideals may exist.

In the final instance, though, what is clear is that notwithstanding an increase in opportunities for women and the growing number of women worldwide who participate in decision making and implementation, the numbers of the poor, particularly women, are increasing. The idea of gender mainstreaming can therefore not be confined to national and international attempts and efforts, but should be globalized in order to impact on the negative effect of economic globalization on the marginalized and excluded.

Notes

1.   For an overview of the position of women within DFA during the apartheid era, see Sadie, Y, 1999, 'Women in foreign relations in South Africa: an exploratory analysis', *Journal of Public Administration*, 34 (3), September.

2.   See also the work of other "difference" feminists, such as Ruddick (1990), Elshtain (1992), Kittay and Meyers (1987) and Elshtain and Tobias (1990).

3.   Despite numerous attempts made by the authors to obtain the 2001 employment profile of DFA, this was impossible. We therefore had to use the 1999 figures. It may be that the profile has changed since then, but based on interviews conducted during early 2002 we have no reason to believe that any dramatic shift has taken place in either direction, i.e., large increases/decreases in the number of female officials employed or women in senior management positions.

4.   Ngcobo's views were echoed by another former female FSI training officer, Ms. Y. Spies (6 March 2002).

5.   This complies with the Beijing Platform of Action (1995) that requires national machineries to promote the advancement of women.

6.   During a Gender Summer School organized by the Center for Gender Studies at the University of Pretoria in January 2002, the issue of gender focal points within government departments (national and provincial) and the role and function of gender officers regularly came to the fore during discussions (both formal and informal). The majority of young (exclusively) black women in these positions complained that they "didn't know what to do," that they were not taken seriously, and that there were hardly any resources available to them in order to pay attention to the objective of mainstreaming gender affairs.

7.   In formulating viewpoints, inputs from, for example, the Commission on Gender Equality are requested.

8.   In an interview with the gender officer of the Department of Trade and Industry, the same sentiments were expressed regarding young professional women entering the service of "they have other priorities" from those of the women who come from a "struggle background" (Matiwana, 28 February 2002).

Chapter 6

Labor, Social Movements, and South Africa's Foreign Economic Policy

Patrick Bond

1. Introduction

South African state elites—primarily President Thabo Mbeki, Finance Minister Trevor Manuel, and Trade and Industry Minister Alec Erwin, backed by African National Congress (ANC) ideologues like Kgalema Motlanthe and Joel Netshitenzhe—have been contesting the terrain of international political economy and defending their version of "globalization" with increasing vigor since the late 1990s. But important groups in civil society are frustrated. For at the time of writing (early 2002), the elites' claims of success have been halting and in crucial regards nonexistent: reform of the World Trade Organization (WTO); World Bank and International Monetary Fund (IMF); access to anti-retroviral drugs on a generic-production basis; universal support for debt cancellation; environmental stewardship at the global scale; and requisite attention to Africa's social, economic, and political needs through the *New Partnership for Africa's Development*.

To understand why progress has been lacking, a sufficiently nuanced reading of the balance of forces requires examination of at least five major currents of argumentation and activism, as differentiated below. From those currents follow different analyses, strategies, tactics, and alliances. By examining both ideological and material positions related to global economic crisis management, we can identify three of these five tendencies, all located in Washington, which aim to bolster the architecture in the interests of the North. In contrast, two other tendencies are much more critical of the status quo, even though they differ about "fixing" or "nixing" the international financial, investment, and trade system. The five positions, from left to right can be labeled, (a) Global Justice

Movements; (b) Third World Nationalism; (c) the Post-Washington Consensus.; (d) the Washington Consensus; and (e) the Resurgent Rightwing (see Table 6.1).

The South African government lines up in the middle three, depending upon circumstances. Indeed, although the philosophical positions associated with the five currents appear ever more clearly delineated, the balance of these forces shifts constantly, with no durable alliances in sight (section two). The unsatisfying status of crisis management, in relation to the trembling architecture of the international economy, was reflected in the inputs and outputs of the November 2001 WTO summit in Doha, Qatar. Notwithstanding the infamous collapse of the Seattle WTO summit in December 1999 due to a refusal to offer consensus by African countries led by Zimbabwe, the trend appears to be one of Third World nationalist conciliation (section three). A key factor has been the comprador roles of Mbeki, and Erwin (section four).

Once the fluid nature of Pretoria's strategy is considered, and the record of failure exposed, this chapter then focuses on differences within key South African civil society forces, especially the Congress of South African Trade Unions and what I will term the independent left. In at least one crucial area—international trade—divisions have been growing to an untenable extent, thereby muting the possibility of a strong progressive backlash to the elites' plans (section five). Reconciliation within the global justice movements will probably only occur through a formula which breaks down global-scale institutions and resurrects national and regional alliances aiming first and foremost at establishing sufficient sovereignty to achieve social justice at home, before again going global when the balance of forces is more amenable (section six).

Table 6.1 Five reactions to the global crisis
an international snapshot (~2002) highlighting South African locations[1]

	Main arguments	Key institutions	Key proponents*
Global Justice Movements	Against globalization of *capital* (not *people*), and for fair (not free) trade, debt cancellation, and a generous social wage	Social/labor movements; environmental advocacy groups; radical activist networks; Regional and national progressive coalitions; Leftwing think tanks; **Treatment Action Campaign, Jubilee South Africa, Cosatu?**	*Achmat*, Amin, *Ashley*, Bello, Bendana, Bordieu, Bove, *Brutus*, Chalmers, Chomsky, Danaher, *Dor*, Galeano, *Gabriel*, George, *Giyosi*, Kagarlitsky, *Keet*, Khor, Klein, Lula, Maathai, *Madisha*, Marcos, *Meer*, Nader, *Ndungane*, Negri, *Ngwane*, Njehu, *Nzimande*, Patkar, *Pheko*, Pilger, *Setshedi*, Shiva, *Tsele*, *Vavi*
Third World Nationalism	For more global integration: i.e., join (not change) the system, but on fairer terms (debt relief, more market access)	Self-selecting Third World governments: Algeria, Argentina, Brazil, China, Cuba, Egypt, Haiti, India, Malaysia, Mexico, Pakistan, Russia, Venezuela, Zimbabwe, and *sometimes South Africa*	Aristide, Castro, Chavez, Mahathir, *Mbeki?*, *Motlanthe*, *Netshitenzhe?*, Mugabe, Obasanjo, Putin
Post-Wash. Consensus	Reform the "imperfect markets" and add 'sustainable development' to neoliberal framework	Most United Nations agencies; International Confederation of Free Trade Unions, governments of France, Japan, and **sometimes South Africa**	Annan, Jospin, *Erwin?*, Jordan, Krugman, *Manuel?*, *Mbeki?*, *Mboweni?*, *Netshitenzhe?*, *Ramos?*, Sachs, Schroeder?, Soros, Stiglitz, Sweeney
Washington Consensus	Slightly adjust the status quo (transparency, supervision, & regulation) and establish bale-out mechanisms to improve stability	US agencies (Treasury, Federal Reserve, USAID), World Bank, IMF, WTO, World Economic Forum, Council on Foreign Relations, centrist Washington think tanks, British and German governments, and *sometimes South Africa*	*Abedian*, *Barrell*, *Bernstein*, Blair, Brown, *Bruce*, Bush?, *Erwin?*, Greenspan, Koehler, *Leon*, *Manuel?*, *Mbeki?*, *Mboweni?*, *Mills*, Moore, O'Neill?, *Ramos?*, *Roodt*, Wolfensohn
Resurgent Rightwing	Restore U.S. isolationism, punish banks' mistakes, and reverse the globalization of people	Populist & libertarian wings of Republican Party, American Enterprise Institute, Cato Institute, Manhattan Institute, Heritage Foundation	Buchanan, Bush?, DeLay Haider, Helms, le Pen, Lott, *Parker*

* South African proponents in boldface.

2. Can Washington Reform?

In most rhetoric, the overriding objectives of those involved in international political-economic reform are the same, namely to reverse skyrocketing income inequality, deep-rooted racial and gender oppressions, global warming and planetary-scale ecological destruction, the spread of AIDS and other public health crises, the burden of Third World debt, worsening terms of trade for the South, currency raids by financial speculators, capital flight, and other structured forms of power and powerlessness. But there are any number of ways to tackle these problems, and the central question is, which ideologies, analyses, alliances, strategies, and tactics are genuinely capable of reversing the world's worsening ills?

The premise of Mbeki and his Pretoria colleagues is that institutions at the commanding heights of the world economy can be reformed to these ends, if an adequate grouping of countries and visionary leaders is assembled. Part of the premise depends upon the notion that the major institutions have already begun the process, under thoughtful leaders like World Bank president James Wolfenson. Have the Bank and IMF made a turn toward "pro-poor" strategies following the September 1999 announcement that Poverty Reduction Strategy Programs would replace structural adjustment? And can the WTO establish a 'development round'—as promised at the November 2001 Doha summit—to change the rules of global trade in the interests of the poorest countries?

Table 6.1 provides a rough political mapping of the balance of forces required to answer such questions. By early 2002, the bloc of neoliberal international elite managers appeared to be holding the Washington Consensus line, notwithstanding the temptation of many on the far right—like George W. Bush—to apply proto-fascist formulae to both geopolitics and economics. The US economy had begun a recession well before the September 11 catastrophe, with potentially devastating consequences for those exporters who had grown dependent upon American hedonistic consumption norms.

Helping to bolster the sole superpower's claim to economic predominance was ally Tony Blair and his chancellor of the exchequer, Gordon Brown. The Federal Reserve Board's chairperson, Alan Greenspan, lowered interest rates urgently, while U.S. treasury secretary Paul O'Neill gave rich individuals and large corporations huge tax cuts to keep these individuals happy and keep them spending. The imposition of tariffs on steel was one indicator of the U.S. state's hypocrisy in pushing "free" trade rules on everyone else, but not itself. The leaders of the Bank, IMF and WTO—James Wolfenson, Horst Koehler, and Michael Moore—maintained their devotion to corporate and banking power, and often specifically US economic interests. Neoliberal apologists appeared generally unmoved by the unfolding economic crisis.[2]

Genuine reform under the leadership of this crew appeared impossible. In the wake of the September 1999 firing of Bank chief economist Joseph Stiglitz, it is hard to take seriously any notion that the Bretton Woods Institutions can make fundamental changes from within. At that point, two years before he won the Nobel Prize in economics, Stiglitz had criticized IMF structural adjustment policies and crisis management in East Asia and Russia. Bill Clinton's treasury secretary, Lawrence Summers, immediately met with James Wolfenson over the latter's desire for a second five-year term, and soon thereafter Stiglitz was dismissed "with a fig leaf," in the words of Jagdish Bhagwati: "a sorry episode." Insiders say that Summers insisted that Stiglitz simply had to leave if the U.S. was to support the Wolfenson reappointment.[3]

The short-lived "post-Washington Consensus" philosophy that Stiglitz introduced was not particularly radical, as it simply posed the need for state intervention in the event of market failure and for more attention to "sustainable development" goals like equity and environmental protection. But the 2001 Nobel award he shared with two other U.S. economists recognized Stiglitz's "information-theoretic" approach to markets, which does fundamentally undermine the neoliberal faith in self-correction, deregulation, and growth.[4] While not a movement builder himself, Stiglitz won a following from other economists who pushed slightly heterodox viewpoints, but entirely from within the general framework of neoliberalism.[5] And there were operational reformers aware of wide-scale market failure. Financier/philanthropist George Soros, at least one national G-7 leader—France's Lionel Jospin[6]—and U.N. secretary-general Kofi Annan all suggested imposition of a "Tobin Tax" on international financial transactions.[7] Bill Jordan of the International Confederation of Free Trade Unions was extremely active, joined by U.S. trade union leader John Sweeney, in pushing for labour-related reforms of the World Trade Organization, as we see below.[8]

Changing the modus operandi of Washington's control system was not merely an abstract theoretical problem. When Argentina defaulted on its foreign debt in late 2001, in the wake of high-profile national bankruptcies in Ecuador (2000) and Russia (1998), even a core neoliberal press outlet, the *Washington Post*, endorsed a bankruptcy option in lieu of squeezing the masses to the point of full-fledged revolution:

> Here is a country that has received two rescue packages in the past year from the IMF, yet still finds itself in a desperate state. The government has already forced domestic creditors to accept lower interest payments and placed a semi-freeze on bank deposits. For Argentina's people, an explicit default on the country's debts would be better than further efforts to stave off the inevitable with tax hikes, which is what the government now suggests.[9]

Just as worrisome to South Africa, a currency crisis emerged when the ANC's allegedly "sound macroeconomic policy" was reduced to rubble during 2000-1: the value of a rand slipped by 60 percent (from US$0.17 to US$0.07, before slightly rebounding to US$0.095) due to both short-term speculation and to outflows of profits and dividends to the new London headquarters of Anglo American Corporation, Old Mutual, South African Breweries, Gencor/Billiton, and Didata. Restoring exchange controls against the unprecedented capital flight, so as to deter rich white people from expatriating their apartheid-era wealth from the New South Africa, proved just too trying a challenge for Mbeki, as a function of the prevailing ideology and power relations discussed below.

The Far Right is absent, for all practical purposes, in South Africa. But in Washington, the resurgent conservatives had gained great momentum when the Supreme Court selected Bush as U.S. president in December 2000. The five justices who outvoted the citizens of Florida and the majority of U.S. voters in that election were all chosen by the new president's father a decade earlier. Bush had a right-wing flank of his own to worry about, led by commentator and perpetual candidate Patrick Buchanan, and a powerful reactionary Republican bloc in the US Congress centered around Tom DeLay, Jesse Helms, and Trent Lott—who all mainly saw the World Bank and IMF as agencies behind a socialist plot to promote cheeky Third World leaders like Robert Mugabe. Internationally, Jorg Haider in Austria and Jean-Marie le Pen in France mirrored this bizarre, reactionary tendency. By 2001, the Far Right was dangerously resurgent, along with the military-industrial complex, thanks to the lunatic-fundamentalist Islamic group Al-Qaeda which hijacked four airplanes on September 11. While on the surface it first appeared as a blow to official U.S. morale, the terrorist attacks soon provided justification for establishing something akin to a police state, which Bush and his big business allies began to hastily construct.[10]

Aside from Mbeki, what were Third World rulers up to at this stage? As Table 6.1 suggests, there were a few nationalist leaders—Jean-Bertrand Aristide, Fidel Castro, and Hugo Chavez in the Caribbean corner of Haiti, Cuba, and Venezuela, respectively—who regularly spoke from the Left. Most notably, perhaps, Malaysian Prime Minister Mahathir Mohamed—an anti-Semitic authoritarian—showed in 1998 that capital controls could be implemented in a major emerging market without the threat of U.S. military intervention. Nigeria's Olusegun Obasanjo made some antisystemic sounds as head of the Group of 77 developing nations and Vladimir Putin appeared anxious to break from the lock step of Russian neoliberalism. Some of the world's most indignant nationalists and anti-imperialist rhetoricians were to be found in Harare, as Robert Mugabe attempted to reinvigorate an exhausted nationalism.[11]

But after adding up a variety of small-scale nationalist projects, the sum is not yet sufficiently impressive at the global scale to merit much attention. The hope that India would lead a Third World revolt against the World Trade Organization—following Zimbabwe's lead in Seattle—was dashed in Doha, Qatar in November 2001.[12] As Washington's economic crisis management evolved into a broader geopolitical "coalition against terrorism," nothing the nationalists tried in the run-up to Doha appeared to work, as we see below. Their most important spokespeople were led, by late 2001, to merely concede the logic and power of Washington's dictates.

Who, then, can catalyze substantial social change in an era of disempowered states, extreme international economic chaos, and additional military-induced suffering? Little hope appeared from those immediately to the left of Washington: the existing set of national rulers and nationalist leaders, conscientious establishment intellectuals and philanthropists, or international agencies. Instead, the row in

Table 6.1 of greatest interest is the global justice movements, whose dynamics are addressed in more detail below. First, however, a reflection of the weakness of the Third World nationalist camp in relation to the combined power of international corporate power, the U.S., and European Union, and comprador trade negotiators like Alec Erwin, can be found in the Doha WTO negotiations in November 2001.

3. A Doha Diversion

Less than two months after the September 11 terrorist attacks, the United States government and its leading corporations were willing to bend over backwards, stylistically, to maintain the pretense of international cooperation. But with respect to content, the Doha agreement amplified the free-trade agenda that had generated such intense unevenness, inequality, ecological destruction, and women's suffering over the previous decades.

Harare-based sociologist Raj Patel explains that the Doha agreement, which adds many new areas of trade and investment liberalization, will have the effect of bullying the world's weakest countries even more:

> The civil services in the poorest countries have been pared to the bone by World Bank structural adjustment policies. Many cannot afford to have even one delegate in Geneva to monitor, negotiate and resist these organizations. Negotiating several issues at once is well beyond the means of most poor countries. The mere demand that these wrecked bureaucracies 'negotiate' a cluster of new issues effectively guarantees their detonation.
>
> Why, then, did developing countries agree to sign? Part of the reason lies in the magic of advertising. The new round hasn't been called a round. Instead what we have is a new brand round, the "Doha Development Agenda." This rebranding idea is one with which we are all familiar: you tinker with the name, but nothing else, in order to make punters believe that you've actually improved things. It has worked for corporate giants, it works for the U.S. government. . . .
>
> In Seattle, Southern governments refused to sign a declaration not because they opposed the entrenchment of neoliberalism and the elite class bias that comes with it, but because they had been roughly treated. Delegates had not been able to enter meetings, and the U.S. negotiating team had rubbed Southern inferiority in their faces. In other words, the signing of the Doha Development Agenda is only a mystery if one thinks that developing country governments have recently taken a principled stand against neoliberalism. They haven't. The refusal to sign at Seattle was not about indignation at neoliberalism, but about the failure to treat elites as they are accustomed.
>
> In Doha, by contrast, United States Trade Representative Robert Zoellick was a dealer, a broker of accord, a merchant of consensus. This new-found humility evidently pushed the buttons of the developing country elite. So they signed. This should come as no surprise. These are the elites that milk and pimp the majority of people in their countries. It's hard to see why putting them in five-star accommodation and making them feel important might make them less venal.[13]

Patel is correct: most developing country governments hadn't taken a principled stand against neoliberalism. And yet, excepting the official South African delegation, their officials grappled with the issues and repeatedly pointed out the obvious: neoliberalism was killing their constituents.

For example, Zimbabwe continued as coordinator of the Africa Group delegation to Doha, and retained alliances with other Third World nationalist regimes. In the run-up to the ministerial summit, the Africa Group (2001) proposed that "patenting of life forms would be prohibited" and that the Trade in Intellectual Property agreement should not "prevent Members from taking measures to protect public health." Thanks in large part to consistent grassroots activist pressure, and the example of the South African struggle against pharmaceutical corporations, the latter demand was, at least, conceded by the North. However, Patel's Doha article again provides a reality check:

> It turns out that the declaration merely clarifies existing provisions in the WTO patents regime, in which public health criteria can already be used to abrogate patent rights. There's nothing new in the Doha declaration to worry the pharmaceutical companies, as the U.S. Pharmaceutical corporate lobby have recently confirmed. In fact, the WTO's rules are so powerful that even rich countries are wary of them. Nothing else explains the Canadian government's swift about-face on the compulsory licensing of Cipro [the antidote to anthrax]. If the Canadians are afraid compulsorily to license because of the precedent this will set for the pharmaceutical industry, it's unlikely that small developing countries stand much of a chance. Only Brazil has moved ahead with a compulsory licensing initiative, despite U.S. threats of legal action. To have the rich countries affirm what was written into an already unjust law is scant victory.

Nationalists comprising the "Like-Minded Group"—the Dominican Republic, Egypt, India, Indonesia, Pakistan, Uganda, and Zimbabwe—plus new friends Cuba, Haiti, India, Kenya, Peru, and Venezuela (2001), offered an eloquent critique of the WTO services agreement that is worth excerpting at length. It appears a rare case of Third World officials speaking truth to power:

> Developing countries have clearly not received the benefits they thought they would. Developed countries continue to be heavily regulated in the form of maintaining trade barriers especially in several sectors of interest to developing countries. For example, technical standards and licensing in certain professional services, is used to effectively restrict entry by developing countries into the industry. . . .
> The regulatory initiatives taken by developing countries would already seem to be having a negative impact on them since many developing countries have adopted regulations that have turned out to be more suited to the needs and level of development of services industries of the developed countries. . . .
> There is the danger that re-regulation as promoted in Article VI could in fact become deregulation [and that this] could be fundamentally incompatible with the requirement or the desire of many governments to provide basic public

services for their people, especially since certain sections of their population may not be able to afford to pay market prices for these services. . . .

Only a few large firms from developed countries and a number of small players dominate many services markets. The top 20 service exporters are mainly from developed countries. . . .

Liberalization under these circumstances of unequal competition has aggravated the alarming divide in supply capacity between developed and developing countries. . . .

Developing countries' small suppliers are also disadvantaged in other ways, such as through discriminatory access to information channels and distribution networks. . . .

Under conditions of liberalization, privatization of services could very easily happen since foreign corporations which are more competitive are likely to enter the new market and take over from the local company. This could have consequences on access to basic services for those who may not be able to afford these commercial prices of services.

In addition, investments, when they come in, have often not been in sectors that could most benefit the host countries. . . .

For the rural sectors in many developing countries, these basic services may not even be provided by the state, but by communities and local authorities which use currently common resources, such as water, minerals, and fuels. . . .

Through marketization, previously available public goods are put out of reach of many when these are commodified in the process of privatization. The experience of several developing countries with structural adjustment already shows that large segments of the population are having serious difficulties gaining access to basic commodities and services at prices they can afford.

But again, as Patel observed, the fine-sounding rhetoric was abandoned under pressure in the final hours. Likewise, a more specific fight picked and lost in Doha—by the Like-Minded Group countries noted above, and El Salvador, Honduras, Nicaragua, Nigeria, Senegal, and Sri Lanka—concerned agriculture:

These talks remain dominated by the EU on the one hand, and the U.S. and Cairns group of exporting countries on the other. As a result, these negotiations have ignored developing country concerns about the problems our small subsistence farmers are facing. . . . Since before Seattle, we have been pushing for a "Development Box" to be included in the Agriculture Agreement, but our proposal has been sidelined. The WTO is supposed to ensure equity in trade, but the present agricultural trading system in practice legitimizes the inequities, for instance, by allowing the dumping of agricultural products from the North. (Friends of the Development Box, 2001)

The Third World bowed to its knees on this occasion, with Pretoria apparently playing the role of "kneepad." South Africa's proliberalization strategy was engineered not only through Mbeki's *New Partnership for Africa's Development* (*NEPAD*), but also through the machinations of Erwin. We can consider each influence in turn.

4. Pretoria's Strategy

An allegedly home-grown, African socioeconomic strategy emerged in 2000-01: the *Millennium Africa Recovery Plan* (with the acronym *MAP*, from mid-2000 to mid-2001); a *New African Initiative* (*NAI*, from July-October 2001); and finally *NEPAD*, launched in Abuja, Nigeria by several African heads of state in October 2001. These different names referred to the same plan, but for various reasons the Abuja meeting settled on *NEPAD*. The timing was auspicious because in the wake of September 11, a general alarm was raised that economic recession and dwindling growth in world trade would marginalize Africa yet further (Goldin and Gelb, 2001). The European Union quickly endorsed *NEPAD*. The Doha summit echoed with the alleged urgency for Africa to get more access to international markets, especially in agriculture. Notwithstanding his continuing AIDS-policy disasters, Thabo Mbeki was seen as Africa's most legitimate, self-confident, and fundamentally pro-Western leader, and a great ally in fending off both Muslim terrorists and cheeky idealists protesting in the North's streets outside elite meetings, allegedly on behalf of Africa.

From the late 1990s, Mbeki embarked upon an "African Renaissance" branding exercise with poignant poetics. The contentless form was somewhat remedied in the secretive *Millennium Africa Recovery Plan*, whose PowerPoint skeleton was unveiled to select elites in 2000, during Mbeki's meetings with Bill Clinton in May, the Okinawa G-8 in July, the U.N. Millennium Summit in September, and a subsequent European Union gathering in Portugal. The skeleton was fleshed out in November 2000 with the assistance of several economists and was immediately ratified during a special South African visit by World Bank president James Wolfenson "at an undisclosed location," due presumably to fears of the disruptive protests which had soured a Johannesburg trip by new IMF czar Horst Koehler a few months earlier.

Thanks to work by a coauthor of South Africa's own disastrous 1996 home-grown structural adjustment program (Stephen Gelb), the content of the 60-page working document was becoming clearer: more privatization, especially of infrastructure (no matter its failure especially in South Africa); more insertion of Africa into the world economy (in spite of fast-declining terms of trade); more multiparty elections (typically, though, between variants of neoliberal parties, as in the U.S.) as a veil for the lack of thoroughgoing participatory democracy; grand visions of information and communications technology (hopelessly unrealistic considering the lack of simple reliable electricity across the continent); and a self-mandate for peace-keeping (which South Africa has subsequently taken for its soldiers stationed in the Democratic Republic of the Congo and Burundi).

By this stage, Mbeki had managed to sign on as partners two additional rulers from the crucial West and North of the continent: Abdelaziz Bouteflika and Olusegun Obasanjo from Nigeria. Unfortunately, both continued to face mass popular protests and widespread civil/military/religious bloodshed at home, diminishing their utility as model African leaders. Later, to his credit,

Obasanjo led a surprise revolt against Mbeki's capitulation to Northern pressure at the World Conference Against Racism in September 2001, when he helped generate a split between EU and African countries over reparations due the continent for slavery and colonialism. Tellingly, even loose talk of reparations was not found in *NEPAD*, and the South African host delegation was furious at Obasanjo's outburst because it nearly scuppered a final conference resolution.

But that incident aside, 2001 was a successful year for selling *NEPAD*. Another pro-Western ruler with a deplorable recent human rights record, Tanzania's Benjamin Mkapa, joined the New Africa leadership group in January 2001 in Davos, Switzerland. There, Mbeki gave the world's leading capitalists and state elites a briefing, which was very poorly attended. A few days later, an effort was made in Mali to sell West Africans to the plan, with on-the-spot cheerleading by Wolfenson and Koehler. The July 2001 meeting of the African Union in Lusaka provided the opportunity for a continent-wide leadership endorsement, once Mbeki's plan was merged with an infrastructure-heavy initiative—the "Omega Plan"—offered by the neoliberal Senegalese president, Abdoulaye Wade, to become the New African Initiative. A few days later, the Genoa G-8 summit offered soothing encouragement. With 300,000 protesters outside the conference accusing the world's main political leaders of running a destructive, elitist club, Mbeki was a useful adornment.

Likewise, Mbeki's October visits to Japan and Brussels confirmed his elite popularity, perhaps because there was no apparent demand for formal monetary commitments. The same month, enthusiastic endorsements of *NEPAD* were published in the *Financial Times* by Johannesburg capital and Washington multilateral banks: the heir to Anglo American Corporation and South Africa's main international think-tank intellectual (Mills and Oppenheimer, 2001), and the highest-ranking Africa officials at the IMF and World Bank (Gondwe and Madavo, 2001).

To sum up the ideological partnership Mbeki proposed, consider the way that the 1980s-90s neoliberal recolonisation of African economic policy is explained in *NEPAD*:

> The structural adjustment programs provided only a partial solution. They promoted reforms that tended to remove serious price distortions, but gave inadequate attention to the provision of social services. As a consequence, only a few countries managed to achieve sustainable higher growth under these programs.

Slippery, this line of analysis, and worth unpacking briefly. One test of robust analysis is to pose the opposite premise, and to see whether the subsequent hypotheses are worth exploring:

- What if structural adjustment represented not "a partial solution" but instead, reflecting local and global power shifts, a profound defeat for genuine African nationalists, workers, peasants, women, children, and the environment?

- What if the structural adjustment programs of the 1980s-90s were the result not of independent Africans searching honestly for 'solutions,' but instead mainly reflected the dramatic shift in power relations at both global scale (where financial and commercial circuits of capital were in ascendance) and within individual African states, away from lobbies favoring somewhat pro-poor social policies and (at least half-hearted) industrial development, toward cliques whose strategies served the interests of acquisitive, over-consumptive local elites, Washington financiers, and transnational corporations?
- What if promoting reforms really amounted to the IMF and World Bank imposing their cookie-cutter neoliberal policies on desperately disempowered African societies, without any reference to democratic processes, resistance, or diverse local conditions?
- What if the removal of serious price distortions really meant the repeal of exchange controls (hence allowing massive capital flight), subsidy cuts (hence pushing masses of people below the poverty line), and lowered import tariffs (hence generating massive reindustrialization)?
- What if inadequate attention to the provision of social services in reality meant the opposite: excessive attention to applying neoliberalism not just to the macroeconomy, but also to health, education, water, and other crucial state services? And what if the form of IMF/Bank attention included insistence upon greater cost recovery, higher user-fees, lower budgetary allocations, privatization, and even the disconnection of supplies to those too poor to afford them, hence leading to the unnecessary deaths of millions of people?
- What if inadequate attention to the provision of social services is not anywhere correlated to the inability of countries to achieve sustainable higher growth, but rather serves as a nice-sounding justification for adjustment with a human face, as UNICEF coined the compromise that *NEPAD* apparently seeks?

If these hypotheses are reasonable, and if the implication is to proceed no further with structural adjustment—human face or not—then a central task of *NEPAD* was posed: to slip around such arguments without reference to their relevance. In doing so, *NEPAD* fit into the globalizers' modified neoliberal project, by which it was even more vigorously asserted, ever more incongruously, that integration into global markets solves poverty, and that therefore an alleged "Development Agenda" should be adopted by the WTO.

There was great neocolonial/comprador trickery afoot when IMF/Bank African leaders Gondwe and Madavo promoted free trade as Africa's savior: the most effective help for self-help will come from trade. Africa needs better opportunities for trade. Yet projections from the last major study (by the World Bank and OECD) of the benefits of the previous liberalization—the Uruguay Round—were a bit less sanguine: Africa would lose billions of dollars in annual output by 2002, as a result of imports swamping the uncompetitive industries which struggle under inefficient scale-economies.

The process of liberalization had actually been underway for a long time, reducing Africa's ability to earn income from trade over the past two decades, and forcing economies to switch from meeting basic needs to generating more— and ever less valuable—export outputs. Given the structure of international commodity trade, the results were inevitably to cheapen imports for already-wealthy Northern consumers, harm millions of small farmers North and South, compel further switching of Southern food production to export cash crops, and concentrate more resources in the clutch of a few oligopolistic firms.

As discussed above, the WTO deal offered to the South in 2001 included fewer restrictions on pharmaceutical patent violation, the potential for slightly freer trade in crops and a few light manufacturing sectors (paid for by yet more opening of African markets), deeper-ranging intellectual property provisions, competition policies drafted in the interests of multinational corporations, and extension of liberalization to water, electricity, banking and other crucial services through the General Agreement on Trade in Services. The reality of international trading power was that both the U.S. and South Africa imposed ever-tougher antidumping penalties against impoverished trading partners.

Gondwe/Madavo confirmed, "The IMF and the World Bank are doing everything possible to play a part [in *NEPAD*]. The initiative expects the IMF and World Bank to make a contribution on the basis of the poverty reduction strategy adopted in 1999." That meant continuing on the path of the Highly Indebted Poor Countries (HIPC) debt-relief initiative, which civil societies and less supine governments have rejected vociferously. With only 13 percent of the promised $100 billion in debt reduction promised at the June 1999 G-8 meeting in Cologne, why should this initiative retain any credibility in late 2001? Mozambican president Joachim Chissano, for instance, publicly complained at that point that the near-total destruction of the cashew-processing industry was the pain the World Bank required for meager gain: a few HIPC breadcrumbs.[14]

Yet for Gondwe/Madavo, *NEPAD* appeared as a crucial means of solidifying existing financial-dependency relations: "Credit is crucial for economic development. That is why, in the longer run, African countries need to retain the trust of investors in their ability and willingness to repay what they borrow. Therefore the IMF, the World Bank, and other development partners are working to help African countries create sound domestic financial sectors and, eventually, integrate into international financial markets." In reality, the IMF and Bank worked for at least two decades, since adopting the Berg Report, to undermine domestic African finance by demanding excessive deregulation at a time of structural adjustment austerity, leading to banking crises across the continent. The words "eventually integrate" are deceitful, given that one of the key dictates of the IMF and Bank was the lifting of capital controls, with virtually no African states daring to put them back on—save Robert Mugabe's Zimbabwe.

Perhaps the most successful of Pretoria's operators in this kind of environment was Alec Erwin, who presided over the U.N. Conference on Trade and Development from 1996-2000 and was mooted as a compromise choice for WTO secretary-general when Michael Moore was considered unsuitable by many Third World countries in 1998. Raised in Durban, Erwin was radicalized in the antiapartheid struggle. He became a heroic trade unionist during the first Durban strikes of 1973, and was regarded as organized labor's premier Marxist intellectual during the 1970s-80s.

By the 1990s, Erwin's politics shifted rapidly rightward, in part because he embraced an intellectual tradition of political economy known as 'Regulation Theory.' Originating in France through the work of Michel Aglietta, Robert Boyer, Alain Lipietz, and others, the theory is based upon institutional analysis and changes in regimes of accumulation from extensive (capital-widening) to intensive (capital-deepening) processes. South African theorists led by Stephen Gelb translated this into a normative strategy for postapartheid economic development, from an inward-oriented Racial Fordist mode of regulating the industrialized economy (blacks doing mass production, whites doing mass consumption), to a Post-Fordist system of export-led growth, small-batch computer-aided production, niche marketing and branding, just-in-time inventory management, more harmonious labor relations (through Quality Circles and Team Concept which help speed up assembly lines), and other 1980s-90s management fads (Gelb, 1987 and 1991; for a critique see Meth, 1990). Neoliberal policies aiming to liberalize finance and trade were part of the package. As Pretoria's trade minister from March 1996, Erwin was especially insensitive to regional concerns over the growing trade deficit and further deindustrialization caused by the S.A./European Union free-trade agreement.

After losing face and the mantle of African leadership in Seattle, Erwin pushed even harder for a new WTO round. In Freetown, Cairo, and Mexico City in 2000-1, he unsuccessfully lobbied African trade officials to support Pretoria's international trade strategy. Finally, Zimbabwe's massive domestic troubles and the retirement of militant nationalist Nathan Shamuyarira offered an excellent opportunity to split SADC members away from the rest of Africa, and to assure that a repeat of the uncooperative African delegation at Seattle did not transpire at the Qatar summit.[15]

As we see below, the role of organized labor and the independent left was not terribly meaningful at Doha. One reason was the remote location and repressive Qatar state's capacity to clamp down on protest. But a more important reason was the division in philosophy (over solidarity), strategy ("fix it or nix it"), and tactics (degrees of militancy) between the two related camps. Was this a momentary cleavage at both global and South African scales, or did the divisions reflect more fundamental problems in the ways in which opponents of neoliberalism organized and operated?

5. Labor and the Independent Left

The social forces which argue for an entirely different approach to international political economy are sometimes termed "anti-globalization"—though that term is slightly absurd—but better described as "movements for global justice" (for more, see Starr, 2000). Table 6.1 lists notable individuals associated with these movements, although the main point is that as an "NGO-swarm"—to cite the Rand Corporation's frightened description—these networks don't have formal leaders who tell followers "the line" or "the strategy." Any such personality list is merely indicative, given the lack of hierarchy in the best segments of the movements, but includes names of internationally-renowned activists, scholars, commentators, and politicians like Samir Amin (based in Senegal), Maude Barlow (Canada), Walden Bello (Thailand), Alejandro Bendana (Nicaragua), Pierre Bourdieu (France), Jose Bove (France), Alex Callinicos (Britain), Camille Chalmers (Haiti), Noam Chomsky (U.S.), Kevin Danaher (U.S.), Eduardo Galeano (Uruguay), Susan George (France), Boris Kagarlitsky (Russia), Marin Khor (Malaysia), Naomi Klein (Canada), Lula Ignacio da Silva (Brazil), Wangari Maathai (Kenya), Subcommandante Marcos (Mexico), George Monbiot (Britain), Ralph Nader (U.S.), Antonio Negri (Italy), Njoki Njehu (Kenya), Medha Patkar (India), John Pilger (Britain), and Vandana Shiva (India). Amongst many South African public figures who are highly regarded in the same circuits are Treatment Action Campaign leader Zackie Achmat, Alternative Information and Development Center director Brian Ashley, anti-apartheid poet and solidarity activist Dennis Brutus, Jubilee South Africa president M.P. Giyosi and secretary George Dor, AIDC trade analyst Dot Keet, Durban social movement leader Professor Fatima Meer, Archbishop of Cape Town Ngongonkulu Ndungane, Soweto civic leader Trevor Ngwane and Virginia Setshedi, SA Communist Party secretary Blade Nzimande, trade analyst Mohau Pheko, liberation-theologian Molefe Tsele, and Neville Gabriel of the SA Council of Churches, and—depending upon the circumstances—Cosatu President Willie Madisha and Secretary Zwelinzima Vavi.

In general, the diverse movements have this in common: *they promote the globalization of people and halt or at minimum radically modify the globalization of capital.* Their demands, campaigns, and programs reflect the work of organizations with decades of experience. Their activists were schooled in social, community, women's, labor, democracy, disarmament, human rights, consumer, public-health, political, progressive-religious, environmental, and youth traditions, spanning an enormous variety of issues, organizational forms, and styles. In the Third World, high-profile justice movements at the turn of the twenty-first century included Mexico's Zapatistas, Brazil's Movement of the Landless, India's National Alliance of People's Movements, Thailand's Forum of the Poor, and the Korean Confederation of Trade Unions.

The most dynamic forces within the movements have arrived at this formula not only because of high-profile battles between protesters and the police protecting elites in London and Seattle (1999); Washington, Melbourne, Prague and Nice (2000); and Quebec City, Genoa and Brussels (2001). In addition, conditions remain that gave rise to "IMF Riots" and massive anti-neoliberal protests across virtually the entire Third World over the past two decades. For many Southern social and labor movements, Seattle was a catalyst to transcend the IMF Riot as knee-jerk protest against neoliberalism. Instead, mass-democratic activist responses have characterized the subsequent protests, which have featured antineoliberal programmatic demands. In some instances, particularly in Latin America (Bolivia and Ecuador), the activism reached a near-insurgent stage; in other sites (South Africa, Nigeria, and India), many millions of workers became involved in mass strikes against neoliberalism; in yet other protests (South Korea, Argentina, Turkey), tens of thousands of protesters took to the streets in waves of militancy (www.wdm.org.uk/cambriefs/DEBT/unrest.htm).

In contrast to these nonviolent movements whose ambition is social justice, the most important reactionary Third World force that emerged at the same time was an ultra-fundamentalist, violent streak within Islam, whose adherents numbered at least 70,000 trained cadres associated with the Al-Qaeda network. Although there was absolutely nothing in common between the justice movements and Al-Qaeda's analysis, vision, objectives, strategies and tactics, there did emerge in the minds of some commentators a kind of "competition" to make an impact—of a very different kind—on the global elite.

For example, James Harding, writing in the *Financial Times* under the provocative title "Clamour against capitalism stilled," anticipated that in the wake of the September 11 terrorist incidents, global justice movements would be "derailed."[16] A spurious reason was "the absence of both leadership and a cogent philosophy to inspire fellowship." One counterpoint was obvious: hierarchical leadership is not necessarily a positive attribute for the kind of broad-based opposition to neoliberalism that is required and that is bubbling up from all corners of Africa and the world. Still, the deathknell of the movement (really many movements) for global justice was sounded by Harding:

> It is riddled with egotism and petty politics. Its actions are sometimes misinformed, sometimes misjudged. It has an inflated sense of its own importance. Its targets keep changing and growing. And it has been robbed of its momentum. Counter-capitalism was not just a movement, it was a mood. Its main platform—the street—is not as open as it was. Its message, always complicated, is now much more loaded. Its audience—politicians, the press and the public—are seriously distracted. And its funding base, already tiny, threatens to shrivel as charitable foundations and philanthropists see their fortunes shrink with the stock market.

All these charges have a grain of truth. But if global justice activists were slightly intimidated by the Resurgent Right's incitement in late 2001, subsequent months and years would see their revitalization, as the problems they identified only became more serious.

For example, in rural Malawi in late 2001, members of social movements and progressive organizations from across Southern Africa gathered at an important workshop to address "the universality of human rights which we strongly affirm to include political and civil, economic and social, workers', cultural and environmental rights." The workshop decried "the international institutions promoting neo-liberal policies for globalization, above all the IMF, World Bank and the World Trade Organization and in this context call for their dismantling." It condemned the "WTO as the key global institution usurping our democratic rights and especially those agreements which have the most serious negative implications for human rights above all, Trade Related Intellectual Property Rights and the General Agreement in Trade in Services" (Southern African People's Solidarity Network, 2001).[17]

Some of the region's most advanced trade unionists would unite with these sentiments, and indeed in militant semi-industrialized settings like Brazil, Korea, Indonesia and Mexico, organized labor moved rapidly to a similar perspective. For Cosatu, the contrast between its own "fix it" (reformist) position—in contrast to the "nix it" (abolitionist) stance of the independent-left social movements—became crystal clear on the eve of the 30-31 August 2001 anti-privatization stay away, as insults flew between leaders of the ANC and the Cosatu/SACP. The front page of *Business Day* carried the following report:

> Cabinet ministers were subsequently dispatched to influential radio and television programs first to "clarify" government positions, but also to "show Cosatu members they are being urged to committing suicide", according to an official involved in the spin-doctoring offensive. Also part of the strategy—championed by Trade and Industry Minister Alec Erwin, Transport Minister Dullah Omar and Public Enterprises Minister Jeff Radebe—was to seek to caution Cosatu members against the possible hijacking of their strike by outside elements such as those protesting at World Bank and International Monetary Fund meetings.[18]

Bizarre as it sounded at first blush, the same newspaper demonstrated the valid underlying rationale for Pretoria's hijack phobia on the following day:

> SA needs to cut import tariffs aggressively, privatize faster and more extensively, promote small business effectively and change labor laws to achieve far faster growth and job creation. This is according to a World Bank report that will soon be released publicly and has been circulating in government.[19]

Like the reported claim by Thabo Mbeki a year earlier, that the Treatment Action Campaign had "infiltrated" Cosatu in its efforts to change government AIDS-drugs policy, it was up to trade unionists to rebut government's delusional paranoia about those allegedly "outside elements" opposed to the World Bank and IMF, through their actions over subsequent months and years.[20] South African workers had, after all, long been acquainted with the Bretton Woods Institutions, not only for the billions of dollars worth of apartheid-supportive lending from 1951-1982, but also for neoliberal economic advice provided in contemporary times.

For example, in addition to mindless promotion of privatization—nearly universally a failure during the late 1990s in South Africa—Bank economists regularly argued that Cosatu members were overpaid. Peter Fallon and a Bank consultant, Nobel Prize laureate Robert Lucas, used a narrow econometric model in their controversial 1997 draft discussion paper (unchanged on final release in March 1998) to argue that over time, "a 10 percent increase in the real product wage would eventually lead to a 7.1 percent decrease in Black employment," and that "employment is reduced through union wage-raising effects by about 6.3 percent."[21] The number crunching was dubious, not just because as in all such exercises, vital political-economic context (such as the 1990s tendency of white businesses to substitute capital for labor, no matter the wage levels) was absent, but also in view of the model's supply-side orientation and lack of attention to demand-induced growth resulting from higher wages. (The demand-side effects would be especially important, were assumptions to be relaxed about the leakage of spending on imported goods that could be made locally, in the event of a strengthening of political will.) One key Fallon/Lucas recommendation was, hence, to "avoid excessive wage increases. . . . The [Employment Conditions] Commission should try to ensure that wage increases do not increase unemployment, which, under present circumstances of very high unemployment, would suggest that real wages be allowed to fall." Fallon and Lucas also endorsed the big-business demand for dual wage rates ("lower wages for young people and for all workers in areas of unusually high unemployment"). In contrast, for upper-echelon government bureaucrats, they generously argued, "it is important that government pay to skilled employees does not fall far behind that of competing sectors"—hence codifying the world's worst apartheid-wage gap.

Cosatu's general secretary at the time, Mbhazima Shilowa, rejected the "so-called gospel of the World Bank that workers should not demand wage increases" and implied that Fallon and Lucas were part of a "lunatic fringe outside SA [claiming] that one of the economy's main problems was alleged inflexibility of the labor market." Shilowa argued that "Labor market flexibility had become discredited among workers who saw it as a euphemism for very few or no regulations at all so employers could hire and fire, pay whatever wages and ensure no worker protection."[22]

The class hostility between Cosatu and the Bretton Woods Institutions was obvious, and a "nix it" position should logically have been adopted. As for the "outside elements such as those protesting at World Bank and IMF meetings," most activists increasingly agreed that the institutions should be shut down, because their existence so decisively exacerbates global uneven development. Without a Bank or IMF acting as cop for the international commercial banks, African governments would have space to default on illegitimate foreign debts, and to turn away from neoliberal economic policies that have done so much harm. Moreover, the development most desperately needed in Africa—paying to build a rural school or hire more village health workers or install a simple water system—generally requires local not foreign currency. So a US$-denominated World Bank loan is unnecessary and indeed dangerous once repayment is required in hard currency.

To illustrate, the Jubilee South movement calls for the Bank and IMF to be abolished, with their capital written down as part of the cancellation of Third World debt. And Jubilee South Africa, the Movement of the Landless in Brazil, the Haitian popular movement, and many other groups have called for a World Bank Bonds Boycott as part of a defunding strategy. The most advanced trade unionists in the North are listening to these calls and acting in solidarity by instructing their pension funds never to buy World Bank bonds. But the debate over fixing versus nixing (closing down) the international institutions continues in South Africa, because when it comes to the WTO, Cosatu's leadership has been drawn in recent years to a myopic "fix-it" stance.

To illustrate the problem, Cosatu ignored the call for a debate on strategy in October 1999 when several dozen key Southern African labor and social movement activists met in Johannesburg. Zwelinzima Vavi then contemptuously denounced that meeting's main resolution: disavowing WTO reform through inclusion of so-called Social Clauses. At the time, COSATU leaders led by SACTWU's Ebrahim Patel believed that they could win trade sanctions against countries whose workplace conditions, rights to union organizing, child labor prevalence, or environmental degradation require punishment. They also gained agreement to impose such Social Clauses in South Africa's own trade agreements from Erwin and big business in NEDLAC. A few weeks later in Seattle, the Cosatu leaders marched in protests outside the WTO summit, calling "Workers of the World Unite!" But then they joined Erwin and Andre Lamprechts from Business SA in the "Green Room" with Clinton's people, where they tried but failed to negotiate a new trade round with Social Clause provisions.

Was it, for Cosatu, a case of "Talk Left (in the streets), Act Right (in the boardroom)"? Sadly, after returning from Seattle in December 1999, Cosatu's delegation continued to call for reform rather than abolition of the WTO. Erwin, meanwhile, was furious about the WTO breakdown, and condemned protesters as Clinton's useful idiots. Just before going to Seattle, Erwin (1999) told Parliament, "We will soon have to give leadership not just to the process of the development of our own economies [in the developing world] but to the equitable development of the world economy. The political capacity to do this and the will to do it in the G7 is weakening despite the power of the social democrats."

At Seattle, Erwin gloated about South Africa's unique corporatist (big government/business/labor) unity. But he then announced he would drop his support for Social Clauses, given how much resistance he was facing from Third World officials. Erwin's subsequent promotion of privatization and a so-called industrial policy—epitomized by vain attempts to attract investments with environment-destroying Spatial Development Initiatives (as in Maputo and Saldanha) and massive, irrational state subsidizes such as the Coega port and Industrial Development Zone—demonstrates the intrinsic bias of corporatism.[23]

The Social Clause controversy is revealing. True, some Southern trade unions support the strategy through their (often subordinate) role in the International Confederation of Free Trade Unions. But many influential Southern social-movement leftists have condemned this approach for leaving in place, and indeed amplifying, the existing antidemocratic structure of the international trading system. Most importantly, critics charge, those advocating Social Clauses have not established whether those most adversely affected by sanctions *want to be* targeted. In contrast, trade sanctions invoked during the anti-apartheid struggle, or anti-junta activism in Haiti during the early 1990s, or ongoing Burmese democracy campaign, *were entirely appropriate*, because the people most affected demanded them as a crucial part of their liberation strategy. In Zimbabwe, comprehensive sanctions against the Mugabe dictatorship have not been invoked because of lack of labor and popular support. Social Clause advocates can only claim a similar power relationship in the case of the Chilean trade unions which requested supportive sanctions during their struggles for better labor laws a decade ago.

To improve the WTO with Social Clauses, independent-left critics continue, will simply heighten imperialist power relations. The point, instead, should be to attack the power that the WTO has to overrule and undermine international agreements and national laws that protect human rights and the environment, and to find genuinely effective means to defend these rights. That requires (a) joining with those Global Justice Movements promoting the abolition of the WTO and a return to earlier trade systems that permitted greater exercise of national sovereignty (including protection where it can be justified on developmental grounds), and (b) establishing alternative mechanisms to punish firms which lower global living and environmental standards (such as corporate dechartering—i.e., denying their right to exist).

One leading South advocacy group, Third World Network of Penang, Malaysia, offers powerful opposition to Social Clauses. The network's main Africa affiliate, Isodec in Ghana, coordinates an Africa Trade Network which has been active across the continent. Eschewing export-led growth, the social movements' alternative development strategy is to promote inward-oriented industrial development based first and foremost upon meeting basic needs, along the lines advocated by Africa's greatest economist, Samir Amin. For U.S. labor, a strategy is emerging which is preferable to tinkering with trade deals and to shining WTO chains: attacking transnational corporations directly, consistent with solidarity-campaigning principles, and passing local restraining legislation against corporations, similar in scope to the 1977 US Foreign Corrupt Practices Act, which penalizes specific firms—not the countries they victimize—for egregious behavior like child labor or toxic dumping.

6. Conclusion: Labor and Social Movement Unity?

Can South African social movements and labor bridge this kind of wedge issue, and move into more durable alliance against neoliberalism, local and global? Varied grassroots organizations—community-based groups, HIV/AIDS support organizations, traditional and ethnic-based movements, progressive churches, women's and youth clubs, environmental groups, and many others—have joined trade unionists in diverse struggles against neoliberalism. Africans are at the helm of many of these movements. In addition to motivating strongly for full debt cancellation across the continent, for example, African initiative is also evident in the grassroots campaign for the return of Nigerian dictator Sani Abacha's billions in looted funds in Swiss and London banks. Early success has helped to break open Swiss secrecy, following similar campaigns over fifteen years waged by citizens' groups and governments in the Philippines and Haiti in relation to the Marcos and Duvallier hoards. In addition, specific World Bank projects in Africa have come under attack by progressive local and international groups, including the Chad-Cameroon pipeline, the Lesotho Highlands Water Project and Namibia's Epupa Dam. Other growing campaigns that link African and international civil society organizations include the environmental debt that the industrial North owes the South, and the campaign to ban "conflict-diamond" trade that contributes to civil war in Sierre Leone and Angola.

Across Africa, such solidarity is being discussed in relation to concrete and potential linkages between social-justice movements of the North and South. An "African People's Consensus" campaign was catalyzed by Jubilee anti-debt, other church, labor, NGO, and community groups in Lusaka in May 1999 and then taken forward at a major Dakar gathering in December 2000 that for the first time linked progressive grassroots and shop floor activists from English, French, and Portuguese-speaking areas of Africa. And likewise, while Thabo Mbeki was gathering international elite support for *NEPAD* and only later checking in on African capitals, a "Southern African People's Solidarity Network" headquartered in Cape Town held regular workshops across the region to generate analysis, establish positions, and coordinate campaigns against neoliberalism and political repression.[24]

Generally these networks of social-justice movements push for "deglobalization" of their nation-states, and for greater regional cooperation, with the aim of reorienting domestic political economies away from the financial and trade circuitry which has been so disempowering these past two decades. Ultimately a "rights-based" philosophy is emerging that stresses decommodification and destratification in the material sphere, women's rights, and social-environmental harmony. The largest deficits are in the spheres of democracy and basic needs, particularly in relation to rural women, and particularly in areas whose production basis should be easy to expand—rural water/sanitation and small-scale irrigation systems, electricity, public works—without debilitating import requirements.

Alliances between the strands of the Global Justice Movements will rely, in part, upon common targets. As the institutional expressions of international financial and commercial capital (led by Wall Street), the IMF, Bank, and WTO provide the movements with an opportunity to both confront power in a concentrated form, and to unmask their deeper institutional meanings within an increasingly rapacious world capitalism. More generally, the Global Justice Movements have sought—and perhaps located—a model of moving from a loose movement network strategy of resistance, through to a broader anti-neoliberal ideology which respects difference, processes, and above all, the humanity of the struggle for liberation.

The Zapatista movement of the southeastern Mexican mountains is sometimes idealized along these lines, in part because its international alliances offer a model of two-way solidarity. But so too, the Zapatistas are distinctly radical democratic in making short-term demands upon their nation-state to deliver the goods—and tellingly, when this is not forthcoming due to neoliberalism, Zapatista self-activity takes forms such as liberating electricity from the pylons that cross Chiapas, invading underutilized ranches and plantations, and declaring municipal autonomy in dozens of sites of community struggle.

These are probably the orientations associated with national political-economic transformation required for South Africa and more desperate African countries to prosper. At the regional and international scales, reduced pressure from neoliberal actors and markets will also be vital. Fortunately, the global-scale agenda is being elaborated through initiatives ranging from mass protests to more surgical activist campaigns, such as the diverse but growing slavery/colonialism-reparations movement, or the World Bank Bonds Boycott noted above, or the successful October 2000 campaign against IMF- and World Bank-imposed user-fees in health and education programs.[25] Regional activists like the Southern African People's Solidarity Network have much more work ahead to identify pressure points that would lesson Mbeki's *NEPAD* impetus.

One of the residual problems for deepening the Global Justice Movements' coherence within the South African setting is the existence of a dysfunctional alliance between the ruling party and the Congress of South African Trade Unions. The SA Communist Party sits uneasily in between. That relationship sabotaged the South African movements' attempts to forge a coherent strategy for the August 2002 World Summit on Sustainable Development (WSSD) in early 2002. Trade union officials walked out of the official UN-sponsored civil society planning for the meeting because of its capture by "anti-government NGOs" and inclusion of indigenous people as a special category. Backed by the SA Council of Churches and SA National Civic Organization, the Cosatu bloc prepared to host the tens of thousands of international delegates with a much less militant orientation. The reason for the abrupt swing was a January 2002 reconciliation with the ANC that perhaps reflected the latter's fear of "outside elements such as those protesting at World Bank and International Monetary Fund meetings." Cosatu agreed to dismantle its plans for ongoing strikes against privatization, whereas the state made promises about inclusivity in policy making and the prospects of a post *Gear* growth summit. However, when the ruling party soon broke its promises over rolling back transport-sector privatization and over free electricity—as ESKOM prepared for privatization—it appeared that the long-term basis for Cosatu's co-option had declined.

In conclusion, although this chapter did not shy away from the main controversies associated with labor and social-movement contestation of foreign economic policy, there are inspiring examples of cooperation. The 2000-2001 Cosatu alliance with the Treatment Action Campaign against both international pharmaceutical corporations and the SA government over access to antiretroviral drugs is one. Another vital instance in which labor plays an even more catalytic role is the defense of life through access to water. Protests by Cosatu, the SACP, NACTU, and allies in August 2001—with threats to continue into the future—were exemplary in that they rejected the commodification and privatization of South African water and other essential state services, on the broadest social grounds, not merely because of job-loss threats. Likewise, representatives of the SA Municipal Workers Union traveled across the world building a case for an international movement against water privatization. They helped inspire and unite social, environmental, and consumer movements from Accra to Vancouver, leading to a proposed World Water Treaty that would prohibit profit making from water.

The stakes will continue to rise. Pretoria's strongest privatization advocates—Mbeki, Manuel, Erwin, and state enterprises minister Jeff Radebe—were unabashed in their contempt for Cosatu's strong social principles in late 2001 and would be so again once the WSSD moment passed. The whole country asked the simple question: How much more abuse must the weaker partner in the Alliance marriage take before finally turning to a place of safety: a "small-a" alliance of labor and independent social movements?

Alliance supporters correctly rebut that the ANC can deliver a few social policy gains to Cosatu, as the parliamentary office has documented. These gains may even counterbalance the perception that trade union leaders are in the Alliance because of its career and class ladder—raised high by Shilowa, Jay Naidoo, Jayendra Naidoo, Erwin, Marcel Golding, Johnny Copelyn, Moses Mayekiso, and so many others whose loyalties shifted 180 degrees once they were drawn into government. But in many other ways, a "small-a alliance" could potentially provide more power and fewer heartbreaking disappointments.

So on the one hand, the idea of Cosatu being "hijacked" by social movements is farcical. But on the other, it does reveal one litmus test of Pretoria neoliberals, in relation to ANC loyalty. Evidently, the centrist and leftist forces within the ANC have conclusively failed in their efforts to paint the neoliberals as the traitors. Critics ranging from Neville Alexander on the left to Peter Mokaba on the right have aired the big-A Alliance debate. While I have no standing to make any insightful additions, it may be worthwhile to conclude by pointing out how far Cosatu leaders must still reach, both in policy and practical political terms, to catch up with the independent social movements.

For South Africa to finally establish sovereignty and democracy, in place of the unsatisfying, continuity-based transition from apartheid to neoliberalism, requires Cosatu to rejoin the most advanced components of the international labor movement, and return to its roots in the independent left. If Cosatu decides to lead, not lag, the global justice movements, rapid progress will continue. Likewise, without a massive worker presence, the movement is doomed. And both are doomed without an explicitly antineoliberal ideology; without a philosophy of solidarity in which those workers and poor people most affected by antineoliberal campaigns are empowered to design them; without strategies which aim not to polish but to abolish the institutions of international economic oppression; and without tactics that are as creative, nonviolent, and militant as they must be to disrupt the terribly uneven development that characterizes contemporary global capitalism.

Notes

1.   Adapted and updated from Bond (2001:94-95).
2.   In South Africa, representatives of overlapping Washington-centric constituencies included not only the neoliberal ANC officials, but also political representatives of big business and white wealth (Tony Leon and Nigel Bruce), high-profile proliberalization bank economists (Danie Roodt and Iraj Abedian), consultants (Reg Rumney), think-tank leaders (Greg Mills and Ann Bernstein), and convivial newspaper editorialists (Peter Bruce and Howard Barrell). Remarkably, although the invariably white male beneficiaries of apartheid were periodically accused of speaking to their own book, the 2000-01 currency crisis led many of them to call, in December 2001, for yet more financial liberalization, paid for by a new IMF loan that would allow yet more apartheid-era wealth to be liberated. *Business Day's* Bruce was an especially avid proponent.
3.   *Left Business Observer*, February 2000.
4.   The main point is that "asymmetry" between market players can lead to large-scale distortions—and hence Stiglitz-style policy prescriptions are generally limited to more transparency, more competition, and a bit more government regulation to eliminate those distortions.
5.   Economists Jeffrey Sachs and Paul Krugman stand out.
6.   There was hope that perhaps he would be joined on the Left of the EU by the German premier Helmut Schroeder, in desperate need in late 2001 of maintaining his Green coalition partnership.
7.   Occasionally, the main South African representatives—Mbeki, Manuel, Erwin, Finance director-general Maria Ramos, and Reserve Bank governor Tito Mboweni— spoke out on the need for international reform.
8.   In October 1998, Sweeney endorsed an $18 billion U.S. taxpayer bailout of the IMF which needed more funds to, in turn, bail out New York and London banks trapped during the 1997-99 'emerging markets crisis.' A year later, he supported the explicitly imperialist U.S. trade strategy organized by Bill Clinton just prior to Seattle, which

fortunately tens of thousands of protesters and the African delegation scuppered. In Seattle, Sweeney marched at least 25,000 U.S. workers *away from*—rather than toward—the convention center confrontation.

9. *Washington Post*, 11 December 2001.

10. Aida Parker and a network of right-wing conspiracy theorists in South Africa were traditionally comfortable among this crowd, as were many Afrikaans *verkramptes*.

11. In South Africa, Kgalema Motlanthe and Joel Netshitenzhe were important nationalists, as was Mbeki on occasion, such as Non-Aligned Movement, G-77, and similar gatherings.

12. At Seattle, the Organization of African Unity caucus issued a statement withdrawing consensus: "There is no transparency in the proceedings and African countries are being marginalized." African trade expert Yash Tandon (1999:18) reported on Zimbabwe's role immediately after the OAU revolt:

Now in panic, the U.S. State Department sent its most skilled negotiators to pacify the Africans. They tried to co-opt Zimbabwe's industry minister [Nathan Shamuyarira] (by now identified as the chief spokesperson for the Africa group) into the process by offering to consider a draft declaration that would satisfy the Africans. This was the first serious effort made by the U.S. to bring in the Africans. However, the Zimbabwe minister was not persuaded, and he refused to join in the "Green Room" consultations.

13. voiceoftheturtle.org/articles/raj_doha.shtml

14. Following the HIPC initiative (1997) came Comprehensive Development Frameworks (1999), Poverty Reduction Strategy Programmes (1999), and the *Nepad* (2000-01). These top-down initiatives culminated at least two decades' worth of other failed or inconsequential reforms, in areas such as environment, gender, transparency, participation, and post-Washington Consensus economics. Together, the long string of reform failures suggest quite conclusively that making the Bretton Woods Institutions and World Trade Organization work for humanity and nature is utopian, given the prevailing balance of forces.

15. Erwin's maneuvers were exposed in the *Mail and Guardian*, 9 and 16 November 2001. His own justifications are spelled out in an interview in *New Agenda*, 3, Autumn 2001.

16. *Financial Times*, 10 October 2001. For a more paternalist and uncomprehending version, see the open letter by Belgian prime minister and European Union president Guy Verhofstadt (2001).

17. To give a flavor of the kinds of Southern African justice movements that make these appeals, this particular gathering—hosted by the Malawi Economic Justice Network—was attended and endorsed by the Inter-African Network for Human Rights and Development; the Alternative Information and Development Center; the Synod of Livingstonia Church and Society Programme; the Malawi Center for Social Concern; the Malawi Civil Society Coalition for quality Basic Education; Coalition Jubilee 2000 Angola; the South African Ecumenical Services for Socio-Economic Transformation; Jubilee South Africa; the Mauritian group Ledikasyon pu Travayer; the Malawi Economic Justice Network; Malawi News; the Mineworkers Development Agency in Lesotho; the National Community Services Programme; the Nkhomano Center for

Development; Mozambique's main trade union federation, the OTM; the Southern African Institute for Economic Research; the Tanzania Association of NGOs and Tanzania Coalition on Debt and Development; Transparency South Africa; the Wits University Municipal Services Project; the Zimbabwe Coalition on Debt and Development; and the Zimbabwe National Students Union.

18. *Business Day*, 27 August 2001.

19. *Business Day*, 28 August 2001.

20. There appeared little basis for the warning against being "hijacked," and not only because Cosatu's organic interests are explicitly opposed to those of the Bank, IMF and WTO. But another reason was the great distance that already existed—due to durable ANC-Cosatu relations—between South Africa's largest trade union movement and core independent left forces. The latter, for example, were among some 20,000 marchers against hypocrisy at the World Conference Against Racism on 31 August 2001, which Cosatu declined to join (in favor of a joint march with the ANC, one third as large, the subsequent day). Those 20,000 comprised the Durban Social Forum, the Anti-Privatisation Forum from Johannesburg, the Jubilee movement, the landless, other critics of services cutoffs, radical Palestinian solidarity activists, and several other small independent-left formations. Cosatu's failure to even seek antiprivatization allies among groups like the Soweto Electricity Crisis Committee—while dragging into its formal People's Summit organizations with no prior history of struggle on the issue (and in one case, a history of investment in Nelspruit's water privatization)—suggests that the litmus test of loyalty to the ANC will still prove an Achilles heel to Cosatu's leftward direction.

21. Fallon and Lucas (1998:ii,iii). For more, see Bond, 2000, pp. 155-191.

22. *Business Day*, 7 April 1998.

23. See, e.g., www.coega.org and Hosking and Bond (2000).

24. www.aidc.org.za

25. www.worldbankboycott.org, www.globalizationchallenge.org.

Chapter 7

The Democratization of Trade Policy—
The SA-EU Trade, Development, and
Cooperation Agreement

Talitha Bertelsmann-Scott

Democratic forms of government have become the norm rather than the exception over the last couple of decades—in 1975 68 percent of all states were under authoritarian rule and yet by 1995 this number had decreased to only 26 percent. This massive increase in democratization coincides with the emergence of the phenomenon of globalization. For some analysts this is no coincidence, as they observe that globalization thrives on economic policies that are more closely associated with democratic governments than any other. But whereas many states are pushed toward democracy by external pressures including globalization and the influence of the World Bank and the IMF, there is not enough global pressure to ensure the democratization of the entire state apparatus. States could remain "democratic" in name only, and not be democratic in practice. There rests a certain onus on governments to ensure that democratization filters right down to all aspects of public life.

In order to avoid the undermining of democracy, new democracies often institute consultative forums in which policy can be formulated in order to achieve consensus with the masses. However, the international climate within which states operate today, which is dominated by the process of globalization, has limited the option for economic policies quite drastically. In order to become an active player in the global market neoliberal economic policies have to be accepted. In addition, the World Bank and the IMF have over the years become even more prescriptive on economic policy making that promotes neoliberal ideologies. This leaves new democracies in a difficult position, as neoliberal policies are seldom reconcilable with the immediate needs of the poor in society.

Foreign trade policy formulation is traditionally further removed from public opinion, in the same way that foreign policy is in general considered the domain of the government and not for ordinary citizens to decide. However, with the global shift toward neoliberal economic policies and the desire of states to reap the benefits of globalization, the liberalization of trade has become the main focus of foreign trade policy for most countries. This liberalization of the economy impacts directly on businesses and where they will be negatively affected they find a seldom ally in labor that fears job losses due to the liberalization of tariffs. This provides the potential for vigorous debate surrounding the extent of liberalization and which sectors are to be protected.

One of the biggest foreign policy decisions that South Africa had to make post-1994, was the nature of its political and economic relationship with its biggest trading partner, the European Union (EU). The negotiations surrounding the establishment of a free trade area between the two parties was debated vigorously in the South African public domain. Numerous conferences, consultative processes, and newspaper and journal articles evaluated the pros and cons of free trade and the desirability of such an agreement with the EU. However, the outcome of the negotiations was to a large extent a foregone conclusion. The offer on the negotiating table was a free trade agreement, supported by cooperation agreements and South Africa's partial accession to the Lomé Convention. The only other option South Africa had was not to conclude a deal, which was no option at all.

Although the South African government used these negotiations to develop an inclusive tradition of policy formulation, the outcome of these consultations were curtailed by a number of international factors, like globalization, the EU itself, and international organizations like the WTO.

This chapter will look at how South Africa attempted to make international trade policy formulation inclusive and democratic and why the outcome of the negotiations were largely predetermined.

The SA-EU Negotiations

For the purpose of this study I would like to identify four key elements of a democracy and look at how they translate into actors in democratic decision making. These elements are participation, representation, transparency, and openness. Although the borders between these are blurred, we can understand these four to translate into parliament, government, a transparent bureaucracy, and the access ordinary citizens have to decision making.

Parliament

During the apartheid years Parliament did not play a significant role in foreign policy or foreign trade policy formulation—this was more or less left to the executive. With the change to a democratic government, Parliament was also given a greater in role in foreign policy formulation.

Apart from debates in the general assembly, two portfolio committees—Foreign Affairs and Trade and Industry—had regular meetings to discuss the developments surrounding the negotiations and for the negotiators to report back to Parliament on their actions.

Dr. Rob Davies who chairs the Portfolio Committee on Trade and Industry, and who often chaired the joint sessions with Foreign Affairs, played a critical role in analyzing the proposed deal, searching for alternative avenues and explaining the implications of the deal to fellow Parliamentarians and ordinary citizens alike. He spoke at numerous conferences and briefed Parliament on developments on regular occasions.

Parliament also played the critical role of ratifying the agreement. On the occasion of South Africa's accession to the Lomé Convention Parliament refused to ratify until certain elements of the deal were clarified by the European Union. So in effect, Parliament checked that the deal reached between the negotiators was acceptable to the people of South Africa.

Levermore et al. (2000:10) note the following on Parliament's role in the negotiation process:

> Firstly, it participated in the discussion surrounding the future of the Lomé and South Africa's possible entry into the African, Caribbean and Pacific (ACP) group, and was an observer at the EU-ACP joint assembly in October 1994. Following the start of the TDCA negotiations, Parliament also maintained regular contact with decision-making bodies within the EU, whilst various chambers (such as Agriculture, Foreign Affairs, and Trade & Industry) were asked by government to produce commentary on the EU mandates. Similarly parliament formed a SACU parliamentary liaison committee, which explored various potential impacts of the TDCA for the BLNS states. The second aspect of Parliament's involvement in the state's decision-making process related to a review it undertook prior to the (South African) ratification of the agreement. The National Assembly's committees on trade and industry, foreign affairs and agriculture and land convened a half-day of public hearings on many facets of the TDCA. The final stage of Parliament's involvement in the TDCA process came when it ratified the agreement in November 1999.

In other words, Parliament in many ways facilitated debate among various stakeholders, not only inside South Africa's borders but also including neighboring countries that will be impacted by the agreement. One could, therefore, conclude that Parliament promoted participation in decisionmaking and acted democratically.

The State

During the negotiations a large number of government departments and bodies were roped in to participate, either directly with the negotiations or to comment on mandates and offers from the European Union.

Departments

The main department responsible for the negotiations was the Department of Trade and Industry, although the chief negotiator, Ambassador Eltie Links, was recruited from the Department of Foreign Affairs. To the outsider it seemed as if the two departments were divided into the "hard" and "soft" negotiators. Whereas Trade and Industry took the hard line and were often relentless during talks, Foreign Affairs had to ensure that on diplomatic level relations between the two parties remained amicable. It was also clear that Foreign Affairs tended to focus on the political implication of a deal—any deal for that matter—whereas Trade and Industry was aware that each concession that was made would have an effect on some businessman somewhere in South Africa and in the European Union.

However, a number of other departments were also involved in the negotiations. Most importantly, the Department of Agriculture played a pivotal role in the negotiations surrounding tariff liberalization in agriculture. In addition they had they unenviable task of having to conclude a wine and spirits and fishing agreement with their counterparts.

Another department involved was the Department of Finance. As Levermore et al. (2000:8) note,

> [Their participation] is mainly due to the trade liberalization measures it advocates through the establishment of the Growth, Employment, and Redistribution macro-economic policy (GEAR).

Significantly, Ambassador Links was previously in the Department of Finance and therefore still maintained close links with his former colleagues.

The wide spread of government departments that were involved in the negotiations ensured that the interests of a large number of South Africans was represented during the talks. However, a glaring omission from government departments was the Department of Labor. It is not clear why this department was not given any specific role during the negotiations or whether there was any objection from Labor to this omission. Presumably it was felt that the Department of Labor's mandate did not extend to the negotiating table. (Also, as discussed below, labor had the opportunity to participate through the NEDLAC forum.) However, it is clear that the interests of labor in South Africa would mostly be affected negatively by a free trade agreement and their position would lean more toward the retention of tariffs and subsidies, rather than neoliberal policies. If the Department of Labor was excluded deliberately for this reason, it casts a shadow over the intentions of the South African government to institute a true consultative process.

Institutions Created by the State

A number of government institutions played an important role in finalizing South Africa's mandate and delivering continuous input to the negotiations.

The most important of these is probably the National Economic Development and Labor Council (NEDLAC). NEDLAC is a tripartite negotiation representing the state, labor, business, and community sectors (see chapter three). There are nineteen business organizations (including Business South Africa and the National African Federated Chamber of Commerce) and three organized labor movements, including the Congress of South African Trade Unions (COSATU). Community sectors are also represented, but only in the Development Chamber and had very little opportunity within the formal NEDLAC structure to raise their opinion.

NEDLAC itself was convinced that it played a pivotal role in the negotiations and one representative even mentioned to the author that they had a ratification right[1]. It was felt that if NEDLAC did not agree with the final agreement there would be no deal. This was, however, denied by the negotiators themselves who confirmed that only Parliament would be able to halt the signing of the deal once the negotiators had completed their task around the negotiating table. Although NEDLAC is seen as a powerful actor in decision-making, the official decision-making power lies with Parliament.

Nonetheless, NEDLAC provided input to the negotiations, as highly skilled people with knowledge of the impact of tariffs and free trade were given the opportunity to engage with government. It also provided an opportunity for labor to raise its concerns in a small forum that had direct access to the talks. However, the overriding impression of NEDLAC's influence over the negotiations has been one of business dominance. Through NEDLAC business leaders pointed negotiators in the direction that would lead to optimal benefits for their companies.

The Department of Trade and Industry made a specific commitment to holding report back sessions with NEDLAC after each round of negotiations. According to Willem Smalberger this was done in order to promote participation, accountability, and the democratic process.[2] It however, also signals the importance attached to business leaders' opinions on progress made within the negotiations.

Levermore et al. (2000: 74) also point to the important role that NEDLAC played.

[N]umerous presentations were made in the strategy formulation stage, when South Africa began to develop its mandate. During the negotiating process, the Trade and Industry chamber met before and after each meeting between the E.U.and South Africa. An important sub-committee (TESELICO) was also established, and was used as a consultative forum for government trade negotiators to liaise with business and labor, whilst monitoring the bi-lateral discussion between the DTI's sectoral divisions.

Another state-created tripartite organization, the *Agricultural Trade Forum*, also met regularly to discuss the agricultural side of the talks. In retrospect the South African negotiators managed to secure somewhat of a negotiating victory in the deal on agriculture, the success of which should also be accredited to the on-going talks between government, farmers, and laborers. Given the significant importance of agriculture to South Africa's economy and overlapping views between business, labor, and government on this area, a strong joint front was developed, which proved far more difficult to crack during negotiations than positions on manufacturing tariffs and quotas. This is an indication that consultation and cohesion among stakeholders has the potential to have some impact, although arguably only an impact on the details, rather than the overall design, of the neoliberal world states have to operate in today.

Finally, the *South African Board on Tariffs and Trade*, the BTT, extensively consulted during the negotiations. Essentially the negotiations boiled down to talks about the dismantling of tariffs and the input of the BTT was crucial. Not only did they have a superior knowledge of South Africa's somewhat complicated tariff structure, but they were also included for their knowledge on rules of origin and the impact liberalization would have on the Southern African Customs Union (SACU).

Levermore et al. (2000:75) argue further that it was at the BTT level that individuals could influence the state's decision-making process. They sought input from a wide selection of role players and received numerous discussions on various aspects of the agreement. These submissions were discussed, and where deemed necessary, passed on to the official negotiators.

The Bureaucracy

In 1994 the state inherited a bulky bureaucracy comprising almost exclusively white government officials that served the National Party government over the last couple of decades. It was clear that a radical shift needed to take place and yet the white population had the expertise on how to run the country, whereas this knowledge was lacking in the previously disadvantaged communities. However, it was not only a question of transforming the people that worked for the state. The old system of divided government with departments for various race groups and homelands was amalgamated into one.

In the first place, the old departments of foreign affairs had to be transformed, or more accurately, the departments of the former TBVC states (Transkei, Boputhatswana, Venda, and the Ciskei) had to be amalgamated into the South African Department of Foreign Affairs. In addition, the old guard that formed part of the National Party had to be moved out of strategic positions and replaced with ANC officials. However, the entire department could not be discarded and replaced as the new government did not have the manpower to do so. Still in need of the expertise and contacts of a number of old officials, the department was slow in changing its face from dominantly white to a representative mix of the South African population. These changes were further complicated by international shifts in focus from realist politics to a recognition that markets mostly dominated political interactions. This meant that the South African Department of Trade and Industry had to be incorporated in the formulation of foreign policy and indeed in representing South African interest at international missions. Although South Africa has not gone as far as Australia that now only has one ministry for both foreign affairs and trade and industry, considerable moves toward closer cooperation between these two departments have been made.

The Department of Trade and Industry (DTI) has arguably been more successful at transforming the face and activities of the department toward a more representative mix of South Africans and also toward a focus on the concerns that the new ANC government was facing. Shifts toward the development of previously disadvantaged sectors of the economy were shadowed by international policies that would encourage sustainable growth and result in job creation at home. Under the apt leadership of Minister Alex Erwin, the department underwent a radical change, but without ever losing sight of its goal and mission.

During the years of negotiations the South African bureaucracy underwent significant changes and upheavals. However, the changes ensured that the bureaucracy that negotiated with the EU was as representative of the South African population as was possible directly after South Africa's transition to democracy. However, a racially representative mix of bureaucrats is still no guarantee that the views of civil society would be adequately represented.

Public Participation

Although the influence that ordinary citizens had on the negotiating process remains difficult to gage, there was no lack of popular interest throughout the long years of negotiation. The rounds of talks received regular and well-informed media coverage and a popular radio station, Radio SAFM, even encouraged listeners to air their views on the talks. Actuality programs on all the major television news stations hosted experts on regular occasions to discuss the details of the negotiations.

Academic interest in the talks was high from the outset, with a number of thesis's focusing on the implications of free trade between the European Union and South Africa on the South African and European economies, the future of the Lomé Convention, regional integration in Southern Africa, and the Southern African Customs Union.

Independent research organizations—both in South Africa and in a number of European countries—were also following the negotiations closely and even did a number of impact studies, although none of these could be conclusive due to the lack of statistical data. A number of conferences were organized in order to share expert views. The negotiators were themselves present at some of these conferences, mostly to share their expertise, but also to gain an understanding of popular opinion. Other NGO's like church organizations were also concerned about the impact the agreement might have and commissioned their own studies and even hosted conferences to discuss the implications.

One particular conference, hosted by the Foundation for Global Dialogue (now the Institute for Global Dialogue), seemingly had a significant influence on the negotiators. The conference was held at a critical juncture when South Africa was examining the European mandate and formulating the response in the form of the South African negotiating mandate. The idea of a trade and development agreement was first mentioned at this conference, discussed among the various experts that were attending, and subsequently became the main thrust of the South African mandate.[3]

After having examined the Parliament's, the bureaucracy's, government's, and civil society's influence on the negotiations one is want to conclude that from the South African perspective the negotiations surrounding the establishment of the SA-EU TDCA were highly democratic. The process was transparent, inclusive, representative, and open. However, the outcome of these talks was to a large extent a foregone conclusion before South Africa even drafted its first mandate. The reasons for this are discussed in the next section.

A Foregone Conclusion?

Despite the democratic claims made by the state, its supposedly transparent institutions, and its widespread consultation with stakeholders, the outcome of the negotiations was to a large extent a foregone conclusion. The details of the talks were reduced to haggling over percentages and quotas, but the fact that the two parties would establish a free trade agreement, supported by cooperation agreements and South Africa's partial accession to the Lomé Convention was clear from the beginning. The only option South Africa had was not to conclude a deal, which really was no option at all.

Democratic and democratization theory leaves little room to explain this, mostly as most theories accept the sovereignty of the state and regard democratic processes as mostly internal to the state. However, this can no longer be the case and there is an urgent need for a reevaluation of theories that exclude global developments. Held (1996) also laments this, as he writes:

> The sovereignty of the nation-state has generally not been questioned. It has been assumed that the state has control over its own fate, subject only to compromises it must make and limits imposed by actors, agencies and forces operating within its territorial boundaries, and by the agents and representatives of other governments and states. . . . The world putatively outside the nation-state—the dynamics of the world economy, the rapid growth of transnational links and major changes to the nature of international law, for example—has barely been examined, and its implications for democracy have not been thought out at all by democratic political theorists.

In his work on models of democracy Held identifies four disjuncture between the sovereignty of the state over policy formulation and the global theatre the state has to operate in, these include the world economy, international political decisionmaking, international law and international culture, and the environment. Two of these are of concern to this study, namely the world economy and the role of international organizations. In addition the very nature of the European Union is examined as another disjuncture to South Africa's foreign trade policy formulation.

Globalization

With the collapse of the Soviet Union and the international shift toward democracy, globalization emerged as a powerful international phenomenon that analysts struggle to define but which affects each and every individual on earth. Most often we understand globalization to be the process by which the world has become increasingly integrated and uniform and a process by which international markets (financial and otherwise) have come to dominate international decision-making.

Identifying globalization as one of the disjunctures, Held (1996) comments as follows:

> [T]he internationalization of production, finance and other economic resources is unquestionably challenging the capacity of an individual state (whether democratic or not) to control its own economic future. At the very least, there appears to be a shift in the costs and benefits of the policy choices before governments, thereby affecting their autonomy; and a disjuncture between the idea of a sovereign state determining its own future and the circumstances of modern economies, marked as they are by the intersection of national, regional and international economic forces.

It is in this climate of globalization that participation in the world economy has seemingly become a prerequisite for economic prosperity and no longer the choice of governments. Free trade plays a great role in promoting globalization. Throughout Thabo Mbeki's presidency—and, in fact, already during the Mandela presidency—government has been quoted as saying that South Africa has to become a global actor. The government almost has no choice in this matter. It is not only South Africa that finds itself in this position, Margaret Thatcher already stated that 'there is no alternative' during her tenure as British Prime Minister. It is, therefore, also that the macroeconomic strategy of the South African government, GEAR, is focused on the liberalization of trade and strategies to become more competitive internationally—which of course limited the possibilities of alternative agreements with the EU.

Interestingly, these limits to national policy making are not the natural by-products of globalization, but are part of a strategy actively pursued by the World Bank, the IMF, and the World Trade Organization. Through Structural Adjustment Programs (SAPs) and the agreements reached within the WTO, countries' ability to make policy choices are curtailed. Bound by these agreements, national governments can do little but follow the current neoliberal paradigm.

> [T]here is a diminishing possibility of using the state to redistribute income (or wealth), to invest in priority sectors, or to maintain full employment, even if electorates want their governments to pursue such objectives. Instead, the instruments of economic policy must be skewed toward encouraging the private sector (domestic and foreign) to do those sorts of things. (Culpeper, 2001:3)

Although a free trade area between the EU and South Africa was presented as a choice South Africa had in establishing itself in the international arena after apartheid isolationism, in reality, South Africa had to accept free trade due to global pressures.

Restrictions Imposed by the European Union

In order to understand the limited options the European Union made available to South Africa during the negotiations, it is important to understand the dynamics of the EU and its relationship with the past apartheid government and the new democratic government. It is also crucial to understand how South Africa fits into the myriad of relationships and agreements the EU has with the rest of the world. These relationships and agreements form a clear hierarchy:

> European Union
> European Economic Area
> Central and Eastern European Countries
> FTA's: Israel, Morocco, Turkey, Tunisia, and Mexico
> Mediterranean Countries
> African Caribbean and Pacific Countries
> Generalized System of Preference
> Other Countries: Most Favored Nation (MFN) treatment

The EU's global trade policy can be envisaged within this hierarchy (Koning, 1997). Right at the top is the E.U. itself, as trade between these countries is completely unrestricted. As one moves down the hierarchy, access to the E.U. markets becomes less and less preferential, with the MFN status—a general concession as determined by the World Trade Organization (WTO)—at the very bottom.

At the time that negotiations were initiated between South Africa and the EU, Pretoria ranked very low on the hierarchy, having had access only to the Union's General System of Preferences. South Africa had become a priority issue for the EU after the signing of the Maastricht Treaty and the establishment of the Common Foreign and Security Policy (CFSP). It would, therefore, only have been natural to move South Africa higher up on the hierarchy. Obviously South Africa could never become part of the EU, but it could fit into the next-best slot of a Free Trade Area.

It is, therefore, quite clear that when talks were initiated between South Africa and the European Union about the future of the relationship between these two parties, South Africa had a limited amount of options. The EU made it quite clear that South Africa would not be granted full membership of the Lomé Convention, which basically only left two further options: the status quo—at the time this was limited access to the GSP with the strong possibility of extending it—or a free trade agreement. As Rob Davies pointed out this arrangements had some serious limitations. "Excluded from the agricultural GSP, for instance, will be such products as red meat, deciduous fruit, wine and grapes; that is, a number of areas where South Africa is currently most competitive." (Davies, 1997) Part of the problem was that South Africa opted for "developed" status within the World Trade Organization and it is this organization that provides the rules for GSP. In other words, in terms of the WTO charter South Africa was not really entitled to GSP but was granted this by special arrangement with the EU.

The second option—which now started to emerge as the only real viable alternative option—was the negotiation of a free trade agreement. At this is then also what emerged from the European mandate for negotiation.

International Organizations

With the advent of globalization the world has also witnessed a massive increase in international organizations. Held (1996) points out that

> The growth in the number of these new forms of political organization reflects the rapid expansion of transnational links, the growing interpenetration of foreign and domestic policy, and the corresponding desire by most states for some form of international governance and regulation to deal with collective policy problems.

One of these organizations is the World Trade Organization (WTO), which was established on 1 January 1995, by the 128 members of GATT, through a ministerial declaration signed in April 1994 in Marrakech, Morocco. It is both an institution to govern international trade and negotiations, and a body of law, which contains and administers a number of legal agreements on how countries should conduct international trade, ranging in specificity from the Agreement on Agriculture to the Agreement on Import Licensing Procedures.

The logic behind this was that if barriers to trade, especially tariff barriers, could be removed, less-efficient industries would no longer be protected. This in turn would encourage countries that have a comparative advantage in a certain product, to produce the bulk of it, leaving others to tend to their own particular product, which enjoys a comparative advantage. According to the advocates of free trade all nations will then be better off: if there are no restrictions then the most that can possibly be produced will be produced and there will be more products to circulate on ground level.

Both South Africa and all the members of the European Union are members of the WTO. This means that a free trade agreement between these two parties had to be negotiated with the WTO rules on FTA's as legal parameters. These rules stipulate that substantially all trade has to be included in such an agreement, which is more often translated as 90 percent of all trade between the two parties. This meant that South Africa could not expect any special favors from Europe within a free trade agreement. A unique relationship outside the form of an FTA was also out of the question, as the WTO stipulates that any concessions offered to another country outside of an FTA will have to be extended to all other WTO members.

The only way in which the EU and South Africa could secure a deal outside the WTO rules was through the securing of a waiver from the WTO—this waiver would have to be granted by all 140 plus WTO members. Many of these states are at a lower level of development than South Africa and would surely have objected to such special treatment. In addition, South Africa had become somewhat of a leader of developing countries in the WTO, encouraging and promoting widespread liberalization as the best avenue toward development (South Africa is ahead of its WTO liberalization commitments). It would have been impossible to sing a different tune in its dealings with the EU. This clearly also limited the range of potential outcomes to the EU-SA negotiations.

Conclusion

Globalization is arguably providing the pressure for states worldwide to resort to democratic forms of government. This is evidenced by the massive increase in democracies and the simultaneous increase in globalization. However, states still carry the task of democratizing the state apparatus. This process is essential for the stability of any democracy. Mass consultation on economic policies has been identified as key to the consolidation of democracy and in the globalized world we live in this also implies the democratization of foreign trade policy. However, it is at this point that a huge contradiction creeps in. Globalization has limited the options for domestic economic policy and has virtually closed the door on all other options but free trade for foreign trade policy. No matter how inclusive foreign trade policy formulation is, the rules of the game have been set and actors are only allowed to read their lines.

However, as has been argued in various chapters in this book, this seemingly inevitable outcome is more a reflection of the narrow conception and practice of "democratizing" foreign policy as instituted in the South African case, than it is a reflection of an objective state of affairs about which nothing can be done. Put differently, if broader forms of public participation were an institutionalized feature of foreign policy making in South Africa, the combined pressure of globalization, restrictions placed on the negotiations by the E.U., and the disciplinary impact of international organizations could be countered, if not neutralized. There lies the rub!

Notes

1.   Numerous interviews with a number of NEDLAC representatives.

2.   Numerous interviews with Willem Smalberger, Department of Trade and Industry. Mr. Smalberger was one of the few, if not the only, official that was involved throughout the negotiations.

3.   In his summation of the proceedings of the conference Rob Davies notes that "[t]he third scenario is the trade and development agreement (TDA). Like everybody else I think that we all heard about this concept for the first time yesterday." In Houghton. 1997. *Trading on Development: South Africa's Relations with the European Union.* Johannesburg.

Chapter 8

Democracy, Development, Security, and South Africa's "Arms Deal"[1]

David R. Black

No dimension of South Africa's foreign and security policy has generated more sustained controversy than the political economy of arms, both in terms of exports and, more recently, purchases. From the earliest days of the post-apartheid era beginning in April 1994, the Government of National Unity (GNU) was dogged by controversy concerning how, and how much, to regulate the international activities of the country's sophisticated arms industry—a legacy of South Africa's decades of growing isolation under apartheid (see Crawford 1999; Batchelor 1998a). How was it possible, commentators wondered, for South Africa to define a policy which simultaneously sustained the viability of this arms industry while remaining true to the African National Congress's professed core foreign policy values of human rights and democracy promotion and the peaceful resolution of disputes? How was this balance to be struck in a context of global oversupply of arms and aggressive competition for markets? The solution which emerged, structured around an extensive review and approval process by a Cabinet committee (the National Conventional Arms Control Committee) brought the country broadly in line with global norms for responsible arms exports, but by no means ended controversial instances of sales to dubious destinations (see Shelton, 1998: 24-27; Batchelor 1998b).[2]

Since December 1999 this ongoing controversy has been supplemented—indeed largely superceded—by mounting controversy over the Government's decision to enter into five major arms purchase transactions with foreign suppliers, for Corvettes, submarines, light-utility helicopters, lead-in fighter trainers, and advanced light fighter aircraft. From an initial estimated cost of R29.8 billion (roughly USD 4.8 billion), the projected cost of the deal has now escalated to R66.7 billion,[3] largely due to the declining value of South Africa's currency, the Rand. This is the "new" South Africa's largest ever public expenditure program and represents a commitment of resources that would, as a commentary from the Institute for a Democratic South Africa (IDASA) notes, purchase "an enormous amount . . . of poverty relief" (IDASA, May 2001: 2.8; also van Zyl and Macdonald, 31 October 2001). Yet in the welter of political and media controversy, focused primarily on the pursuit of suspected instances of conflict of interest and corruption, as well as the ANC government's hamfisted efforts to manage the affair politically, several of the more substantial and enduring implications of this Strategic Defense Procurement Package (hereafter the "arms deal") have been relatively neglected.

In this chapter, I will focus on three such sets of implications. These concern the prospects for democratic deepening and consolidation in South Africa; the prominence of the arms industry as a locus of development strategy in the context of globalization; and the reinscribing of conventional assumptions and discourses concerning sovereignty and state security. The analysis is informed by interrelated debates concerning the "democratization of foreign policy," the political economy of the "competition state" in semi-peripheral contexts, and critical security studies respectively. Overall, the case of South Africa's arms deal demonstrates that it would be a serious mistake to underestimate the degree of change in the new South Africa, notably pertaining to security and defense policy: there are many features of this story that would have been simply inconceivable in the old, militarized, secretive, and authoritarian era. Nevertheless, it also highlights the limited character of democratic life in the new South Africa; the limiting effects of globalization on development policy choices; and the degree to which decisionmakers in the "new" South Africa have come to accept in practice conventional defense and security assumptions which effectively privilege the security of states over people. In short, it underscores the distance South Africa has traveled, in Vale and Taylor's (1999) terms, from "something (potentially) special" to "just another country."

The Story So Far . . .

The story of the arms deal begins with the National Defense Review, which was debated and adopted by South Africa's Parliament in April of 1998. The Defense Review, in turn, was to elaborate upon the policy framework set out in the Defense White Paper, adopted unanimously by Parliament in May of 1996. The latter had been quite revisionist, if not radical, in its insistence on the centrality of the security of *people* as the country's first priority, and indeed was posited by one of the key participants in its preparation, Laurie Nathan, as a potential "agenda for state demilitarization" (Nathan 1998). The Review did not dispute this prioritization, but was less visionary and more prosaically focused on fleshing out such matters as "posture, doctrine, force design, force levels, logistical support, armaments, equipment, human resources, and funding" (Defense

Review, 1998: chapter 1.7). The Review process, which began in February of 1996, involved extensive consultations including several national consultative conferences and regional workshops attended by a wide cross-section of "stake-holders," ranging from the "defense establishment" to "civil society" as well as government. When completed, representatives of all parties in Parliament apparently greeted the Review enthusiastically.

Included in it was a discussion of Force Design (chapter eight) that laid out four broad options, each incorporating models of re-equipment for the South African National Defense Force (SANDF). There was widespread agreement that such a discussion was quite urgently needed, since there had been a precipitous decline in defense (and especially capital) spending between 1989 and 1995, from R19.6 billion to R10.5 billion in constant 1995 prices (see Batchelor, 1998a:104). Much of the existing equipment of the SANDF, particularly of the navy and air force, was rapidly approaching or had already reached obsolescence. But what sort of military, and military weaponry and equipment, did South Africa need given the fact that (as the White Paper discussed) the greatest threats to South Africa's people arise from underdevelopment, various socioeconomic problems, and violent crime, and that it faced no credible conventional military threat in the medium term at least (see Nathan 1998:45-46)? The Defense Review neatly side-stepped this issue by taking as its point of departure that its force design should focus on the military's primary function—defense against military aggression—and then taking a "threat-independent [essentially hypothetical] approach" to posit a force structure that could effectively respond to a range of imagined military threats (see CAMS, Sept. 2000:3-5). In other words, the options discussed were unconnected with any *real*, conceivable military threat to the country. The associated costs were presented in broad terms, and without any discussion of their budgetary requirements. Indeed, the Review explicitly noted that "[t]he approval of a force design by the parliamentary defense committee, Cabinet or Parliament does not constitute blanket approval for all implied capital projects or an immutable contract in terms of the exact numbers or types of equipment" (Defense Review, 1998: chapter 8.8). Yet it was these options, and in particular the Review's preferred Option One, that formed the basis for the procurement package subsequently negotiated by the government.

In November 1998, the Cabinet announced that it had considered a report from the subcommittee on the Procurement Program for the SANDF, recommending six core defense procurement programs and including recommendations on core suppliers. Cabinet authorized the subcommittee and the Minister of Finance to enter into further negotiations for an affordable final package with the preferred suppliers. In December 1999, the government contracted for five major arms transactions involving: three diesel-electric submarines and four corvettes from German consortia; thirty Italian Augusta light utility helicopters; nine Swedish/British advanced light fighter aircraft (Gripen) with an option to acquire nineteen more in 2004; and twelve British Aerospace (BAE) Hawk fighter trainer aircraft with an option to purchase twelve more in 2002 (see Cilliers, 2001; CAMS, Sept. 2000; and Jacobs et al., 2001: 23-26). The whole package, plus some additional weapons systems subsequently slated for purchase, are outlined in Table 8.1. The estimated cost of nearly R30 billion was supposed to be more than compensated for by the extraordinary proposition that the deal would generate R104 billion in economic "offsets" or benefits, and 65,000 jobs. Both claims were subsequently acknowledged to be both uncertain and substantially inflated.

The deal encountered early objections from a coalition of non-governmental organizations, which coalesced as the Coalition Against Military Spending (CAMS), on grounds that the package made no sense in the absence of a credible military threat, and that the vast sums involved would be far better spent addressing South Africa's profound human security challenges. Nevertheless, it did not become a major public issue until the auditor-general produced a report in September 2000 questioning various aspects of it, notably concerning the choice of tenders and subcontracts. This prompted a further investigation and report by Parliament's Standing Committee on Public Accounts (SCOPA), a committee which by (post-1994) convention operated on an essentially nonpartisan basis under an opposition party chair (in this case, the Inkatha Freedom Party's [IFP's] widely respected Gavin Woods). SCOPA's own report, issued in October 2000, alleged certain "questionable proceedings" and called for a joint investigation by four statutory investigating bodies: the Public Protector, the Office of Serious Economic Offences, the Directorate of Public Prosecutions, and the Special Investigating Unit (a 'corruption busting' unit headed by the indefatigable Judge Willem Heath). The SCOPA report was adopted by Parliament without debate in November. Then the ANC's senior leadership woke up to the potential implications of what Parliament had approved. There followed an extraordinary round of communications, involving the Speaker, Frene Ginwala, Vice-President Jacob Zuma, SCOPA Chair Gavin Woods, and ultimately President Mbeki himself. The net effect of this was to exclude the controversial Judge Heath from participation in the Joint Investigating Team (JIT) investigation,[4] while casting doubt on the independence of the Speaker from the ANC Executive. VicePresident Zuma went so far as to accuse SCOPA of launching "a fishing investigation to find the corruption and dishonesty you assume must have occurred" (Jacobs et al., 2001: 24). Not long thereafter the ANC Chief Whip, Tony Yengeni, removed the independent-minded chair of the "ANC Study Group" within SCOPA, Andrew Feinstein, from the Committee and replaced him with party loyalist Vincent Smith ("Is Smith just doing his job?", 1-7 March 2002). In March 2001, Yengeni himself became the subject of accusations in the press of having received a luxury Mercedes-Benz 4 X 4 from the European Aeronautics Defense and Space Company (EADSC), one of the successful bidders for a tender in the arms deal. It later transpired that EADSC had supplied up to 30 cars to South African "VIPs." Yengeni was arrested in October 2001 on charges of corruption, with an alternative charge of fraud, along with forgery and statutory perjury (Jacobs et al., 2001: 25), whereupon he resigned his position as Chief Whip. As various commentators have noted, it is remarkable that he remained in his key parliamentary post until this very late date.

Meanwhile, the JIT conducted an extensive investigation, issuing its report in November 2001. The report exonerated "government" (narrowly interpreted as the political leadership) from all "improper or unlawful conduct," leading to accusations from opposition politicians of a "whitewash" (see IDASA, Dec. 2001:9). However, the report was also very critical of certain aspects of the deal, including the inadequacy of evaluation systems for some contracts, inconsistent application of criteria for "offsets," and the existence of a clear conflict of interest involving the Department of Defense's Chief of Acquisitions, Mr. S. "Chippy" Shaik (IDASA, Dec. 2001:3-5). Finally, after more controversy and increasingly intractable party-based divisions within SCOPA, Committee Chair Gavin Woods resigned in February 2002, charging in documentation accompanying his resignation that the JIT report "was generally poor and superficial" (*Cape Times*, 26 Feb. 2002; also Feinstein, 1-7 March 2002). As of this writing, the saga continues to unfold.

Three aspects of the deal have dominated the public/media controversy. The first concerns the suspicion and indeed reality of instances of conflict of interest and corruption. The "deployment" of 30 luxury vehicles by EADSC has already been noted. The charges of conflict of interest revolve primarily several prominent "black empowerment" enterprises, notably the linked African Defense Systems (ADS) and Futuristic Business Solutions (FBS), which together won some of the most lucrative subcontracts associated with the arms deal. After leaving Parliament, the former Minister of Defense and an ex-Umkhonto we Sizwe (MK)[5] commander, the late Joe Modise, became a director of several companies pursuing business opportunities associated with the deal. The older brother of SANDF Procurement chief Chippy Shaik, Schabir Shaik, and another ex-MK commander closely linked to Modise,[6] Lambert Moloi, were the controlling officers of ADS. These figures were at the nexus of what the press dubbed "MK Inc" ("Cadres Cash In," 4 May 2001), and while only Chippy Shaik was identified by the JIT report as having been strictly speaking in a conflict of interest position, the others certainly appeared to violate the spirit if not the letter of conflict of interest rules. ("Say it ain't so, Joe", 15 March 2002)

Closely related to this focus was the question of whether various inside maneuvers associated with the deal had resulted in the artificial inflation of its cost, and more broadly whether taxpayers were getting "value for money." Media attention was focused, for example, on the Cabinet's decision to select the British Aerospace (BAE) Hawk as the new fighter trainer, over the newer, lighter, and cheaper (reportedly half the price) Italian-designed Aeromacchi. It was noted that "[s]ix months before being named the preferred supplier, British Aerospace sponsored numerous overseas trips for Cabinet Ministers, MP's and government officials and donated R5 million to the ANC's MK Veterans Military Association," and that "rumors abound" about numerous business links between Modise and BAE (see "To fight the good fight," 27 May 2001). The implication was that insider influence, as well as administrative weaknesses, had led to the negotiation of a deal which was more expensive than necessary, to the direct benefit of certain well-connected interests.

Third, attention was focused on the ANC's clumsy and somewhat paranoid attempts to manage the affair and limit dissent—a striking instance of the Mbeki government's persistent inability to develop an effective and coherent media strategy (see Cilliers, 2001). The moves to exclude Judge Heath from the JIT investigation, tainting the impartiality of the respected Speaker of Parliament; the removal of Andrew Feinstein from SCOPA and the committee's politicization along partisan lines; the failure to remove Tony Yengeni from his post as party whip until charges were laid; these and other interventions and non-interventions added fuel to the controversy, and heightened an atmosphere of mutual suspicion between the senior decision makers in government and the predominantly white-controlled mainstream print media.

Three comments can be made regarding these focuses of controversy. First, as unsavory as the various irregularities highlighted by press investigations are, it does not appear that they are particularly out of the ordinary for major arms deals globally. Nor (as the JIT report found) does it appear that corruption or conflict of interest affected the core decisions taken in the procurement program, or extended, on the whole, beyond the level of relatively minor officials and functionaries.[7] Second, it is not surprising that the ANC leadership has been rather defensive, indeed paranoid, about mass media coverage, given that in President Mbeki's words, "[w]e are faced with the virtually unique situation that, among the democracies, the overwhelmingly dominant tendency in South African politics, represented by the ANC, has no representation whatsoever in the mass media"[8] (Mbeki, Jan-Feb 2001). Nor is it surprising that this mass media would focus on issues of increasing corruption, mismanagement, and political authoritarianism, since this is what many white South Africans have long believed is the likely trajectory of their country under black majority rule. On the other hand, it is not helpful for the government to routinely label critics in the press and the DP opposition as racist ("Maduna slams 'racist' critics", 19 Nov. 2001). As with so many key issues in South Africa, then, this one has been "read" through a race-inflected prism—part of a worrying and destructive trend. But third, these issues, though not insignificant, are essentially side shows effectively distracting attention from the more fundamental questions to which the deal gives rise, including issues of democracy, development, and security. It is to these issues, then, that this paper now turns.

The Challenge to Parliamentary Democracy and Societal Democratization

Through the past decade, there has been considerable debate internationally concerning efforts to "democratize" foreign policy and the roles of Parliament and civil society, respectively, in this process (see, for example, Neufeld, 1999; Nossal, 1995). Similarly, in the early years of the postapartheid era, there was considerable excitement surrounding the possibility of South Africa's Parliament, populated as it was by numerous activists and veterans of struggle, emerging as a vital force for democratization deeply linked to South African (civil) society (CSAS, 1995). There was a certain (not entirely coincidental) irony about this new emphasis on democratizing foreign policy: it arose at a time when many were arguing that democratic political institutions were increasingly marginalized in the context globalization and what Robert Cox has characterized as the "internationalization of the state" (Cox, 1987:253). The arms deal illustrates some of the substantial problems and limitations associated with the aspiration toward democratizing foreign policy, in the South African case at least.

With regard to Parliament itself, this case serves to underscore the weakness of processes of parliamentary oversight and accountability, even as they pertain to a public procurement process of this magnitude and significance (see IDASA, May 2001 and Dec. 2001). The first, and perhaps most extraordinary, fact is that following Parliament's approval of the Defense Review in April 1998, with its highly notional and schematic presentation of proposals for Force Design and rearmament, the Cabinet did not feel it necessary to return to Parliament for specific approval of any of the elements of the arms deal that they subsequently negotiated. Nor did Parliament insist on its right to be consulted. Thus, aside from Pan-Africanist Congress MP Patricia de Lille's unsubstantiated charges of kickbacks associated with the commercial negotiations in September 1999, Parliament was completely marginal to the core decision-making processes concerning what to procure and how to procure it. The result was a rushed and secretive negotiation process, leading to decisions which lacked a clear legislative mandate and the scrutiny and legitimacy which Parliamentary investigation provides.

When the Standing Committee on Public Accounts did become involved from September 2000 on the basis of the auditor-general's report, this was very late in the game—akin to bolting the barn door after the horses had fled. Moreover, its scrutiny was fundamentally limited to an after-the-fact investigation of the financial management of the deal. Indeed, the (heretofore) nonpartisan operating principles of the Committee were based on the premise that "[t]he political affiliation of ministers or senior civil servants is of no consequence in determining whether financial regulations [its purview] have been transgressed or not" (Feinstein, 1-7 March 2002). Thus, core questions— for example, whether the weapons system made sense in strategic, developmental, or financial terms, and what their opportunity costs were relative to other urgent public priorities—were never debated in any parliamentary forum.[9]

In addition, facing its first really major test on an issue of such political magnitude and sensitivity, SCOPA's nonpartisan operating principles quickly broke down, and the committee began functioning along party-political lines with the majority ANC faction operating in close consultation with the party's senior leadership in pursuit of damage limitation. It remains an open question as to whether the committee's previous modus operandi can be restored—although the chances of this would seem to be slim on issues of comparable significance. Those familiar with party politics in other parliamentary systems will be unsurprised by this development. Nevertheless, SCOPA's partisan politicization has worrying implications in a one-party dominant system like South Africa's. Moreover, the disciplining and centralizing tendencies which are inherent in Parliamentary systems are reinforced in the South African case by the country's adoption of proportional representation, and its prohibition against Members of Parliament "crossing the floor" to join a party other than the one from which they were elected. Together, these provisions have tended to strongly reinforce the dependence of individual MPs on senior party leaderships and to increase the political risks of independent thought and action, particularly within the governing party (Southall 2000:155-8). The centralizing trends of which these tendencies are a part help to explain the fact that the ANC's party membership has declined from roughly 300,000 in 1999 to around 89,000 today ("ANC Party Membership Plummets," 19 March 2002).

This picture should not be overstated. There are some parliamentary committees which are still highly effective, and inclined toward vigorous critical scrutiny and initiative. Often these committees cooperate closely with groups in civil society, both in terms of research and the generation of specific policy and legislative proposals (February interview, 4 March 2002). A case in point is the Joint Standing Committee on Defense which, in close consultation with what may be described as "anti-militarist" societal organizations, has vigorously defended the principle of full parliamentary oversight of arms sales and twice turned back weaker legislation to institutionalize the National Conventional Arms Control process (Lamb interview, 26 Feb. 2002). Nevertheless, as the case of Andrew Feinstein indicates, the leadership of these committees is highly vulnerable if they become too critical of their party leaders' initiatives.

Moreover, parliamentary committees continue to suffer from serious resource limitations in terms of both research and administrative support. A case in point is the SCOPA which, under Gavin Woods' leadership, took on the task of scrutinizing the vast and complex arms deal with the assistance of precisely one researcher. Under these circumstances, it is hardly surprising that the more effective committees develop something close to a symbiotic relationship with groups in civil society, such as IDASA or the Center for Conflict Resolution at the University of Cape Town. Since these groups are largely externally funded, and must maintain a certain degree of critical distance from public officials, such relationships introduce important dilemmas on both sides.

Beyond this, the arms deal has underscored the quite profound and striking marginalization of thoughtful critical voices in civil society. The more fundamental objections of the Coalition Against Military Spending (CAMS), incorporating NGO's ranging from women's groups to faith groups to the Jubilee 2000 Campaign for debt cancellation to the (AIDS) Treatment Action Campaign, have already been noted.[10] These and more research-oriented "think tanks", along with parliamentarians, had substantial opportunities to make representations to the defense review process. In the past, many of these civil society groups were allies of the ANC in the struggle against apartheid. They also tend to be strong advocates of a more positive, transnationally oriented "regionalist" approach in South African foreign policy. The perspectives they represent may yet have a major impact on the arms deal, as a constitutional court case is brought against the government by Terry Crawford-Browne and his organization, Economists Allied for Arms Reduction, on grounds that it: broke financial laws in entering into loan agreements; acted irrationally and unconstitutionally in going ahead with the deal; and refused to heed the plight of poverty-stricken South Africans, as it is constitutionally obliged to ("NGO goes to court", 21 Nov. 2001; Crawford-Browne interview, 26 Feb. 2002).[11] Yet in the review itself, their perspectives were hardly discernible, certainly on the big questions. As CAMS has put it: "in the drafting of the Defense Review, which was done by the Department of Defense, little cognizance was taken of views expressed in the conferences and workshops by those opposed to the views of the military-industrial complex." (CAMS, Sept. 2000: 3)

Two points arise from these observations. First, they underscore the tendency of projects to "democratize" foreign and security policy through extensive consultative processes to descend into exercises in legitimation which, for the most part, have relatively little impact on substantive policy *outcomes*. Rather than enhancing the quality of democratic life, such exercises can have the perverse effect of increasing the sense of powerlessness and alienation which is a widespread if not universal feature of contemporary state-based democracies (see Neufeld, 1999, and Nossal, 1995). Second, however, they beg the question of *why* these more critical voices had so little impact, either on the defense review or in the subsequent public controversy concerning the arms deal. While there are many potential explanations for this, the political significance of the deal as a key instrument of development/industrial policy, and the resilience of dominant assumptions concerning the need for a strong *state* security capacity, together provide a large part of the answer.

The Arms Deal and the Arms Industry in the Context of Globalization

The ANC and government officials have insisted that the real reason for proceeding with the arms procurement package was that "without replenishment of the main arms of service of the SANDF, its operational capabilities would have been structurally impaired, undermining the country's security and the Constitutional requirement for such a capacity" ('An Investment to Safeguard Democracy', Jan-Feb 2001). In other words, the government undertook this package based on considerations of *national interest* and *constitutional obligation*. These arguments are further probed in the next section. Notwithstanding these claims, however, a pivotal aspect of the government's argumentation for the deal was the "offsets" it would generate, resulting in investment and jobs for South Africa(ns). The main contractors were required to indicate in their tenders the economic benefits they would commit themselves to providing to South Africa. These took two forms: (1) direct benefits to local military contractors to whom aspects of the work were subcontracted, referred to as "Defense Industrial Participation" (DIP); and (2) nonmilitary trade and investment in South Africa to which the tenders committed themselves, termed "National Industrial Participation" (NIP). As noted above, initial estimates of the benefits accruing from these offsets ran as high as R104 billion in trade and investments and 65,000 jobs (IDASA, May 2001).

These figures, it has subsequently transpired, were highly exaggerated. To cite just one example, the German submarine consortium contracted to produce three new diesel-electric submarines has said that contrary to Cabinet documents suggesting that 16,251 jobs would be created through its sub-contracting activity in the Coega harbor and stainless steel plant, the actual figure is 4,000, of which 3,000 will be during construction only (CAMS, Sept. 2000: 9). Moreover, it is not clear how much of the NIP funds associated with the package as a whole constitute new investments that would not have been undertaken regardless of the deal. It has also been pointed out that the penalties for defaulting on offset provisions, set at around 10 percent, are light enough that in many cases, they can easily be absorbed within the profit margins of the projects in question. In short, there is a great deal of uncertainty surrounding the degree to which the offset commitments will actually materialize (see IDASA, May 2001). Too little attention was given in advance of the negotiations to assessing the international experience with such agreements, much of which appears to be quite sobering (Lamb interview, 26 Feb. 2002; Williams interview, 12 Feb. 2002).

Even if the benefits have been exaggerated, however, it seems clear that one of the major reasons why the Cabinet as a whole was persuaded to support the deal was that it would directly benefit industrial development and job creation in South Africa. It was, in short, a valuable instrument of industrial policy, closely linked to the long-term viability of South Africa's arms industry through sub-contracts and strategic linkages.

There is considerable evidence that relying on the defense industry as an instrument of industrial development is a highly flawed strategy, particularly in a semiperipheral country with high levels of unemployment. With specific reference to South Africa, this is because the investment and jobs created are highly capital intensive; the benefits are regionally concentrated in the country's industrial heartland of Gauteng; the sector is relatively skill intensive, meaning it absorbs a disproportionately large share of highly skilled workers in a context of serious skills shortages economy-wide; the employment benefits accrue disproportionately to white men, thereby widening gender and racial inequalities; and research and development costs are likely to continue to escalate because of the import dependence of much of the activity in the sector (see COSATU, 6 Feb. 2001; and Willett, 1995). Why, then, would the South African government have viewed the industrial offsets as a major selling point for the deal?

In part, the answer lies in considerations of prestige. Long before the arms deal was embraced, the ANC government was apparently persuaded of the importance of maintaining and promoting South Africa's arms industry, despite its declining significance in terms of manufacturing output, exports, and jobs (see Kynoch, 1996; Batchelor 1998b). Some key members of Cabinet—notably the Minister and Deputy Minister of Defense—regarded having "world-class" technology embedded in this highly sophisticated industry as important in itself, symbolizing South Africa's achievement and potential. They seem to have won over both former President Mandela and President Mbeki.

More substantially, however, it seems likely that the government was persuaded of the value of this instrument of industrial policy due to the paucity of viable alternatives. Here, the context of globalization is important. In 1996 the GNU, in pursuit of more rapid rates of economic growth through the attraction of larger volumes of private investment, shifted its development course from the more social democratic Reconstruction and Development Program (RDP) to the neoliberal Growth, Employment, and Redistribution (GEAR) strategy. It thus embraced a market-oriented program of macro-economic restructuring, marking a sharp departure from South Africa's strong historical emphasis on highly interventionist (albeit racialist) approaches to economic development and an activist industrial policy (see Marais, 1998; Hentz, 2002, chapter 5). In this highly controversial break with the ANC alliance's own historic preference for a more-or-less socialist development strategy, the government embraced the global economic orthodoxy of the day, and the model of the neoliberal "competition state" (see van der Westhuizen, 1999; Cerny, 1997).

As is well known, the results have been disappointing. Growth rates have struggled to keep pace with rates of population increase and unemployment has remained stubbornly high (around 45 percent), as new job creation has been offset by the hundreds of thousands of jobs lost in the restructuring process ("New survey puts SA jobless rate at 45 percent", 1-7 March 2002). More to the point of this chapter, however, this shift in development strategy meant that government effectively surrendered many of its traditional interventionist levers of industrial and development policy—not least the extensive network of state-owned enterprises which are now being haltingly privatized. Military spending was one of the relatively few government-controlled levers that continued to be viewed as legitimate, most importantly by the interests in advanced capitalist countries that set the terms of the globalization debate. Indeed, as soon as it became clear that South Africa was planning an extensive program of military reequipment and modernization, the country was apparently inundated by European governments (mostly social democratic) and enterprises peddling weapons systems (Crawford-Browne interview, 26 Feb. 2002; Cilliers, 2001).[12] This undoubtedly became a significant push factor in persuading the government to move toward a hasty decision on the deal.

Moreover, the procurement package could be seen as the key to securing the medium-term viability of key elements of the South African arms industry—still largely state-controlled through Armscor (responsible for acquisitions and overall coordination) and Denel (responsible for R & D and production). In a global industry marked throughout the 1990s by rapid restructuring and transnational strategic alliances, particularly in Europe (see Shelton, 1998:5-7), the deal strongly reinforced the growing range of linkages between South African arms producers and major European counterparts. Besides the direct benefits of the subcontracts, therefore, the deal could be seen as a reinforcing South African access to the European market, and as enhancing the possibility of South African companies serving as production platforms in alliance with European firms for global arms exports (Crawford-Browne interview, 26 Feb. 2002). It is thus plausible that whatever the personal stake of 'MK Inc' in the government choosing the BAE Hawk over the Aeromacchi fighter trainer, for example, a key consideration was the strategic linkage that it would reinforce with BAE.

Beyond the direct investment, employment, and strategic benefits that the government was able to secure through the arms deal, however expensive and overstated, it also offered a means of advancing a more specific and highly salient economic development priority: black empowerment (interview with foreign diplomat, 27 Feb. 2002). In short, as discussed earlier, the government was able to direct substantial commercial benefits to a small but highly prized group of African-controlled enterprises. In the market-oriented context of GEAR, promoting a successful class of black entrepreneurs had become a major government priority; yet ironically, GEAR also reduced the range of means at the government's disposal to do so. Once again, the arms deal offered the country's political leadership an extraordinary opportunity to directly advance this objective, to the great material benefit of, among others, ADS, FBS, and their principals.

In short, and ironically given its historic opposition to the militarization of South African society under apartheid, the ANC government has hitched its industrial policy wagon firmly (though not exclusively) to the global arms trade and the cotinued viability of South African exporters therein. This is not a "good" policy choice, given the high cost of the jobs produced and sustained, its tendency to reinforce import dependence and inequalities based on region, race, and gender, its absorption of an excessively large share of highly skilled personnel, and its implications for "crowding out" urgently needed social spending (see COSATU, 2001; Willetts, 1995). However, it looks considerably better when, in the context of globalization and market-oriented restructuring, many of the formerly feasible industrial and development policy alternatives are effectively ruled "out of bounds."

Nevertheless, as noted at the outset of this section, industrial policy and black empowerment arguments could not have served in themselves to justify such a massive public expenditure. Decision-makers in South Africa had to be persuaded that it was indeed both appropriate and important for South Africa to maintain a stout, traditional military defense capability against external attack—the traditional core function of the military.

The Reinscribing of Traditional Assumptions Regarding Sovereignty and State Security

How is it that the arms deal was consummated without a plausible strategic rationale for the capabilities purchased—or even a meaningful public debate on their appropriateness? Why did all parties in Parliament provide enthusiastic support for the Defense Review, in which the force design which is now in the process of being implemented was first posited? Why have civil society critics of the deal, raising more profound questions about South Africa's *real* security needs and priorities, been largely marginalized? And what are the *real* security implications and costs of the deal?

In answer to these questions, one must take account of the continued weight of "taken-for-granted" assumptions about the desirability, indeed necessity, of a robust military-defense capability to defend a traditionally conceived, state-based "sovereignty," as emphasized by scholars of critical security studies (e.g., Booth and Vale, 1995; Vale, 2002; P. Williams, 2000). In short, not only has military rearmament been championed by a formidable coalition of old and new forces within the South African state and political economy, including senior figures from the old MK and SADF along with the state-owned defense industries (Kynoch, 1996:445-7), but that this "pitch" has found a highly receptive audience in a South African political culture marked by deeply entrenched militarist/realist assumptions.

The starting point for this discussion is the absence of any credible military threat to the Republic of South Africa and its people—defense against which is posited as the primary function of the SANDF in both the White Paper and the Defense Review. Nor, in the postapartheid era, is any sort of alliance role drawing the South African military into an extra-regional war (such as occurred during World Wars I and II) at all conceivable. The most compelling and therefore most frequently used rationales for the maintenance of a substantial South African military capability include the maintenance of civil order in times of crisis (including, for example, deployment to Kwazulu-Natal in the explosive context of the 1994 transitional elections—see Kynoch, 1996:454); border patrol in the face of mass movements of migrants and refugees; peace support operations, predominantly in Africa; coastal/fisheries patrol of South Africa's extensive coastal zone and those of its neighbors; and disaster relief within and beyond South Africa's borders, as in the admirable rescue efforts of SANDF personnel during the floods of 2000 in Mozambique. None of these functions are uncontroversial; indeed all (save perhaps the last two) present South Africa's military and political decision makers with some extremely difficult scenarios and dilemmas.[13] It is not surprising, therefore, that the military establishment's strong preference in terms of force design was for a return to its traditional core function of defending against military attack. Yet the expensive hardware contracted for in support of this role, including jet fighters, Corvettes, and submarines, seems on its face quite excessive and even inappropriate for the more plausible uses to which South Africa's military capacity could be put. It also underscores the fact that there is a good deal more defense spending to come, as the core capabilities of the military which *are* relevant to its most plausible applications (mostly associated with the army) come up for renewal and replacement.[14] At the very least, the merits and timing of such major purchases deserve to be debated, and their opportunity costs in terms of socio-economic spending foregone assessed.

As the foregoing sections have demonstrated, these debates have not really occurred, certainly since the omnibus Defense Review process was undertaken. Indeed with hindsight, what is striking is the apparently enthusiastic all-party reception the Defense Review got when it was brought before Parliament. Similarly, it is striking that the public controversy surrounding the deal has hardly touched on the core question of whether the package makes any strategic sense in the first place, and only marginally more on what its opportunity costs are.[15] Nor has it focused on the deal's link to a reinvigorated arms industry as a dubious cornerstone of industrial/development strategy.

These striking silences in the dominant public and media debates strongly indicate that, as retired Colonel Rocky Williams, a key participant in the Defense Review, has put it, most South Africans continue to operate within a modernist framework that takes sovereignty as its primary referent. Moreover, he notes, South Africa is "quite a martial country" with a long history of warfare, the upshot of which is that many of the country's people "like armies" and want a strong, well-equipped defense force that can "kick ass" (interview, 12 February 2002). Among the country's significant political parties, this militarist orientation is probably least strong within the ANC alliance (though it has always had strong champions among ex-MK cadres in government and beyond it). Thus, one foreign diplomat in Cape Town has observed that the mainly "white parties" (in particular, the Democratic Party and the New National Party, as well as the Zulu-based IFP) probably initially interpreted the arms deal as evidence of the growing "maturity" of the ANC, recognizing the "fact" that the strength of the nation was based on its "ability to project power" (interview, Cape Town, 26 February 2002). It is not surprising, then, that the focus of their attacks has been around questions of mismanagement, political authoritarianism, and corruption, versus the question of whether the deal made strategic sense to begin with.

What, then, are the *real* security implications of the arms deal? Inevitably, of course, the answers are speculative. They can be divided somewhat artificially into two: implications for the region as a whole, and for South Africa itself. For the region as a whole, it is likely to reinforce the idea among South Africans and their neighbors that "South Africa" is continuing to live "up against" its neighbors, rather than with and among them (Vale, 2002). The Mbeki government has been highly sensitive to regional anxieties, and has been careful to work within regional multilateral fora in virtually all of its Southern African initiatives. Nevertheless, it is hard for neighbors not to see South Africa as harboring hegemonic aspirations when the latter spends three times as much on its military as all of the other SADC states combined (CAMS, Sept. 2000: 13), and when its technological domination is being strongly reinforced by current procurement projects. The arms deal also invites them to continue to think of the region in terms of a collection of sovereign states with both a right and an obligation to defend their sovereign prerogatives through the maintenance of a robust military capability. And, when they seek to re-equip in support of this end, the reinvigorated South African defense industry stands ready to supply them with many of the weapons they seek ("SA should help regional defense industry", 17 Aug. 2000).[16] In this manner, South Africa's arms deal and the force design which underpins it serve to obfuscate the fact that the most profound security threats in the region are sub- and transnational, arising from the shared realities of poverty, disease, environmental degradation, oppressive governance, and the like.

Domestically *and* regionally, then, the costs of the arms deal must be considered in terms of spending foregone on programs addressing the roots of human insecurity and regional instability. As a result of the arms deal, defense spending in South Africa will have increased by almost 36 percent in real terms between 2000 and 2003 (van Zyl and Macdonald, 2001:5; also CAMS, Sept. 2000: 12). This makes it among the fastest growing of government spending priorities, significantly outstripping spending growth in areas which are consistently identified as top public and governmental priorities, such as social services or the criminal justice system (COSATU, Feb. 2001). Too little attention has been given to the programs which have been slowed or foregone, with potentially profound human security implications, as a result of the billions of rands being allocated to arms procurement—and to the fact that this process in South Africa is likely to encourage emulation in neighboring states. To cite only the most dramatic and disturbing case in point, while South Africa moves quickly forward with the implementation of its arms deal, it continues to prevaricate on the provision of antiretrovirals to AIDS-infected pregnant women, at the certain cost of literally thousands of premature deaths of the country's children.[17] Which, it may justifiably be asked, is the more urgent security priority for South Africa today?

Conclusions

The extent of change in the security policy of the new South Africa should not be underestimated. At one level, the arms deal strongly underscores this. Aside from the most obvious point that the SANDF no longer constitutes an instrument of destructive destabilization of the country's neighbors, the arms deal has been undertaken in the wake of a decade of precipitous cuts to the defense budget, which fell from over 4 percent of GDP in 1989 to well under 2 percent today. These cuts have been accompanied by the integration of former liberation and homeland army personnel into the SANDF, and the insertion of ex-liberation army fighters into senior leadership posts. As the Defense Review *process* indicates, civil-military relations have been reconstituted on a dramatically more open and transparent footing, certainly compared with the highly militarized and secretive situation that prevailed in the 1980s.

Moreover, the vigorous and sustained scrutiny of the arms deal by public and mass media institutions alike, and the very public controversy which has surrounded it, strongly indicate that South Africa has become a much more open and democratic society than ever before. However much critics might charge that the JIT report was a 'whitewash', for example, the fact they have felt perfectly at liberty to do so, and that such an extensive investigation occurred *at all*, indicate a dramatic shift in the modus operandi of South African politics in the postapartheid era.

Nevertheless, at a deeper level the deal also serves to underscore the extent to which the South African government has come to operate like "just another country". Like many established liberal democracies, its democratic institutions and processes are relatively weak and limited in their powers of investigation, oversight, and accountability, while executive dominance is strong and arguably increasing. Moreover, while more critical voices in civil society have many more opportunities for input into policy *processes,* their impact on *outcomes* remains minimal. Like most other semiperipheral countries, South Africa has accommodated itself to the imperatives of globalization and market-oriented restructuring, resulting in increased societal polarization and a reinforced developmental salience for the arms industry. Finally, the country's policy debates and outcomes reflect the profound resilience of traditional realist assumptions concerning the necessity for, and purpose of, a robust military-defense capacity. This is so despite the force of arguments that the country cannot be secure unless its people are secure, and that this can only occur within an open regionalist framework—neither of which are advanced by the country's current arms deal. While it is perhaps unfair to expect the new South Africa to have fulfilled the ambitious aspirations embedded in many early postapartheid debates toward becoming a different sort of country, pursuing an alternative security paradigm within and beyond its borders, it is nevertheless a source of regret.

Table 8.1: Revised Weapons Purchase Program
September 1999

Weapons	Preferred supplier	Type	No.	Cost (Rands million)	Delivery period
Corvettes	German Corvette Consortium		4	6 917	2003-2005
Submarines	German Submarine Consortium	Class 209 Type 1400 diesel-electric	3	5 354	2005-2007
Maritime helicopters	GKN Westland, UK		4	787	2005
Light utility helicopters*	Augusta, Italy	A 109	30	1 949	2003-2005
Light fighter aircraft	SAAB Sweden & BAe, UK	Dual-seat Gripen JAS39	9	4 740	2006-2008
Trainer aircraft	Bae, UK	Hawk dual-seat lead-in fighter trainer	12	2 370	2005
		Total Tranche 1		**22 117**	
Light fighter aircraft	SAAB Sweden & BAe, UK	Dual-seat Gripen JAS39	19	8 662	2008-
Trainer aircraft	BAe, UK	Hawk-dual seat lead-in fighter trainer	12		2008
		Total tranches 1& 2		**30 779**	
		Additional weapons purchases proposed			
Ground based air defence systems				10 000	
Armoured vehicles					
Battle tanks	France/UK	GIAT Le Clerc/Challenger	95	3600	
Grand total				**44 379**	

Source: Coalition Against Military Spending (CAMS) Background Information, September 2000.
* This item was omitted from the list quoted in the medium-term expenditure estimates for 2000/01.

Notes

1.   The author gratefully acknowledges the support of the Social Sciences and Humanities Research Council of Canada in the preparation of this chapter, the timely and capable research assistance of Andrew Grant, and helpful comments from James Hentz and Paul Williams on an earlier draft.

2.   There have also been weaknesses in terms of implementation. In particular, despite a requirement that the NCACC report annually to Parliament on South Africa's arms exports, as of March 2002 it had not done so since 1999.

3.   This figure includes interest costs and is liable to further escalation in light of adverse currency trends, interest charges, and other inflationary pressures. See van Zyl and Macdonald, 2001: 4.

4.   Jacobs, et al., wryly note that '[i]t did not go amiss that Heath had fallen foul of certain [ANC] political leaders.'

5.   The ANC's military wing during the apartheid era.

6.   He was Modise's brother-in-law and his aide de camp after 1994.

7.   This conclusion, however, remains tentative, as evidence of conflicts of interest are continuing to emerge: see "Say it ain't so Joe", 15 March 2002.

8.   Presumably meaning press outlets that are typically supportive of the ANC.

9.   It is important to place this point in some comparative perspective. For example, in as established a liberal democracy as Canada, Parliament's role in approving major procurement packages has been described by defense policy scholar Dan Middlemiss as "negligible at best, non-existent in the sense of making a specific approval for a specific procurement program" (Personal communication, 11 April 2002). As in the arms deal, such oversight as there has been has virtually always come after the fact, and has often been focused on narrow procedural matters through scrutiny of the Reports of the Auditor General to the Public Accounts Committee. In this sense, South Africa's recent experience closely follows long-standing Canadian practice. However, the failings of parliamentary practice in established liberal democracies like Canada should not be used to justify comparable weaknesses in South Africa, given the high aspirations and more recent provenance of the latter. Also on the Canadian case, see "MP's as nobodies on Parliament Hill", 18 March 2002. I am indebted to Jim Hentz for stressing the need for comparative perspective.

10.   Whether these groups speak for the majority of South Africans is doubtful, as discussed in the final section of this chapter. This, however, is beside the points made below.

11.   The strong and autonomous role of the Constitutional Court, empowered by an unusually progressive Bill of Rights, is a feature of South African political life which is likely to continue to have substantial and generally progressive—the controversial— social repercussions in the context of South Africa's democracy.

12.   Given the moral dubiousness of the global arms industry, it is easy to see why South Africa was seen as such a desirable customer. Not only was the package a large and lucrative one, but the purchaser could not be accused of human rights violations or be construed as an imminent threat to regional peace and security.

13.   On peace support operations, for example, see R. Williams, 2000.

14.   As shown in Table 8.1, the government has already signaled its intention to add major capital spending programs for the army to those it has already undertaken in the context of the original arms deal.

15. Though for an excellent effort to stimulate and inform a debate on opportunity costs, see van Zyl and Macdonald, 2001.

16. Although Africa is a secondary market for South African arms, owing primarily to its limited buying power, Peter Batchelor has noted that all SADC states except the Seychelles have purchased (mostly small) arms from South Africa since 1996 (Batchelor, N.D.; see also Khanyile, 2000). This does not include arms shipped clandestinely from South African sources to nonstate combatants in the region and beyond. On the latter, see Batchelor, 1998b: 60.

17. I am indebted to a foreign diplomat based in Cape Town for drawing my attention to this particular frame. This is not to suggest that there is a direct causal link between the arms deal and the failure to supply antiretrovirals to HIV-positive pregnant women: as observers of South African politics know, the politics of AIDS in South Africa is very much more complicated. What the comparison underscores is the opportunity cost of arms spending, and the strange alacrity with which it is accepted as compared with other, arguably far more urgent, spending priorities.

Chapter 9

The Challenge of Transnational Democracy and the Southern African Development Community

Pierre du Toit

The national state is widely predicted to be in decline, and according to one forecast, is likely to continue to exist as one set of institutions alongside other corporations (Van Creveld 1999). The rise of new intergovernmental organizations can be attributed, in part, to the inability of territorially bound states to deal with certain problems. Typically, these problems emerge from sources outside specific national boundaries, and can be described as being larger than the jurisdiction of the state. The decline of the state as a salient corporation means that new functional equivalents have to be found, because states have been the dominant sites of both security and democracy for many decades. The focus of this chapter is to examine the issue of democratizing such larger intergovernmental bodies, using the case of SADC as an example. The democratic qualities, or lack of, of SADC will be considered with reference to the access to decision making available to one of its members, South Africa, and with respect to one case, the military invasion of Lesotho in September 1998.

Theoretical Framework

National states emerged as the dominant political units in Europe, not by way of amicable social contracts between consenting individuals, but through a ruthless process of elimination, conducted by means of war. Of the 500 or so independent political units in the Europe of 1500, only 25 remained by 1900, all of them national states (Tilly 1975, p. 15). State leaders eliminated rival contenders through the superior capacity for social control which state organization made possible. The gradual and simultaneous capacity for extracting resources from, and regulating the social relationships of a resident population within a fixed territory, redistributing these resources in pursuit of specific policy objectives, mostly in preparation for, or the conduct of war, and thus penetrating society through special purpose organizations in the form of bureaucracies which were both distinctive and autonomous from other social units is a well documented feature of statebuilding in Europe (Finer 1975; Finer 1997; Migdal 1988; Tilly 1990).

The important point here is to note that (by the end of the eighteenth century only) the end result was for states to achieve a virtual monopoly on force, at the expense of the subject populations (Finer 1974, pp. 83-88; Mann, 1988, pp. 116, 117). This was followed in the nineteenth century with the marked democratization of the European state, in part as a response to pressure from subject populations for more rights (Tilly 1975, p. 38), and in part as an incentive offered by state leaders to increase the legitimacy of the states' demands for ever higher taxes (Ardant 1975). Crucial to the expansion of the legitimacy of the democratized state was its claim to provide public goods to its citizens, in return for compliance with its tax requirements. From the outset, the first and foremost public good which the state could offer derived from its monopoly on force. It could provide protection, in the form of physical security to its citizens in return for compliance, or it could withhold protection, or even use its coercive monopoly against its citizens as an alternative to voluntary compliance. This monopoly was and is obviously open to abuse (Tilly 1985).

The predicted eclipse of states, as argued from the perspective of the dynamics of the political economy of globalization is, as Peter Evans has shown, neither persuasive, nor a foregone conclusion (Evans 1997). Far more compelling is the argument posed from the perspective of security. Martin van Creveld traces this decline in the ability of states to provide the most basic of public goods, physical safety, to their loss of the monopoly on war, and the loss of the monopoly on coercive means (Van Creveld 1991).

Security Problems and the Security Dilemma

The crucial link between security and democracy lies in the ability of the state to provide security to all its citizens on an equitable basis. In a democratic state, the coercive monopoly of the state is used to provide protection to all citizens, as a basic right. This is achieved when the public and private domains can be legally demarcated, and the public domain becomes the terrain for the provision of collective goods such as welfare, social, political, and economic rights. Security, in the form of physical protection, is provided for every citizen against every other one, against the arbitrary actions of the state, and against threatening actions from beyond the borders of the state. This protection can be provided by the agencies of the state itself, (police and military forces) or can be privatized.

Privatized security is tolerable in democratic states up to a point. As long as private agencies are authorized and licensed by the state, and act under the general auspices of the laws of the state, they may be permitted. However, security cannot be privatized entirely, as it extends only to those customers who can pay for it (Shaw 1997). Democratic states are compelled to provide protection to all citizens, and equitably so. This can only be done if the personnel of the state augment the security provided by the private sector.

The measure of the failure of the state to provide such protection is when the *security dilemma* arises within the state. This condition emerges when intermingled or adjacent groups of people start to sense that they have to take care of their own security. This condition can arise through a number of circumstances, one of which is a substantial weakening of the state. The dilemma emerges, according to Posen, when "what one does to enhance one's own security causes reactions that, in the end, can make one less secure" (Posen 1993, p. 28). When groups perceive the state not to be capable, or willing, to provide security, and they act on their own volition, security again becomes privatized, or communalized, in a sense. Such security, however, further undermines the basis for democracy though the spiral of destabilizing countermeasures it elicits. These countermeasures are likely to emerge when the offensive and defensive capabilities of groups responding to their own insecurity, cannot be distinguished by other, proximate groups, and when offensive countermeasures, especially by the second-order category of insecure actors, appear to be more effective (Posen 1993, p. 28). This creates the incentive to seek security through preemptive actions.

Size, Security, and Democracy

The destabilizing spiral of events triggered by the security dilemma can, as Kaufmann has shown, lead to state collapse or disintegration once a crucial threshold of escalation has been passed. This two-step threshold entails, firstly, the recognition that "once violence (or abuse of state power by one group that controls it) reaches the point that ethnic communities cannot rely on the state to protect them, (and) each community must mobilize to take responsibility for its own security" (Kaufmann 1996, p. 147). The second step in the Kaufmann threshold is crossed "[o]nce a majority of either group comes to believe that the killing of non-combatants of their own group is not considered a crime by the other" (Kaufmann 1996, p. 159). Both Posen and Kaufmann have argued forcefully that the inability of the state of Yugoslavia to solve the multiple security dilemmas that emerged after 1990 within the state has eventually lead to its demise and break-up into smaller units. These small mini states of Slovenia, Croatia, and Bosnia are now being built into new units of security, and also as units of democracy. The small size of these units, do however, hold important implications for the quality of democracy they are able to deliver.

Where the state is considered a viable but still inadequate site for providing security and at the same time, for serving as a site for democracy, additional or alternative units come into consideration. Conceptualizing the evolution of institutional forms beyond the conventional territorially defined, territorially fixed and mutually exclusive state has produced a number of vague notions, such as the "virtual state," the "defective state" and the "region state." Some of the more prominent institutional changes have been the emergence of smaller units which result from the fragmentation of states along the lines of ethnic solidarities. Both Posen and Kaufmann have argued forcefully that the inability of the state of Yugoslavia to solve the multiple security dilemmas that emerged after 1990 within the state eventually led to its demise and break-up into smaller units. These small mini states of Slovenia, Croatia, and Bosnia are now being built into new units of security, and also as units of democracy. However, security need not be pursued only by ever smaller political units. The security dilemma can also be addressed by constructing larger units. Where the security dilemma emerges between sovereign states in the international arena, the argument has been advanced that security can be gained through larger institutional configurations such as *security regimes* (Jervis 1978). Leaving aside the specific character of these international regimes, the general point can be made that states whose citizens are threatened by forces, including non state actors, from outside their borders may resort to establishing larger units of authority in order to regain security.

The response to security problems appears to be that of both a fragmentation into units smaller than the territorial state, and a coalescence into larger units. The interrelationship between size, and the nature of jurisdictions, on the one hand, and the requirements of security and democracy, on the other, therefore needs to be conceptualized in more detail. Such greater conceptual depth can be found in the work of Robert A. Dahl and Edward R. Tufte. In their book *Size and Democracy* they raise the issue of trade-offs between two aspects of democracy which appear to be inversely related to the size of the democratic unit. Democratic theory, according to them, sets two criteria for the ideal political unit. The first is *citizen effectiveness*: "citizens acting responsibly and competently fully control the decisions of the polity." The second is *system capacity*: "the polity has the capacity to respond fully to the collective preferences of its citizens" (Dahl & Tufte 1973: 20). In the ideal Greek city-state these criteria were met through direct democracy (for citizen effectiveness) and an autonomous, self-sufficient, and small city-state (for system capacity). Democratic practice changed when the much larger national state became the unit of democracy, resulting in a reduction in the extent to which both criteria could be met simultaneously. Large powerful states could, as sovereign units, at least initially claim to be autonomous, but these entities required indirect forms of participation from citizens numbering millions, thus compromising citizen effectiveness. Continued evolution of the global economy, in particular, right into the present era of globalization has further undercut the autonomy, and thus system capacity, of even these very large units of democracy.

The overall thrust of the analysis by Dahl and Tufte is that while small homogeneous units (such as Slovenia and Croatia) may be most appropriate for meeting the requirements of citizen effectiveness, there is no optimal size unit for achieving system capacity (Dahl & Tufte 1973:109). They argue that different problems (relating to capacity) can be dealt with effectively by different size units. One category of problems may require larger units "[if], because of its boundaries, a political system lacks authority to secure compliance from certain actors whose behavior results in significant costs (or loss of potential benefits) to the members of the system, then the boundaries of the political system are smaller than the boundaries of the political problem" (Dahl & Tufte 1973:129). The repertoire of examples is familiar: air and water pollution, nuclear proliferation, contagious diseases, monetary instability, and the exploitation of the resource commons such as oceans and continental shelves. The following strategic responses are available to units whose boundaries are too small to deal effectively with a given problem.

One option is to adjust unilaterally by not taking any action, but just bearing the costs of the behavior from beyond the boundaries of the system. The second is for the system to engage with the relevant other units in a process of mutual accommodation, reached through a process of negotiation. The third strategic option is to cooperate with adjacent units in order to establish new larger units, specifically designed to address the particular problem at hand and entrusted with a corresponding mandate and jurisdiction. These enlarged institutions may range from expanded unitary states to federations and confederations (and, we may add, international regimes).

At the other end of the spectrum are the instances where boundaries of units may be too large. "If the application of uniform rules throughout a political system with given boundaries imposes costs (or loss of benefits) on some actors that could be avoided (with no significant cost to others) by non-uniform rules, then the boundaries of the political system are larger than the boundaries of the political problem" (Dahl & Tufte 1973, pp. 133,134). The strategic options open to such units appear now in a reverse sequence to those of units that are too small.

The first option is, once again, for the unit to adjust unilaterally, to bear and absorb the costs of such deleterious behavior. The second is to seek mutual adjustment, through a negotiated settlement. The third is to create new, smaller decentralized subunits, small enough to include only the disadvantaged people within their jurisdiction. The various constitutional formulae of decentralized unitary states, federations, and confederations feature again. The final option is to establish completely new, smaller, sovereign territorial states, whose members come exclusively from the ranks of the disaffected.

Clearly, given the range of problems facing many contemporary states, the pressure is created to construct both larger and smaller units. Even a single-problem issue such as security can generate pressure toward both smaller (ethnic mini states) and larger (security regimes/communities) units. Dahl and Tufte are keenly aware of this condition and conclude with the proposition that democratic theory should abandon the search for an optimal size unit. Instead, it should take as given that a multiplicity of units should serve to enhance system capacity, and that the task should be one to find the optimal number of units appropriate to democracy in any particular setting. In an impressively prescient conclusion, they present a view on the future configuration of democracy highly appropriate to an international context characterized by both state decline and an increasingly globalized economy:

> Rather than conceiving of democracy as located in a particular kind of inclusive, sovereign unit, we must learn to conceive of democracy spreading through a set of interrelated political systems, sometimes though not always arranged like Chinese boxes, the smaller nesting in the larger. The central theoretical problem is no longer to find suitable rules, like the majority principle, to apply within a sovereign unit, but to find suitable rules to apply among a variety of units, none of which is sovereign. (Dahl & Tufte 1973:135)

Every one of the variables noted above is relevant to the Southern African transition and the security problems attendant to it. Smaller units, in the form of nine provinces, are an integral aspect of South Africa's new democratic constitution. A larger unit in the form of the Southern African Development Community has also been reconstituted, and has very rapidly evolved into a regional body attempting to deal, among others, with security issues. The democratic quality of this larger unit of security is open to question, and will be examined in this chapter.

Toward Cosmopolitan Democracy

How can citizen effectiveness be advanced within intergovernmental organizations such as SADC? The cosmopolitan model of democracy proposed by David Held offers some guidelines (Held 1992:34, 35). Firstly, Held proposes that such intergovernmental organizations be democratized to the level of becoming regional parliaments, with the European Parliament as the pre-eminent leading example. This entails that members be directly elected from constituencies that traverse national boundaries, by an electorate of the transnational unit, and that the elected members campaign on the basis of transnational issues. In short, this model presupposes the rapid evolution of a transnational political party system. Such an electorate can gain further control over decision making in this transnational polity through general referendums about controversial transnational issues. Secondly, international functional organizations can be democratized through having elected supervisory boards. Thirdly, a "cluster of political and civil rights" with which to shape, steer, and constrain democratic decision making has to be entrenched. These rights have to be written into the constitutions of both national and intergovernmental parliaments, with international courts given adequate jurisdiction to hear cases from litigants from every member state. Fourthly, where intergovernmental organizations tend to include both democratic and undemocratic states as members, a two-chamber system of representation can be instituted. Held proposed this for representation at global level only, that is, for a reformed UN, but it can also be applied too less inclusive regional bodies. One chamber is to represent all members, and the other only those who qualify as democracies, with the latter being given preeminence over the former. Which of these proposals are relevant to the further democratization of SADC? A brief overview of SADC structures is appropriate to answering this question.

SADC Structure: Size, System Capacity, and Citizen Effectiveness

The evolving institutions of SADC have been monitored and analyzed elsewhere (Breytenbach 2000; Bruce 1998; Cilliers 1996, 1999; Van Aardt 1997a, 1997b), and will be described only very briefly in this section, with special reference only to those features which bear on the democratic criteria of citizen effectiveness and system capacity.

The predecessors of the Southern African Development Community (SADC) namely the Frontline States (FLS), its informal substructure, the Inter-State Defense and Security Committee (ISDC), and Southern African Development and Co-ordination Conference (SADCC) were all closely engaged with security issues, albeit as part of the antiapartheid conflict. The 1992 SADC Treaty principles commits all members to the pursuit of both democracy and security, and the areas of cooperation singled out in Article 21(3) focus on development priorities.

The major bodies within SADC have certain features relevant to the internal democracy of the organization. The Summit of Heads of State, the Council of Ministers, and the Standing Committee of Officials all require a quorum of two-thirds of its members. Decisions have to be taken by consensus, which entails that every member state can exercise a veto. The Summit and Council are democratically constituted (in the sense of representing voters indirectly) to the extent that the heads of state and the relevant ministers are properly democratically elected.

The controversial Organ on Politics, Defense and Security initially was to operate on the levels of heads of state, as well as ministerial level and also with a level of technical assistance, with the ISDSC as the informal substructure of the Organ. In the various proposals for reform, such as the 1996 Gaborone draft, internal decision making at the level of heads of state would still conform the SADC format of two-thirds of members constituting a quorum, and decisions to be reached by consensus. The much-disputed issues of the status of the Organ within the overall structure of SADC and that of the Chair of the Organ were apparently resolved in November 1999. It was then agreed to situate the Organ below the SADC Summit of Heads of State, with a Troika (past, present, and incoming chair) Organ chair, assisted below them by a ministerial committee comprising both Foreign Affairs and Defense ministries, with below them the ISDSC (*Business Day*, 2 November 1999).

Some of the bodies within SADC have a direct bearing on enlarging system capacity in order to deal with security matters. In every case they entail the construction of *larger* units for dealing with security problems such as the proliferation of small arms into the region. Whether such larger capacity has in fact been achieved, is not the focus of this chapter. The ISDSC has sub-committees on Defense, Public Security, and State Security, and is chaired by Ministers of Defense on a rotational base, with the host country providing the secretariat for the deliberations of the meetings. The ISDSC has also recently become involved in establishing an infrastructure for regional peacekeeping.

The Southern African Regional Police Chiefs Cooperation Organization (SARPCCO) is another specialist body focusing on security matters. Established within the framework of the ISDSC, SARPCCO consists of police chiefs within the region, facilitates cross-border police cooperation, and has become the de facto subregional arm of the International Criminal Police Organization (Interpol). Its supreme body is the Council of Police Chiefs (CPC) which meets annually. This body also meets with the relevant police ministers of the region in order to get political endorsement for their decisions, so as to facilitate implementation of their decisions.

The Lesotho Invasion

How effective and how adequate are the democratic features of SADC in securing citizen control over decisions taken in this polity? A partial answer can be sought by examining the experience of one country, South Africa, in one case, the military intervention in Lesotho in 1998. How much control did the citizens of South Africa have in this decision making process?

The first level of citizen participation is indirectly, through representatives engaged in decision making within the regional body itself. Was there compliance with the SADC procedures? South Africa invaded Lesotho on September 22, 1998 with a 600-member force. Later that day 200 members of the Botswana Defense Force joined them. The South African government claimed that the invasion had been requested by the Lesotho government, and had also been extended to Mozambique and Zimbabwe, and that Lesotho was requesting assistance in accordance with SADC agreements. Therefore, they claimed, the actions were taken under the auspices of SADC. An SADC meeting on September 21 was reported to have mandated such an intervention. The following objections have been raised against this interpretation.

Firstly, the said meeting of 21 September was attended by South Africa, Zimbabwe, Botswana, and Mozambique only, which did not constitute a quorum (Cilliers 1999:15). At the properly constituted SADC Summit held in Mauritius on 12-13 September South Africa declared that Lesotho was not on the meeting's agenda (Makoa 1999:69). Secondly, the SADC pronouncement on the meeting did not explicitly, or according to Mark Malan, even implicitly mandate military intervention. It only expressed concern at the turmoil inside Lesotho, and praise for South Africa's attempts at mediation, as well as for the initiatives to investigate claims of corruption in the election process (Malan 1999:93). Thirdly, even had the internal decision making procedures been upheld, the action did not occur with the authorization of the UN Security Council, especially with regard to Article 53 (Malan 1999:94). The action therefore clearly contravened current international law.

The second level of participation by citizens is at the level of the member state itself. Are there effective democratic procedures which allow citizens to control decisions about the military invasion of another country? In the case of South Africa the national constitution does have such provisions, again allowing indirect citizen participation. Section 201 of the 1996 constitution allows military forces to be deployed outside the borders in defense of the country or in the fulfillment of an international obligation. Should this be done, the President is required to inform Parliament, within seven days of the deployment of the troops, of the purpose of the action, the place where they are engaged, the number of troops involved, and the expected period for which they will be thus occupied. If Parliament is not in sitting at the time, an appropriate Committee of Parliament must be thus informed.

These requirements were promptly met with the Lesotho invasion. On September 22, the day of the invasion, the acting President, Mr. Mangosuthu Buthelezi, informed Parliament that the invasion was undertaken in response to a request for help from the Lesotho premier Pakalitha Mosisili. Buthelezi claimed that it was a military intervention conducted under the auspices of SADC, with the objective to thwart an impending military coup. He declared that the South African forces' aim was to stabilize the political and military situation after which they would be withdrawn (*Business Day*, 23 September 1998). He pledged to give further briefings to the cabinet and to opposition leaders during the course of the day.

The Further Democratization of SADC

The Lesotho case reveals a number of shortcomings in the democratic quality of SADC. Firstly, the access of citizens to decisions reached at SADC level is highly contingent upon the democratic quality of their own national constitutions. South Africans at least have indirect access to the process via section 201. Citizens in undemocratic member states such as Swaziland and the DRC do not even have these limited constitutional devices at their disposal. Secondly, the democratic quality of decision making within SADC is also contingent upon the democratic quality of the member states. The SADC Summit, and Council for example, can be considered a democratic representation of the citizens of the region only to the extent that they have been properly elected themselves. In Swaziland and the DRC these are entirely absent, while Zimbabwe, Zambia, and Mozambique have all held elections which have been accused of being procedurally suspect. Thirdly, confusion and lack of clarity about when SADC is acting in accordance with international law, and when it is acting in accordance with its own internal procedures, have to be dealt with effectively.

Moving away from the Lesotho case, what can be recommended for the further democratization of SADC, along the line proposed by Held? Firstly, the establishment of a regional parliament is probably the least likely immediate prospect. The democratic fundamentals that need to be in place for such a process to evolve include a regional political party system, a national constitutional order in which the identity of citizen is salient, a democratic political culture in which the distinction between public and private goods is understood, the distinction between public and private spheres of jurisdiction is enacted, and where the concept of rule of law is internalized. Regional or cosmopolitan democracy presupposes building blocks comprising of strong autonomous states, and strong democratic regimes.

Secondly, the democratization of functional bodies within SADC through the establishment of elected supervisory boards runs into similar obstacles. Elected supervisors can only be forthcoming from member states that have valid electoral processes up and running in their own countries.

Thirdly, Held raises the issues of the enactment of "cluster of political and civil rights" with which to guide democratic decision making, and with which citizens could gain access to a court system. The evolution of such a doctrine and practice of rights again presupposes a legal and constitutional order where the rule of law prevails, where the principle and practice of contract is unchallenged, and where the identity of citizenship, on both a regional and national basis, is salient. One proposal for facilitating the process of building a Human Rights doctrine and practice is that an Institute for Democracy and Human Rights be established, with a mandate to report directly to the SADC Heads of State or to the Organ (Cilliers 1999:77).

The practical problem pertaining to the functioning of such an institute, as with the other two avenues of democratization mentioned above, is that the member states of SADC differ hugely in the extent to which they are democratic at the national level. Some are just more removed from a human rights culture and practice than others. While the SADC Treaty holds as a principle the "Sovereign equality of all member states," in democratic terms, some are vastly more equal than others. How does one deal with this structural problem? The proposal by Held is to establish a two-tier level of representation, and by implication, a first-class and second-class category of membership. At the lowest level an inclusive body/chamber represents all members, and at the second level only democratic qualifiers are assembled. This democratic chamber will then be suitably qualified to partake in the further democratization of the organization, such as electing supervisory boards for functionally specific bodies. The fiction of an equality of members, as it bears on their democratic attributes, therefore will have to be discarded.

Conclusion

SADC is an evolving intergovernmental regional organization trying to get to grips with among others, security issues for which the boundaries of the various member national states are too small. In this sense the larger unit tries to enhance the system capacity of the new political unit. The trade-off thus far is a decrease in citizen effectiveness. To extend this effectiveness at the level of the regional organization the body will first have to deal with the most salient difference within their members' ranks: the extent to which they are functioning democracies.

Chapter 10

Democratic Participation in Foreign Policy and Beyond: An Outline of Options

Janis van der Westhuizen and Philip Nel

In the introductory chapter we drew attention to the conceptual need for a more expansive definition of both democracy and foreign policy. We also underscored the degree to which the search for an expanded definition of foreign policy and the democratization of foreign policy making are complementary processes. A democratic foreign policy making process should therefore be seen to be accountable insofar as the citizens' right to participate in the making of government policy is institutionalized individually and collectively; provides for public contestation about different publicly known policy options, and ensures that chosen policies genuinely address the real—rather than perceived or presumed—concerns of the public at large. Above all, it should be focused on the broad array of what we in the introduction termed "policies beyond the state."

Statecraft in the twenty-first century increasingly requires a more sophisticated and multidimensional repertoire of capabilities for effective governance both domestically and transnationally. Given the growing number of issue areas and interest groups operating at the "intermestic" level of analysis (that is, the integration of domestic and international spheres) questions about the way in which state elites make domestic expectations about the state's role compatible with external pressures have become more salient. Paradoxically, despite the unprecedented degree of global informational, communicative and transport access, perceptions of powerlessness and democratic impotence—despite democracy's "third wave"—remain.

This book provides abundant evidence that South African citizens have good reasons to share in this sense of powerlessness and impotence. There are three different, but ultimately related processes contributing to this sense of im-

169

potence. On the one hand, South Africans are experiencing rapidly the full brunt of what Cox termed the "internationalization of the state" with profound consequences for traditional, territorially based, assumptions of democracy. On a normative level this process implies that the very definition of what it means to be a democratic South Africa is not so much a homegrown conception, but one that is inculcated by a set of powerful international norms that prescribe identity, interests, and policy options. This leads to a reversal of the expected role of the state: instead of externally representing the interests of the people, the ruling state elite have now become the agents through which these powerful international norms and their supportive practices are conveyed and sold to the domestic audience. This has fundamentally altered the nature of foreign policy, and in itself justifies a major rethink of how analysts think and argue about foreign policy. It also means that we have to reconsider what the prospects and limits of public/democratic participation in these circumstances are. At the very least, it necessitates a much more critical and guarded engagement on the part of the citizenry with the policies of the state. In fundamental ways this state is no longer "their" state.

The second process has been alluded to in the introduction. It has to do with the numerous policy domains that have taken on a transnational dimension or focus. Engagement with foreign policy thus has a much broader scope that it did when the subfield of foreign policy analysis had its field day in the 1960s and 1970s. With this dispersal of transnational issues has also come a dispersal of authority, in some cases away from the state and toward private actors, both for-profit and not-for-profit actors. The result is that citizens very often do not know where the power nodes of specific issue areas lie, and therefore do not know whom to influence or where to push to try and secure their interests.

Finally, the singular failure of the South African state (ever since its formation in 1910, but also since its democratic turn in 1994) to adequately provide avenues for democratic participation in policy making has exacerbated the sense of powerlessness and impotence. In these circumstances it comes as no surprise that South Africans seem to be increasingly apathetic about transnational issues, and prefer to leave such matters in the hands of the state elite and their organic intellectuals. One can understand why this state elite prefers policy-making behavior that excludes the public from meaningful participation. Faced with their own sense of impotence in the face of real and assumed losses of policy autonomy, state agents rationally prefer to jealously protect their remaining policy competencies and to play their cards close to their chests. Of course, the South African state is not alone in coping with this dilemma. In fact, the restricted conception of democracy we discussed in the introduction, which explicitly limits the prospects of public participation, seems to have become one of those constitutive norms that proscribe statehood in today's world.

Globally, there seems to be a grassroots backlash against these three processes. Those who doubt this need look no further than the protests that have now become an established feature of the global conference circuit since Seattle, c. 1999. Nevertheless, periods of "restricted" or "thwarted" democracy are not historically unique, but often reflective of a more dynamic process involving market expansion and accompanying social turmoil. Against this backdrop, the ANC-led government has, like many other social democratic governments (i.e., Tony Blair's "moral" foreign policy) sought to pursue human rights driven foreign policy underpinned by a greater degree of democratic participation than previous South African governments. As various chapters in this book have demonstrated, living up to these commitments has proven difficult and South Africa's record on this score remains patchy. Yet, Pretoria's dilemmas are not unique and may well be shaped indirectly by the degree of democratization—of what appears to be—an incipient global polity.

The potential for greater openness and democratization of our embryonic global polity is not irreversible. In fact, the processes engendering these dynamics can just as easily close or reduce democratic pressures as much as they can be enhanced. In short: the democratization potential inherent within globalization can be both an opportunity as well as a threat. Rather than attempting to assess the outcome of these changes, we try to simply gauge the pulse of a volatile transnational attempt to (re-) configure world order on the basis of an elementary set of indicators of change. The purpose of this chapter is to briefly review some oft-overlooked options at the disposal of various different actors, beyond the routine procedures of conventional foreign policy analysis. These options are constrained by the prevailing structural and normative features of the global system, and we restrict our list to options that are possible within these confines. In a more comprehensive list than the one we present, one could also include options that relate to the thorough transformation of the existing global order, and the role that democratic participation can play in this regard. The influence of transregional norms toward democratization also requires further analysis. For example, in the case of Mercosur, pressures from other states effectively forestalled a military coup in April 1996 which would have thwarted Paraguay's emerging democracy (Patomäki & Teivainen, 2002:48-49). Similarly, NEPAD may yet trigger democratic pressures as is suggested by a group of Kenya businessmen who told President Daniel Arab Moi, "in no uncertain terms" that "he was not even attempting to uphold the principles of the New Partnership for Africa's Development (Nepad)" (*Business Day*, 11 June 2002). Before we turn our attention to such transformational strategies, it is important that both the benefits and disadvantages of options that operate within the confines of the prevailing order are understood. This is the limited goal that we have set for this chapter.

Needless to say, what follows is neither an exhaustive analysis of all the potential types of reaction nor of all distinct elements that can be contained under each reaction type. The four types, namely co-optation, concession, reformism, and depoliticization refer to the relationship between various efforts and campaigns by social movements (some egalitarian, others less so) to infuse a more socially oriented liberalism and the way in which the established order (dominant states, transnational elite classes, multinational corporations, and international institutions) has responded to those projects.

Options

Co-optation

As a reaction to growing pressure for democratic participation, co-optation as a variant of corporatism, seeks to defuse conflict by granting a variety of functional groups, typically labor alongside big business, privileged access to policy-making networks within the state.[1] Constituting the so-called "golden triangle" this trio of stakeholders has been crucial to sustaining a degree of stability and consensus for economies undergoing periods of democratic transition, in Europe after the Second World War and the developing world, notably Latin America in the 1970/80's and South Africa in the 1990s. As a kind of crisis management mechanism, corporatism tends to be more successful as a temporary measure and more likely to enjoy a greater degree of credibility in countries with participating associations demonstrating very large proportions of specific categories of workers registered with labor unions (Ottaway, 2001:269).

Corporatist practices are not only evident in national or even regional contexts, but at the global level of analysis as well. As Marina Ottoway (2001) has demonstrated, much like states at the domestic interface, international institutions and transnational corporations are being challenged by the growing ubiquity of NGO and social movement networks, reflecting the concern with justice and equity (as well as the environment) which was the driving force for the first wave of socialist movements. Not unlike the labor movement which critiques the socioeconomic consequences of industrialization, NGOs and social movements critique the very condition that gave rise to their own prominence: globalization. Global corporatism is therefore a response to the persistent challenges from NGOs and TSMs in order to hold multinational corporations accountable to higher standards regarding environmental, labor, and human rights practices. The UN Global Compact and World Commission on Dams are two particularly novel examples.

The Global Compact

Proposed by the UN Secretary-General Kofi Annan on 31 January 1999 to the World Economic Forum, the Global Compact (GC) aims to engage corporations and international labor and NGOs to promote adherence to good corporate practices—based on nine universal principles[2]—by committing to the advocacy of the GC in mission statements and annual reports on the assumption that greater attention will be paid to these concerns by corporations. Companies are also expected to post on the GC website at least once a year efforts made to fulfill these expectations and partner with the UN projects to help developing economies marginalized by globalization. Since July 2000, 4000 companies worldwide have signed up, while 1,000 are being targeted for inclusion within three years[3] (Ruggie, 2001:372).

Proponents of the GC proclaim the potential of the project as a learning forum and interorganizational network to submit case studies of corporate responsibility with the expectation that "good practices will help drive out bad ones through the power of dialogue, transparency, advocacy and competition" (Ruggie, 2001:373). Given the difficulty of generating the necessary consensus within the General Assembly to develop a meaningful code of conduct and the financial and logistical requirements to enforce such a code, the GC is not a regulatory mechanism but rather as an opportunity for dialogue, "helps companies to internalize the relevant principles so that they can shape and re-shape corporate practices as external conditions change" (Ruggie, 2001:374).

Critics however, contend that in the eighteen months of the GC's existence, it has failed to publish a single case study of sustainable practices; [4] while the GC proclaims to be transparent, the names of most participating companies are secret and many of the known signatory firms to the GC, such as Aventis, Rio Tinto, Unilever, and Norsk Hydro, stand accused (by NGOs) of Compact violations[5] (Bruno & Karliner, 2002). Insofar as these charges can be sustained, the essentially corporatist goals of the GC are quite apparent. For example, Bruno and Karliner (2002:5) contend that although the UN acknowledges its inability to monitor the companies in the Compact, and relies upon NGOs to do so, NGOs "are not permitted to know the names of the companies they would monitor."

World Commission on Dams

Formed in 1988, the World Commission on Dams (WCD) emerged in the after-math of widespread dissatisfaction with the environmental degradation, impact upon local communities, threatened species, and agricultural disruption which often followed the construction of mega-dams. Pitted against governments, construction and power-supply companies and banks, antidam activists claimed to speak for communities whose land would be flooded and pro-dam prota-gonists who highlighted the benefits: access to irrigated land and electricity. Often portrayed as a conflict between greedy corporations and downtrodden locals, the mounting costs of such stalled projects prompted the need to find a solution (Ottaway, 2001:281).

Emerging as a mediator between opposing groups, the World Bank, after commissioning a study to assess the impact of the dam projects it had financed, provided the initial finance to set up the WCD. The latter was the outflow from a meeting between the World Bank and the World Conservation Union (IUCN), the largest international network of environmental groups. Failing to agree, the environmentalists, corporations, international agencies, and the Bank agreed to establish the WCD to further discussions and analyze problems. Its "mandate" would be terminated in June 2000 after a report had been submitted to the Bank, the IUCN and the "international community". Remarkably, as Ottaway (2001: 282) argues

The WCD had a 'mandate', but there was no 'mandating' authority. Its recommendations could not be binding on any party. It was a group of individuals backed by a network, and it took upon itself the task of making recommendations on the issue with no power to enforce them.

Co-optation constitutes as much of a threat as an opportunity to the development of a global polity. At first blush ensuring that civil society enjoys easier access to global policy processes is to be welcomed. However, global corporatist practices run into a variety of negative consequences. For one, civil societies participating in global tripartite councils are not necessarily representative in any meaningful sense of the term. Usually those groups are self-selected on the basis of their capacity to mobilize, to be heard, their own willingness to participate, and the opinions of international organization officials regarding who should be included. This is less of a problem in the case of ad hoc, voluntary tripartite organizations, which issues recommendations. It becomes problematic when such entities are empowered to make binding decisions (Ottaway, 2001:285). Another difficulty relates to the asymmetry of power relations between civil society organizations, international organizations, and/or big business and governments. The larger the disparity between stakeholders, the less pluralist such processes are likely to be. Finally, the formalization of civil society interaction often requires a greater degree of bureaucratization on the part of the latter; a process which effectively undercuts the flexibility and capacity to mobilize which gives NGOs their punch. As Ottaway (2001:277) concluded regarding the attempt to make NGO participation a more formal affair in the UN Economic and Social Council (ECOSOC):

> In the end, the attempt to enhance NGO presence at the UN achieved little. It increased the number of NGOs with consultative status but did not produce a dramatic change in their role and influence. It divided them in separate categories, carefully regulating the number of words they could write and the number of minutes they could speak. The cost of inclusion was not more democracy but more bureaucracy.

Nevertheless, these concerns should not overshadow the upside to emerging corporatist modes at the transnational level. Such arrangements do infuse a greater degree of pluralism to global debates, can ensure that more information could be brought to bear on issues, and dissiminate such information among a larger number of civil society groups—as proved critical through the Internet in the case of the stillborn Multilateral Investment Agreement (MIA)—while participation also means that a new basis for leverage is created: the threat of withdrawal and possible "delegitimization" of such arrangements.

Concession

Patterns of concession refer to instances where the established order has given in to demands for greater global equity either on the basis of human rights or environmental concerns. While such concessions may be important to the people or environment affected by them, they do not necessarily lead to fundamental change, nor do they necessarily challenge the established order. In fact, cynics who discount even the potential for this limited degree of agency would contend that such concession, admittedly made under duress, were precisely aimed at preventing larger campaigns or issues drawing attention to, or challenging the inequitable distribution of, what Susan Strange called the structural power of the global system.

To illustrate, compare the relative success with which the International Campaign to Ban Landmines (ICBL)—in collaboration with a number of smaller states and "middle powers" in particular—developed a novel diplomatic process through which international agreement to ban landmines was secured even in the face of open opposition from the U.S. and others (China, India, Russia).

In contrast, although the campaign for debt forgiveness shared a number of strategic similarities with the ICBL, the process has been a decidedly protracted and stalled affair with piecemeal and very limited series of debt-relief programs. Firstly, both the landmines and debt campaigns were initiated through civil society activism. Secondly, embedded norms constituted the basis for mobilization. In the case of the Ottawa Process, proponents grafted a norm in favor of a landmines ban upon an earlier norm against "unnecessary suffering" and "superfluous injury". Similarly, the antidebt campaign also grafted on an older, more established norm—the Doctrine of Odious Debts. However, unlike landmines, debt is a much more complex, less tangible concern and thus not an "easy sell" in terms of social mobilization and human drama, as landmines were. Moreover, the debt issue was quite simply perceived by South African policy makers—especially the Finance Ministry and Reserve Bank—as way too much of a risk, given the potential financial costs Pretoria may have to bear if the world's capital markets saw it as a 'rebel' (Van der Westhuizen, Taylor & Nel, 2001:123). Thus unlike the landmines issue, which did not truly challenge the structural nature of the global political economy, in the case of debt relief for South Africa, Pretoria did not only disassociate itself from the Jubilee 2000 movement, but actively sought to discourage any efforts to that effect (Van der Westhuizen, 2001).

Reformism

Activists purporting to "put a human face on globalization" by agitating for higher labor, environmental, or human rights standards could also be classified as "reformers". Their ultimate goal does not extend toward large-scale transformation of the existing capitalist order, but merely its reformation as befits social forces attempting to infuse a more socially responsible liberalism. We highlight one such set of social forces to stand for the many others: ethical consumerism. Be it in the form of activist shareholders, the portfolio managers of "socially responsible" investment funds, or simply consumers who decide to boycott a product or service perceived to abide by less scrupulous standards, ethical consumerism is not novel: Ghandi used consumer boycotts in support of Indian independence and other anti-imperialist boycotts in 1905; U.S. labor movement boycotts in the struggle for trade unions were first published in 1913, while anecdotal evidence by the *Ethical Consumer* suggests boycotts of sugar from plantations employing slave labor during the abolitionist campaigns of the early nineteenth century in the United States.

By 1974 academic texts identified "socially responsible" consumers, but it was not until environmental issues, apartheid South Africa, and animal testing moved up the social agenda in the 1980s that the politics of consumption e-merged with growing frequency (Harrison, 2001). Recount the controversy over Nestle's sales of infant formula in the developing world in the late 1970s; the Union Carbide pesticide disaster in 1984 in Bhopal, India; and of course the massive anti-apartheid based, consumer boycott that targeted a host of foreign MNCs (Barclays Bank's share of the student loan market, for example, declined from 27 to 15 percent) (Klein, 2001).

By the 1990s, consumer boycotts escalated, from the first anti-sweatshop campaigns in the mid-1990s, campaigns against Nike, Wal-Mart in the U.S., and Monsanto, for not disclosing which of its products were genetically engineered, have spilled over to concerns about multinationals operating in developing coun-tries with scant regard for human rights.

In part, the growth of the 'corporate ethics crusade' was triggered by three considerations. Firstly, a growing sense of disillusionment—by the mid-1990s—that the post-Cold War era and the onset of democratization—failed "to turn any economic frog into a spry and wealthy prince" as Ethan Kapstein (2001:107) put it. Secondly, since governments have been hamstrung by an unfolding regulat-ory regime beyond their traditional policy framework, the ethics movement has found targeting big business directly a far more efficient strategy than via domestic policy networks. And thirdly, by the sheer potential for capitalist reformism, given that besides MNCs and the transnational capitalist class, the culture ideology of consumerism constitutes the third pillar of contemporary capitalism (Sklar, 1997).

Not unlike concession or co-optation, reformism may add to emancipatory potential as much as it could detract from it. Ethical consumerism faces a number of dilemmas in this regard. For example, is it desirable for firms to take on ethical issues in the first place? Could human rights crusades not become commodified and thus leave only those human rights that are "profitable" better protected? Secondly, to what extent could OECD consumers be forcing MNCs from late industrializers especially the developing world to abide by ethical standards?[6] Expecting similar environmental, labor and human rights standards may drive workers to the informal economy with even lower standards, if any

(Kapstein, 2001:106). Indeed, instead of consumer-activism becoming a truly global mode of counter-hegemonic resistance, it could even undermine nascent North/South coalitions. Parochial or reactivist moves can easily be masked by seemingly cosmopolitan motives when, as Epstein (2001:109) suggests, Western consumers reject cheap imported garments not because of cheap labor in Indonesia, but because multinationals were undermining textile employment in South Carolina. In short, two dilemmas haunt ethical consumerism. The first is deflecting the charge that ethical concerns merely impose the values of one group on another. The second requires undoing Marx's ghost: "the only thing worse than exploitation is not being exploited at all." Ethical consumers may have prevented Pakistani child laborers from producing sweatshop soccer balls, but not from stopping those children from becoming prostitutes after the multi-nationals' departure.

Despite these obstacles ethical consumerism remains a powerful instrument through which firms can be held accountable, especially if the governments in which they operate are not amenable to change or even influence, as Western students' boycott of Pepsi succeeded in getting it to withdraw from Myanmar in 1997 or a number of MNCs to divest from apartheid South Africa in the mid-1980s.

Yet even postapartheid South Africa has seen the rise of one of the most powerful transnational networks, the Treatment Action Campaign (TAC) mobilizing both domestically and abroad in cooperation with a host of other NGOs to challenge the ANC-led government's ideosyncratic policy on HIV/AIDS. Not only has this social network succeeded in forcing foreign pharmaceutical firms to abandon their plans to take the South African government to court because of its stated intent to develop generic AIDS drugs in contravention of international patent law, but the TAC has consistently used domestic courts to force the South African government to provide the necessary drugs to prevent mother-to-child transmission of HIV. Consistent with Keck and Sikkink's (1998) evaluation of success for specific transnational advocacy networks, the success of the TAC may in large part be attributable to two factors: firstly because the issue in question involves bodily harm against vulnerable individuals (especially women and children) and secondly because the chain of responsibility is direct (the very reason why the HIV/AIDS debate has become so incomprehensibly ideosyncratic in South Africa). And, consistent with their model, Pretoria's HIV/AIDS stance has caused the country's image irreparable harm globally, because the two factors—bodily harm and causality—are concerns that transcend unique cultural or social contexts.

In short: once a firm has become subject to ethical scrutiny, it is often forced to react, either by declaring its ethical commitments or by taking substantive steps in this regard (i.e., Nike increasing wages in Indonesia). Critics often lament that codes of conduct are often unenforceable or monitored by NGOs whose independence is ultimately compromised as they become co-opted into such mechanisms. Yet, the real value of such codes is that they open the door to holding those firms accountable which would otherwise be much more difficult.

In other words, such codes create a norm against which action can be measured. Moreover, ethical consumerism directed against one brand or firm often has spillover effects on others, forcing anticipatory compliance from competitors.

Depoliticization

Despite a growing interest in the globalization/democratization nexus, the crucial role played by the global media has yet to become a more prominent feature in both academic and policy-making circles. Not unlike any of the other three indicators of change discussed above, it is the media in and of itself which performs a pivotal role in terms of the degree to which globalization *creates* opportunities for greater democratization of the existing world order or could just as easily *close* spaces for greater democratic participation. Our use of the term "depoliticization" refers to this enigma: does the media highlight the way in which power and wealth is distributed by drawing attention to issues that need to be placed on the agenda for global governance, a process of politicization; or does it play a depoliticizing role? In other words, do the media refrain from such an overtly political role in terms of not only content and style, but possibly ownership as well?

Undoubtedly, the consolidation of a democracy expressed resolutely in terms of political culture is fundamentally shaped by the quality of its media in terms of independence, fairness, and critical oversight of political life. Similar expectations hold for the media in the development of a more democratic process of global governance. Without it, potential pluralist processes may become captive to co-optation; the risk of delegitimizing institutions, which fail to sanction stakeholders who abrogate commitments, disappears, while attempts to hold corporations and states accountable through ethical consumerism would be useless without an independent media to spread the word. Simply put, the degree to which globalization engenders progressive change across all our indicators rests fundamentally upon the extent to which the global media responsibly serves an incipient global civil society inasmuch as national media enhances domestic civil society and democratic participation.

World society, however, remains marked by two particularly troubling features heightening processes of depoliticization, namely patterns of global media ownership and the prevailing model of journalistic practice.

The growth of global mass media can be attributed to two significant factors. Firstly, as deregulation and privatization became the vogue in the 1980s, the mass media and especially in the broadcasting sector, non profit, public services made way for larger, commercial television and radio services, ultimately driven by considerations of advertising revenue. Secondly, technological advance especially in broadcasting and satellite services expanded the geographical reach not only of broadcasters, but also book, magazine, and newspaper publishers, not to mention the invariable expansion of the Internet (McChesney,

1997:1). In combination, these factors, political/economic and technological helped create the markets of scale and associated distribution networks fundamental to the emergence of the Information Age as the next industrial revolution (Murphy, 2002).

Today, a few global media giants dominate nearly all sectors of media. The first tier of nine gigantic conglomerates with global reach is dominated in terms of 1997 sales revenue by Time Warner ($24 billion); Disney ($22 billion); Bertelsmann ($15 billion); Viacom ($13 billion) and Rupert Murdoch's News Corporation ($11 billion); Sony ($9 billion); TCI (Tele-Communications Inc.) ($7 billion 1996); Universal (Seagram, $7 billion); and NBC (General Electric, $5 billion, 1996). A second tier of three or four dozen corporations fill regional or niche markets in North America, Europe, Latin America, and Asia which produce the overwhelming majority of the world's film production, TV shows, cable channel ownership, book and magazine publishing and music. [7] How such concentration of ownership could affect news content is startling considering the following examples. Time Warner owns Turner Broadcasting which owns CNN; News Corp. is the owner of and significant partner in a number of newspapers, television stations, and satellite broadcasting systems, including STAR TV and Sky TV; while Disney owns ABC, General Electric owns NBC, and Westinghouse owns CBS. Apart from NewsCorp, which is based in Australia, all these corporations are based in the United States (Shah, 2002:1).

Reinforcing the dominant culture ideology of globalization, namely consumerism (Sklar, 1997) mass media privileges "soft" media content which essentially packages entertainment as news: which celebrity is sleeping with whom, who won the lottery and ever-expanding lifestyle supplements and diminishing "hard" news or political analysis. Problematically, how the prevailing model of journalism—which assumes neutrality and letting the "facts" speak for themselves—fails to undo or even draw attention to this predicament, is well captured by Shah (2002):

> It is a model that results in journalism that describes events with little analysis, relies upon polls and statistics to show social trends but without providing historical context, and provides no vehicle of expression for ordinary people at the grass roots level. It is precisely the type of journalism that serves the interests of the owners of the global mass media firms because it avoids asking deeper questions about the exercise of power, the dispensation of social justice, and the prospects for cultural survival.

Undeniably, the globalization of the media has strengthened moments of democratic opening through transnational satellite projections of the Tiananmen Square massacre as much as it has often shaped public opinion and hence public pressure against, for example, the continued NATO bombing campaign in Kosovo, the U.S. campaign in Afghanistan, or the Israeli's military response to Palestinian suicide bombings. Yet in the absence of such drama and sensationalism, the question remains whether media content is shaped by an implicit political bias and depoliticization in which, "consumerism, the market, class inequality and individualism tend[s] to be taken as natural and often benevolent, whereas political activity, civic values and anti-market activities tend to be marginalized or denounced" (McChesney, 2002:7).

Even this very broad typology of relationships between campaigns by social movements and the established order of dominant states, transnational elite classes, multinational corporations, and international institutions remains highly tentative as the changing contours of international relations after the events of September 11, 2001 clearly suggest. Yet, considering the extent to which many fear that the expansion of American conservatism under Bush may ultimately influence international norms to favor stability over democracy, the need to enshrine democratic practices not only within the state but also beyond becomes all the more imperative.

Notes

1.   According to Schmitter's (1974) classic definition, corporatism is "a system of interest representation in which the constituent units are organized into a limited number of singular, compulsory, non-competitive, hierarchically ordered and functionally differentiated categories, recognized or licensed (if not created) by the state and granted a deliberate representational monopoly within their respective categories in exchange for observing certain controls on their selection of leaders and articulation of demands and supports."

2.   Drawn from the UN Declaration on Human Rights, the International Labour Organization's (ILO) Fundamental Principles and Rights at Work and the Rio Declaration on Environment and Development, these are "respecting the protection of internationally proclaimed human rights; non-complicity in human rights abuses; freedom of association and the effective recognition of the right to collective bargaining; the elimination of all forms of forced and compulsory labor; the effective abolition of child labor; the elimination of discrimination in respect of employment and occupation; a precautionary approach to environmental challenges; greater environmental responsibility; and encouragement of the development and diffusion of environmentally friendly technologies" (Ruggie, 2001:377, n.2).

3.   Electricity supplier ESCOM seems to be the only South African company listed on the Global Compact. See www.unglobalcompact.org.

4.   On the one-year anniversary of its launch, the GC was to publish its first set of corporate case studies in July 2001. In July, it was announced that these case studies would only be released at the Learning Forum in London, October 29-30, 2001. However, at the Learning Forum, UN officials discovered that "none of the company submissions conformed to the case study guidelines suggested by the Global Compact Office" and that about half "did not make reference to any of the nice GC principles" (Bruno & Karliner, 2002:6).

5.   While CorpWatch itself listed most of these companies in an earlier Report, *Tangled Up in Blue*, September 2000 (www.corpwatch.org/un), it accused the Global

Compact Office of sustaining secret membership or at best being inconsistent with the release of such names (Bruno & Karliner, 2002:5).

6.   We are indebted to Chris Jones, University of Wales, Aberystwyth who raised these two points in his critique on an earlier paper by Van der Westhuizen.

7.   For a full list and detailed description of these corporations, see McChesney (1997).

Bibliography

"An Investment to Safeguard Democracy" (2001), *ANC Today*, Vol. 1, No. 1, 26 Jan.-1 Feb., www.anc.org.za/ancdocs/anctoday/2001/at01.htm.

"ANC party membership plummets'" (2002), *Daily Mail and Guardian*, 15 March.

"Cadres Cash In" (2001), *Financial Mail*, 4 May.

"Is Smith just doing his job?" (2002), *Weekly Mail and Guardian*, 1-7 March.

"Maduna slams 'racist' critics of arms deal" (2001). *The Star*, 19 November.

"MP's as nobodies on Parliament Hill" (2002), *The Globe and Mail*, 18 March.

"New survey puts SA jobless rate at 45%" (2002), *Weekly Mail and Guardian*, 1-7 March.

"NGO goes to court to stop R66bn arms deal" (2001), *The Star* (Johannesburg), 21 November.

"SA should help regional defence industry" (2000). *The Star* (Johannesburg), 17 August.

"Say it ain't so Joe" (15 March 2002), *Daily Mail and Guardian*, 15 March.

"To fight the good fight" (27 May 2001), *Sunday Times*, 27 May.

Abrahamsen, R. (2000) *Disciplining Democracy: Development Discourse and Good Governance in Africa*, London: Pluto Press.

Adorno, T. (1995) *Negative Dialectics,* New York: Continuum.

Africa Group (2001), "Proposals on TRIPS for WTO Ministerial," http://www.twnside.org.sg, 19 October.

African National Congress (1994) *Foreign Policy Perspective in a Democratic South Africa*, Johannesburg: African National Congress.

African National Congress (1996) *The State and Social Transformation—Discussion Document*, Johannesburg: African National Congress.

Ajam, T. (1997) Home Affairs and Foreign Affairs, in *The second women's budget*, edited by D. Budlender, Cape Town: IDASA, pp. 37-49.

Almond, G. A. & Powell, G. 1996, *Comparative politics. A theoretical framework*, Harper Collins, New York.

Almond, G. A. (1950) *The American People and Foreign Policy*, New York: Harcourt Brace.

Antonio, R. (1983) "The Origin, Development and Contemporary Status of Critical Theory," *The Sociological Quarterly*, vol. 24, no. 3, pp. 325-51.

Antonio, R. J. (1981) "Immanent Critique as the Core of Critical Theory: Its Origins and Developments in Hegel, Marx and Contemporary Thought," *British Journal of Sociology*, vol. 32, no. 3, pp. 330-45.

Ardant, G. (1975) "Financial Policy and Economic Infrastructure of Modern States and Nations" in *The Formation of National States in Western Europe*, edited by C. Tilly, Princeton, N.J.: Princeton University Press, pp. 164-242.

Ashforth, A. (1990) *The Politics of Official Discourse in Twentieth Century South Africa*, Oxford, UK: Clarendon.

Bachrach, P. (1967) *The Theory of Democratic Elitism: A Critique*, Boston: Little, Brown.

Bachrach, P. (1975) "Interest, Participation, and Democratic Theory," in *Participation in Politics - Nomos XVI*, edited by J. Roland Pennock and John W. Chapman, New York: Lieber-Atherton, pp. 39-55.

Ball, T. and Pocock, J. G. A. (eds.) (1990) *Conceptual Change and the Constitution*, Lawrence: University Press of Kansas.

Barber, B. (1984) *Strong Democracy: Participatory Politics for a New Age*, Los Angeles: University of California Press.

Barber, B. (1996) *Jihad vs McWorld: How Globalisation and Tribalism are Reshaping the World*, New York: Ballantine Books.

Barber, B. (2000) "Can Democracy Survive Globalization?" *Government and Opposition*, vol. 35, no 3: 275-301.

Bardes, B. A. and Oldendick, R. (1978) "Beyond Internationalism: The Case for Multiple Dimensions in Foreign Policy Attitudes," *Social Science Quarterly*, vol. 59, pp. 496-508.

Batchelor, P. (1998a), "South Africa's Arms Industry: Prospects for Conversion," in *From Defence to Development*, edited by J. Cock, Cape Town: David Philip.

Batchelor, P. (1998b), "Arms and the ANC," *The Bulletin of the Atomic Scientists*, vol. 54, no. 5, pp. 56-61.

Batchelor, P. (no date), "South Africa's Arms Trade and the Commonwealth: A Cause for Concern?" Unpublished manuscript.

Beetham, D. (1994) "Key Principles and Indices for a Democratic Audit," in *Defining and Measuring Democracy*, edited by D. Beetham, London: SAGE.

Bendix, R. (1977) *Nation-Building and Citizenship*, Berkeley: University of California Press.

Berlin, I. (1969) *Four Essays on Liberty*, Oxford, U.K.: Oxford University Press.

Birch, A. H. (1993) *The Concepts and Theories of Modern Democracy*, London: Routledge.

Black, D. (1999). "The Long and Winding Road: International Norms and Domestic Political Change in South Africa," in *The Power of Human Rights: International Norms and Domestic Change*, edited by. T. Risse, S. C. Ropp, and K. Sikkink. New York: Cambridge University Press, pp. 78-108.

Bohman, J. (1996) *Public Deliberation: Pluralism, Complexity and Democracy*, Cambridge, Mass.: MIT Press.

Bohman, J. and Rehg, W. (eds) (1999) *Deliberative Democracy: Essays on Reason and Politics*, Cambridge, Mass.: MIT Press.

Bond, P. (2000) *Elite Transition: From Apartheid to Neoliberalism in South Africa*, London, Pluto Press and Pietermaritzburg, University of Natal Press.

Bond, P. (2001), *Against Global Apartheid: South Africa meets the World Bank, IMF and International Finance*, Cape Town, University of Cape Town Press.

Bond, P. (ed.) (1991), *South Africa's Economic Crisis*, Cape Town, David Philip and London, Zed Press.

Booth, K. and P. Vale (1995) "Security in Southern Africa: after Apartheid: Beyond Realism," *International Affairs*, vol. 71, no. 2.

Bratton, M. and van de Walle, N. (1997) *Democratic Experiments in Africa: Regime Transitions in Comparative Perspective*, Cambridge, U.K.: Cambridge University Press.

Braybrooke, D. (1975) "The Meaning of Participation and of Demands for It: A Preliminary Survey of Conceptual Issues," in *Participation in Politics*, edited by J. R. Pennock and J. W. Chapman (Nomos XVI), New York: Lieber-Atherton, pp. 56-88.

Breytenbach, W. (2000) "The Failure of Security Cooperation in the SADC Region: Explanations for the Suspension of the Organ for Politics, Defence and Security," *South African Journal of International Affairs*, vol. 7. no. 1, pp. 85-96.

Bruce, D. (1998) "The Role and Achievements of the Southern African Regional Police Chiefs Cooperation Organization (SARPCCO)," *ISSUP Bulletin*, no. 4/98, pp. 1-10.

Bruno K., & Karliner J., CorpWatch/Tides Center, (January 2002) "Greenwash + 10: The UN's Global Compact, Corporate Accountability and the Johannesburg Earth Summit". www.corpwatch.org.

Budge, I. (1996) *The New Challenge of Direct Democracy*, Cambridge, U.K.: Polity Press.

Burawoy, M. (1985) *The Politics of Production: Factory Regimes Under Capitalism and Socialism*, London: London: Verso.

Burgin, E. (1993) "Congress and foreign policy: The misperceptions" in *Congress Reconsidered*, edited by L. Dodd & B. Oppenheimer, Washington, D.C., Congressional Quarterly Press.

Business Day, June 11, 2002. "NEPAD: Revolution in accountability". www.bday.co.za/bday/content/direct/1,3523,1104014-6096-0,00.html

Butler, J., Rotberg, R. and Adams, J. (1977) *The Black Homelands of South Africa: The Political and Economic Development of Bophuthatswana and KwaZulu*, Berkeley: University of California Press.

Camp, R. (ed.) (1996) *Polling for Democracy: Public Opinion and Political Liberalization in Mexico*, Wilmington: SR Books.

CAMS (Coalition Against Military Spending) (2000) "Coalition Against Military Spending (CAMS) Background Information September 2000," unpublished mimeo.

Caspary, W.R. (1970) "The Mood Theory: a Study of Public Opinion and Foreign Policy," *American Political Science Review*, vol. 64, no. 2, pp. 536-47.

CEDAW *(Convention for the Elimination of all Forms of Discrimination)*, undated. First South African Report. Office of the President.

Centre for Southern African Studies (1995) *Parliaments and Foreign Policy: The International and South African Experience*, A Conference Report, Bellville: CSAS Special Report.

Cerny, P. (1997) "Paradoxes of the Competition State: The Dynamics of Political Globalization," *Government and Opposition*, vol. 32, no. 2, pp. 251-74.

Checkel, J. (1998) "The Constructivist Turn in International Relations Theory," *World Politics*, vol. 50, pp. 324-48.

Chikane, F. (2001) "Integrated Democratic Governance: A Restructured Presidency at Work," issued by the Office of the President and Vice-President of the Republic of South Africa.

Chittick, W. O., Billingsley, K. R. and Travis, R. (1995) "A Three-Dimensional Model of American Foreign Policy Beliefs," *International Studies Quarterly*, vol. 39, pp. 313-31.

Cilliers, J. (1996) "The Evolving Security Architecture in Southern Africa," *Africa Insight*, vol. 26, no. 1, pp. 13-25.

Cilliers, J. (1999) *Building Security in Southern Africa—an update on the evolving architecture*, Halfway House: Institute for Security Studies.

Cilliers, J. (2001) "A deal that just won't go away," *Traders*, vol. 7.

Cohen, C. (1971) *Democracy*, Athens: University of Georgia Press.

Cohen, J. and Rogers, J. (1983) *On Democracy*, Harmondsworth, U.K.: Penguin.

Converse, P. (1964) "The Nature of Belief Systems in Mass Publics," in *Ideology and Discontent*, edited by D. Apter. New York: Free Press.

COSATU (2001), "The arms deal and job creation,"
www.cosatu.org.za/docs/2001/armsdeal.htm

Cox, R. (1987) *Production, Power, and World Order*, New York: Columbia University Press.

Cox, R. (1994) "Global Restructuring: Making Sense of the Changing International Political Economy", in *Political Economy and the Changing Global Order*, edited by R. Stubbs & G. Underhill, Toronto, Ontario: McCleland and Stewart Inc.

Cox, R. (1996) "Social Forces, States, and World Orders" in Cox, R. with Sinclair, T. *Approaches to World Order* Cambridge, U.K.: Cambridge University Press.

Crawford, N. (1999) "How Arms Embargoes Work," in *How Sanctions Work: Lessons from South Africa*, edited by N. Crawford and A. Klotz London: Macmillan Press.

Crawford, N. and Klotz, A. (eds.) (1999) *How Sanctions Work: Lessons from South Africa*. Basingstoke, U.K.: Macmillan.

Crozier, M., Huntingdon, S., and Watanuki, J. (1975) *The Crisis of Democracy: Report on the Governability of Democracies to the Trilateral Commission* New York: New York University Press.

Cuba, Dominican Republic, Haiti, India, Kenya, Pakistan, Peru, Uganda, Venezuela and Zimbabwe (2001), "Assessment of Trade in Services," Special Communication to the World Trade Organization, 9 October.

Cuba, Dominican Republic, Haiti, India, Kenya, Pakistan, Peru, Uganda, Venezuela and Zimbabwe (2001) "Assessment of Trade in Services," Special Communication to the World Trade Organisation, 9 October.

Culpeper, R. (2001) *Development Economics: A Call to Action.* A Draft paper prepared for the discussion at the UNRISD meeting on *"The Need to Rethink Development Economic,"* 7-8 September, Cape Town.

Cunningham, J. and Moore, M. (1997) "Elite and Mass Foreign Policy Opinions: Who Is Leading This Parade?," *Social Science Quarterly*, vol. 78, no. 3, pp. 641-56.

Dahl, R. (1956) *A Preface to Democratic Theory*, Chicago: University of Chicago Press.

Dahl, R. (1971) *Polyarchy*, New Haven, Ct.: Yale University Press.

Dahl, R. (1989) *Democracy and its Critics*, New Haven, Ct.: Yale University Press.

Dahl, R. (1998) *On Democracy,* New Haven, Ct.: Yale University Press.

Dahl, R. and Tufte, E. (1973) *Size and Democracy*, Stanford, Calif.: Stanford University Press.

Davies, R. (1997) "Analysis of the negotiation process: critical areas, contradictions and commonalities" in *Trading on Development*, edited by R. Houghton, Johannesburg: Foundation for Global Dialogue.

De Tocqueville, A. (1966)[1835] *Democracy in America,* two volumes (translated by George Lawrence and edited by J.P. Mayer and Max Lerner). New York: Fontana.

Deegan, H. (2002) "A Critical Examination of the Democratic Transition in South Africa: The Question of Public Participation," *Commonwealth and Comparative Politics,* vol. 40, no. 1, pp. 43-60.

Defense Review (1998), *South African Defence Review*, Pretoria: Department of Defense, http://www.mil.za/Articles&Papers/DefenceReview/

Department of Foreign Affairs (1996) *South African Foreign Policy Discussion Document*, issued by the Department of Foreign Affairs, Pretoria.

Department of Foreign Affairs (1997) "Background Document Delivered by the Ministry of Foreign Affairs at the Parliamentary Media Briefing Week: South Africa''s New Place in the World," February 11.

Department of Foreign Affairs (2000) Foreign Minister Zuma "Media Statement on Minister Zuma''s Closing Address to the Security Council," New York, February 1.

Department of Foreign Affairs (DFA) (2001b) *Annual Report 2000/2001*, Pretoria, Department of Foreign Affairs.

Department of Foreign Affairs (DFA). (2001a) *Strategic Plan 2000-2005*, Pretoria, Department of Foreign Affairs.

Department of Foreign Affairs (1995) *Policy Guidelines by the Minister and Deputy Minister of Foreign Affairs*, 1995, published by the DFA, Pretoria.

Diamond, L. (1988) "Roots of Failure, Seeds of Hope" in *Democracy in Developing Countries: Volume 2, Africa*, edited by L. Diamond, J. Linz, and S. Lipset, Boulder, Colo.: Lynne Rienner: pp. 1-32.

Diamond, L. (1993) "Three Paradoxes of Democracy," in *The Global Resurgence of Democracy*, edited by L. Diamond and M. Plattner, Baltimore, Md.: Johns Hopkins University Press.

Diamond, L., Linz, J. and Lipset, S. (eds.) (1988) *Democracy in Developing Countries: Volume 1, Persistence, Failure, and Renewal*, Boulder, Colo.: Lynne Rienner.

Diamond, L; Linz, J. & Lipset, S. 1995. *Politics in Developing Countries: Comparing Experiences with Democracy*. Boulder, Colo.: Lynne Rienner Publishers,

Dominguez, J. (1981) "Public opinion on international affairs in less developed countries," in *From National Development to Global Community: Essays in Honour of Karl Deutsch*, edited by R. Merritt and B. Russett. London: George Allen & Unwin: pp. 184-205.

Du Pisani, A. (1988) *What Do We Think? A survey of white opinion on foreign policy issues*, No. 4. Johannesburg: SAIIA.

Du Pisani, A. (1990) *What Do We Think? A survey of white opinion on foreign policy issues*, No. 5. Johannesburg: SAIIA.

Eichenberg, R. (1998) "Domestic Preferences and Foreign Policy: Cumulation and Confirmation in the Study of Public Opinion," *International Studies Quarterly*, vol. 42, pp. 97-105.

Elbadawi, I. and Hartzenberg, T. (eds.) (2000) *Development Issues in South Africa*, London: Macmillan Press.

Elman, M. (1999) "The Never-ending Story: Democracy and Peace," *International Studies Review*, vol. 1, no 3, 88-103.

Elshstain, J and Tobias, S. (1990) *Women, Militarism and War: Essays in Politics, History and Social Theory*. Savage, Md.: Rowman and Littlefield.

Elshstain, J. (1992) "The power and powerlesness of women". In *Beyond Equality and Difference: Citizenship, Feminist Politics, Female Subjectivity*, edited by G. Bock and S. James, London: Routledge.

Elster, J. (1988) "Introduction," in *Constitutionalism and Democracy*, edited by J. Elster and R. Slagstad, Cambridge, Mass.: Cambridge University Press, pp. 1-17.

Elster, J. (1999) "The Market and the Forum: Three Varieties of Political Theory," in *Deliberative Democracy: Essays on Reason and Politics*, edited by J. Bohman and W. Rehg, Cambridge, Mass.: MIT Press, pp. 3-34.

Elster, J. (ed.) (1998) *Deliberative Democracy*, Cambridge, Mass.: Cambridge University Press.

Erwin, A. (1999), "Address to Parliament on the Challenges of Globalization at the 'Millennium' Debate Occasion," Cape Town, 19 November.

Evans, P. (1997) "The Eclipse of the State? Reflections on Stateness in an Era of Globalization," *World Politics*, vol. 50, pp. 62-87.

Falk, R. & Strauss, A. (2001) "Toward a global parliament," *Foreign Affairs*, vol. 80, no. 1, pp. 212-20.

Fallon, P. and Lucas, R. (1998) "South Africa: Labor Markets Adjustment and Inequalities," World Bank Southern Africa Department, Washington, D.C.

Faure, M. and Venter, A. (2000) "Electoral systems and accountability: a proposal for electoral reform in South Africa," in *Elections and Democracy in Southern Africa*, edited by H. Kotzé and B-E. Rasch, Oslo, Norway: Norwegian Institute of Human Rights, pp. 69-92.

Feinstein, A. (2002), "The last rites have been read," *Weekly Mail and Guardian*, 1-7 March.

Finer, S. (1974) "State-building, state boundaries and border control," *Social Science Information*, vol. 13, no. 4/5, pp. 19-126.

Finer, S. (1975) "State- and Nation-Building in Europe: The Role of the Military," in *The Formation of National States in Western Europe*, edited by C. Tilly, Princeton, N.J.: Princeton University Press.

Finer, S. (1997) *The History of Government From the Earliest Times, volume 3, Empires, Monarchies and the Modern State*, Oxford, U.K.: Oxford University Press.

Finnemore, M. (1996) *National Interests in International Society,* Cornell University Press, Ithaca, N.Y.

Finnemore, M. and Sikkink, K. (1998). "International Norm Dynamics and Political Change," *International Organization* vol. 52, no. 4, pp. 887-917.

Fiskin, J. (1997) *The Voice of the People: Public Opinion and Democracy* (expanded to include new "Afterword"), New Haven, Ct.: Yale University Press.

Fite, D et al. 1990. "Gender Differences in Foreign Policy Attitudes" *American Politics Quarterly*, vol. 18, no. 4, pp. 34-42.

Foyle, D. (1997) "Public opinion and foreign policy: elite beliefs as mediating variables," *International Studies Quarterly* vol. 41, pp. 141-69.

Friedman, M. (1963) *Capitalism and Freedom* Chicago: University of Chicago Press.

Friedman, S. (1991) "An Unlikely Utopia: State and Civil Society in South Africa," *Politikon*, vol. 19, no. 1, pp. 5-19

Friends of the Development Box (2001) "Press Statement," Doha, 10 November.

Fung, A. and Wright, E. O. (2001) "Deepening Democracy: Innovations in Empowered Participatory Governance," *Politics & Society*, vol. 29, no. 1, pp. 5-41.

Gelb, S. (1987), "Making Sense of the Crisis," *Transformation*, no. 5, pp. 33-50.

Gelb, S. (ed) (1991), *South Africa's Economic Crisis*, Cape Town: David Philip.

Geldenhuys, D. (1982) *What Do We Think? A survey of white opinion on foreign policy issues*, No. 1. Johannesburg: SAIIA.

Geldenhuys, D. (1984) *The Diplomacy of Isolation: South African Foreign Policy Making*. New York: St. Martin's.

Geldenhuys, D. (1984) *What Do We Think? A survey of white opinion on foreign policy issues*, No. 2. Johannesburg: SAIIA.

Geldenhuys, D. (1986) *What Do We Think? A survey of white opinion on foreign policy issues*, No. 3. Johannesburg: SAIIA.

Gill, S, (1995) "Theorizing the interregnum: the double movement and global politics in the 1990s" in, *International Political Economy: Understanding Global Disorder*, edited by B. Hettne, Cape Town: SAPES.

Gilligan, C. (1982) *In a Different Voice: Psychological Theory and Women's Development.* Cambridge, Mass.: Harvard University Press.

Gills, B., Rocamora, J., and Wilson, R. (1993) *Low Intensity Democracy: Political Power in the New World Order.* London: Pluto Press.

Goldin and Alan Gelb (2001), "Attacks on US Hurt Africa," *Financial Times,* 10 October.

Gondwe, G. and C. Madavo (2001), "New swipe at fighting poverty," *Financial Times,* 7 October.

Good, K. (1997a) *Realizing Democracy in Botswana, Namibia and South Africa* Pretoria: Africa Institute.

Good, K. (1997b) "Development and Democracies: Liberal Versus Popular," *Africa Insight,* vol. 27, no. 4, pp. 253-257.

Gourevitch, Peter (1978). "The Second Image Reversed: The International Sources of Domestic Politics," *International Organization* vol. 32, no. 4, pp. 881-912.

Government Communication and Information System (GCIS) (1998) *South Africa Yearbook 1998,* Pretoria, GCIS.

Gramsci, A. (1971) *Selections From the Prison Notebooks* London: Lawrence and Wishart.

Greenberg, S. (1987) *Legitimating the Illegitimate: State, Markets and Resistance in South Africa,* Berkeley: University of California Press.

Haas, M., Jiwalai, R. and Kuroda, Y. (1996) "Democratic Foreign Policy Decision-making: Comparing Japan and Thailand," *Journal of East Asian Affairs,* vol. 10, no. 2, pp. 223-61.

Habermas, J. (1979) *Communication and the Evolution of Society* Boston: Beacon Press.

Habermas, J. (1987) *The Philosophical Discourse of Modernity* Cambridge, U.K.: Polity Press.

Habermas, J. (1990) *Moral Consciousness and Communicative Action* Cambridge, U.K.: Polity Press.

Habib, A. (1997) "From pluralism to corporatism: South Africa's labour relations in transition," *Politikon: South African Journal of Political Studies,* vol. 24, no. 1, pp. 57-75.

Halliday, F. (1998) "Gender and IR: progress, backlash, and prospect," *Millennium,* vol. 27, no. 4, pp. 834-49.

Hancock, W. (1937). *Survey of British Commonwealth Affairs: Problems of Nationality 1918-1936.* Oxford, U.K.: Oxford University Press.

Hansard, 24 April 1997, cols. 1855-1929.

Harriott, H. (1993) "The Dilemmas of Democracy and Foreign Policy," *Journal of Peace Research,* vol. 30, no. 2, pp. 219-26.

Harrison R. (2001) "The rise of ethical consumerism," www.ethicalconsumer.org/Ecnewssite/pages/philosophy/riserise.htm

Hartley, T. and Russett, B. (1992) "Public Opinion and the Common Defense: Who Governs Military Spending in the United States?" *American Political Science Review,* vol. 86, no. 4, pp. 905-15.

Held, D. (1992) "Democracy: From City-States to a Cosmopolitan Order?" *Political Studies,* vol. XL, pp. 10-39.

Held, D. (1996) *Models of Democracy* (second edition), Cambridge, U.K.: Polity Press.

Helleiner, G. (2001) "Markets, politics and globalization: Can the global economy be civilized?" *Global Governance,* vol. 7, no. 3, July–September.

Heller, P. (2001) "Moving the State: The Politics of Democratic Decentralization in Kerala, South Africa, and Porto Alegre," *Politics & Society,* vol. 29, no. 1, pp. 131-63.

Hentz, J. (2002) *Cooperation Among States: South Africa and the Logic of Cooperation in Southern Africa*, Virginia Military Institute: unpublished manuscript.

Hill, K. and Hinton-Andersson, A. (1995) "Pathways of Representation: A Causal Analysis of Public Opinion-Policy Linkages," *American Journal of Political Science*, vol. 39, no. 4, pp. 924-35.

Hinckley, R. 1998, "Public Attitudes Toward Key Foreign Policy Events," *Journal of Conflict Resolution*, vol. 32, pp. 295-318.

Hirschmann, D. (1987) *Changing attitudes of black South Africans toward the United States of America*, Grahamstown: Institute of Social and Economic Research, Rhodes University.

Holsti, K. (1988) *International Politics: A Framework for Analysis* (5th edition), Prentice-Hall, Englewood Cliffs, N.J.

Holsti, O. & Rosenau, J. (1981) "The foreign policy beliefs of women in leadership positions", *The Journal of Politics*, vol. 43, no. 2, pp. 24-33.

Holsti, O. (1992) "Public Opinion and Foreign Policy: Challenges to the Almond-Lippman Consensus," *International Studies Quarterly*, vol. 36, pp. 439-66.

Holsti, O. (1996) *Public Opinion and American Foreign Policy*, Ann Arbor: University of Michigan Press.

Holsti, O. and Rosenau, J. (1980) "Does Where You Stand Depend on When You Were Born? The Impact of Generation on Post-Vietnam Foreign Policy Beliefs," *Public Opinion Quarterly*, vol. 44, pp. 1-22.

Horkheimer, M. (1974) *Eclipse of Reason* New York: Seabury Press.

Horkheimer, M. (1995) *Critical Theory: Selected Essays* New York: Continuum Books.

Hosking, S. and P. Bond (2000) "Infrastructure for Spatial Development Initiatives or for Basic Needs? Port Elizabeth''s Prioritisation of the Coega Port/IDZ over Municipal Services," in *Empowerment through Service Delivery*, edited by M. Khosa, Pretoria: Human Sciences Research Council.

Hoyt, P.D. (2000) "Bureaucratic politics and the foreign policy process: the missing element of process," *The Journal of Political Science*, vol. 28, pp. 1-20.

Huntington, S. (1968) *Political Order in Changing Societies*, New Haven, Ct.: Yale University Press.

Huntington, S. (1991) *The Third Wave: Democratization in the Late Twentieth Century*, Oklahoma: University of Oklahoma Press.

Hurwitz, J. and Peffley, M. (1987) "How Are Foreign Policy Attitudes Structured? A Hierarchical Model," *American Political Science Review*, vol. 81, pp. 1099-119.

Hutchful, E. (1995-96) "The civil society debate in Africa," *International Journal*, vol. 51, pp 54-57.

IDASA (2001), "Democracy and the Arms Deal: A Submission to Parliament," Mimeo, Cape Town.

Isaacs, M. (1998) "Two Different Worlds: The Relationship Between Elite and Mass Opinion on American Foreign Policy," *Political Communication*, vol. 15, pp. 323-45.

Iyengar, S. and Kinder, D. (1987) *News That Matters: Television and American Public Opinion*. Chicago: University of Chicago Press.

Jackson, R. (1990) *Quasi-States: Sovereignty, International Relations, and the Third World*, Cambridge, U.K.: Cambridge University Press.

Jacobs, S. et al. (2001), *Real Politics, the Wicked Issues*, Cape Town: IDASA.

James, W. & Caigure, D. (1996) "The New South Africa: Renewing civil society," *Journal of Democracy*, vol. 7, no. 1, pp. 56-66.

Jensen, M P. (1987) "Gender, sex roles and attitudes toward war and nuclear weapons" *Sex Roles*, vol. 17, nos. 5 and 6, pp. 121-30.

Jentleson, B. (1992) "The Pretty Prudent Public: Post Post-Vietnam American Opinion on the Use of Military Force," *International Studies Quarterly*, vol. 36, pp. 49-74.

Jentleson, B. and Britton, R. (1998) "Still Pretty Prudent," *Journal of Conflict Resolution*, vol. 42, no. 4, pp. 395-417.

Jervis, R. (1978) "Cooperation under the Security Dilemma," *World Politics*, vol. 30, no. 2, pp. 167-214.

Jordan, D. and Page, B. (1992) "Shaping Foreign Policy Opinions: the Role of TV News," *Journal of Conflict Resolution*, vol. 36, no. 2, pp. 227-42.

Kapstein E. (2001) "The Corporate Ethics Crusade," *Foreign Affairs* September/October, pp. 105-19.

Kaufmann, C. (1996) "Possible and Impossible Solutions to Ethnic Civil Wars" *International Security*, vol. 20, no. 4, pp. 136-75.

Keane, J. (1988) "Despotism and Democracy: The Origins and Development of the Distinction between Civil Society and the State, 1750-1850," in *Civil Society and the State*, ed. J. Keane, London: Verso.

Keck M. and Sikkink, K. (1998) *Activists Beyond Borders: Advocacy Networks in International Politics*, Cornell, N.Y.: Cornell University Press.

Keet, D. (2000) "The challenges facing African countries regarding the WTO trade regime since the third ministerial meeting in Seattle," *IGD Occasional Paper*, no. 25.

Keim, D. (1975) "Participation in contemporary democratic theory," in *Participation in Politics: Nomos XVI*, edited by J. Pennock and J. Chapman, New York: Lieber-Atherton, pp. 1-38.

Kelly, R. et al. (1991) "Gender and managerial/leadership styles". *Women and Politics*, vol. 11, no. 2, pp. 25-36.

Kennan, G. (1950) *American Diplomacy: 1900-1950*, Chicago: University of Chicago Press.

Khanyile, M. (2000), "Arms: Morality and Reality," *Africa Insight*, Vol. 39, Nos. 3-4, pp. 24-31.

Kittay, E & Meyers, D. (1987) *Women and Moral Theory*, Ottowa, Canada: Rowan and Littlefield.

Klein N. (2001) *No Logo*. London: Flamingo

Klotz, A. (1995). *Norms in International Relations: The Struggle against Apartheid*, Ithaca, N.Y.: Cornell University Press.

Knopf, J. (1998) "How Rational is the 'Rational Public'?," *Journal of Conflict Resolution*, vol. 42, no. 5, pp. 544-71.

Koning, A. (1997) "The EU's Trade and Development Policy" in *Trade and Development*. Cape Town: Galvin & Sales.

Korany, B. (1986) *How Foreign Policy Decisions Are Made in the Third World: A Comparative Analysis*, Boulder,Colo.: Westview Press.

Kotzé, H. (1992) *Transitional Politics in South Africa: an Attitude Survey of Opinion-Leaders*. Centre for International and Comparative Politics, University of Stellenbosch, Stellenbosch, Research Report no. 3 of 1992.

Kotzé, H. (1996) "The new parliament: transforming the Westminster heritage" in *South Africa: designing new political institutions*, edited by M. Faure, M. & J. Lane, London: Sage, pp. 252-68.

Kotzé, H. (1997) *Take us to our leaders: the South African National Assembly and its members*, Konrad Adenauer Stiftung (KAS) Occasional Papers, Johannesburg, KAS.

Krog, A. (1998) *Country of my Skull*, Johannesburg: Random House.

Kull, S., Destler, I.. and Ramsay, C. (1997) *The Foreign Policy Gap: How Policymakers Misread the Public*, Center for International and Security Studies, University of Maryland, Baltimore.

Kymlicka, W. and Norman, W. 1992, "The Social Charter Debate," *Network Analysis* No 2, University of Ottowa, Canada.

Kynoch, G. (1996) "The 'Transformation' of the South African Military," *The Journal of Modern African Studies*, vol. 34, no. 3, pp. 441-57.

Lapid, Y. (1989) "The Third Debate: On the Prospects of International Theory in a Post-Positivist Era," *International Studies Quarterly*, vol. 33, pp. 235-54.

Lauren, P. (1988). *Power and Prejudice: The Politics and Diplomacy of Racial Discrimination*. Boulder, Colo.: Westview.

le Pere, G. and van Nieuwkerk, A. (2002) "The Evolution of South Africa's Foreign Policy, 1994-2000," in *Power, Wealth and Global Justice: An International Relations Textbook for Africa*, edited by Pa. McGowan and P. Nel, Cape Town: UCT Press, pp. 248-66.

le Pere, G. et al. (compilers). (1996) *Concluding Report: Recommendations of the Working Group on a Foreign Affairs Advisory Council*, Foundation for Global Dialogue (FGD) Occasional Paper No 3, Braamfontein: FGD.

Levermore, R, Gibb, R and Cleary, M. (2000) "The SA-EU TDCA: an analysis of decision-making procedures and processes in South Africa," SAIIA Report No. 15.

Lewis, P. (1992) "Political Transition and the Dilemma of Civil Society in Africa," *Journal of International Affairs*, vol. 46, no. 1, pp. 31-54.

Liebenberg, I. et al. (eds) (1994) *The Long March: The Story of the Struggle for Liberation in South Africa*, Pretoria: HAUM.

Lippmann, W. (1925) *The Phantom Public*. New York: Harcourt, Brace.

Locke, J. (1690/1947) *An Essay Concerning the True Origins, Extent, and End of Civil Government*. New York: Harper.

Louis, W. (1984) "The Era of the Mandates System and the Non-European World," in *The Expansion of International Society*, edited by H. Bull and A. Watson. Oxford, U.K.: Clarendon, pp. 201-13.

Maggiotto, M. and Wittkopf, E. (1981) "American Public Attitudes Toward Foreign Policy," *International Studies Quarterly*, vol. 25, pp. 601-31.

Makoa, F. (1999) "Foreign Military Intervention in Lesotho's Elections Dispute: Whose Project?" *Strategic Review for Southern Africa*, vol. 21, no. 1, pp. 66-87.

Malan, M. (1999) "Can they do that? SADC, the DRC, and Lesotho," *Indicator SA*, vol. 15, no. 4, pp. 90-5.

Mandela, N. (1993) "South Africa's future foreign policy," *Foreign Affairs*, vol. 72, no. 5: 86-97.

Mann, M. (1988) "Nation-States in Europe and other Continents: Diversifying, Developing, not Dying", *Daedalus*, vol. 122, no. 3, pp. 115-140.

Mansbridge, J. (1980) *Beyond Adversary Democracy*, Basic Books, New York.

Manual for National and Provincial Departments (1997) *Mainstreaming gender considerations in policies and programmes*. Pretoria: Government Printers.

Marais, H. (1998) *South Africa Limits to Change: The Political Economy of Transition*, Cape Town: University of Cape Town Press.

Martin, L. (2000) *Democratic Commitments: Legislatures and International Cooperation*, New Haven, Ct.: Princeton University Press.

Marx, K. (1970) *Critique of Hegel's Philosophy of Right*. Cambridge, U.K.: Cambridge University Press.

Marx, K. (1973) "The Civil War in France" in Marx, K. and Engels, F. *Selected Works, Volume II,* Moscow: Progress Publishers, pp. 178-244.

Marx, K. and Engels, F. (1973) "Manifesto of the Communist Party" in Marx, K. and Engels, F. *Selected Works, Volume I.* Moscow: Progress Publishers, pp. 98-137.

Masiza, Z. (1999) "Silent Citizenry: Public Participation and Foreign Policy Making," Centre for Policy Studies, *Policy Brief,* vol. 15, pp. 1-6.

Mathews, J. T. (1997) "Power Shift," *Foreign Affairs,* vol. 76, no. 1, January/February, pp. 50-66.

Mattes, R., Davids, Y. and Africa, C. (2000) *Views of Democracy in South Africa and the Region: Trends and Comparisons,* No. 2 in "The Afrobarometer Series," produced by The Southern African Democracy Barometer, Cape Town.

Mbeki, T. (2001) "Address by the President of South Africa, Mr. Thabo Mbeki, at the University of Hong Kong, December 12, 2001," Pretoria: The Presidency.

Mbeki, T. (2001), "Welcome to *ANC Today*," *ANC Today,* vol. 1, no. 1, 26 Jan.-1 Feb., http://www.anc.org.za/ancdocs/anctoday/2001/at01.htm.

Mbeki, T. (2002) Address of President Thabo Mbeki at the 90th anniversary of the African National Congress, 6 January 2002.

McChesney R. (1997) "The Global Media Giants: The Nine Firms That Dominate the World" Extra! November/December 1997 on www.fair.org/extra/9711/gmg.html

McChesney R. (2002) "The Political Economy of Global Media," www.uaf.edu/journal/morrison/McChesney.html

McGlen, N & Sarkees, M. (1993) *Women in Foreign Policy.* New York: Routledge.

McKeon, R. and Riockan, S. (eds.) (1951) *Democracy in a World of Tensions: A Symposium,* Chicago: Chicago University Press.

Meiskins Wood, E. (1995) *Democracy Against Capitalism: Reinventing Historical Materialism* Cambridge, U.K.: Cambridge University Press.

Meth, C. (1990), "Productivity and South Africa's Economic Crisis," Unpublished research monograph, Durban, University of Natal Department of Economics.

Meth, C. (1990), "Productivity and South Africa's Economic Crisis," Unpublished research monograph, Durban, University of Natal Department of Economics.

Migdal, J. (1988) *Strong Societies and Weak States, State-Society Relations and State Capabilities in the Third World,* Princeton, N.J. University Press, Princeton.

Miller, C. (1991) "Women in international relations? The debate in inter-war Britain," in *Gender in international relations,* edited by R. Grant and K. Newland, Bloomington: Indiana University Press.

Mills, G. (1996) "South Africa's Foreign Policy Priorities: A 1996 Update," *CSIS Africa Notes,* no. 180, January.

Mills, G. (1998) "French policy-making in Africa," *South African Journal of International Affairs,* vol. 6, no. 1, pp. 59-65.

Mills, J. and J. Oppenheimer (2001), "Partnerships only way to break cycle of poverty," *Financial Times,* 1 October.

Monroe, A. (1979) "Consistency Between Public Preferences and National Policy Decisions," *American Politics Quarterly,* vol. 7, no. 1, pp. 3-19.

Moore, D. (1996) "Reading Americans on Democracy in Africa" From the CIA to 'Good Governance'," *European Journal of Development Research,* vol. 8, no. 1, pp. 123-48.

Moravcsik, A. (1993) "Introduction: Integrating International and Domestic Theories of International Bargaining". In *Double-edged Diplomacy: International Bargaining and Domestic Politics,* edited by P. Evans, H, Jacobson, & R. Putnam, Berkeley: University of California Press, pp. 3-42.

Morgenthau, H. (1973) *Politics among Nations: The Struggle for Power and Peace* (fifth edition). New York: Alfred Knopf.

Moser, C. (1993) *Gender Planning and Development: Theory, Practice and Training,* London: Routledge.

Murphy C. (1994) *Industrial Organization and Social Change: Global Governance Since 1850.* Cambridge, U.K.: Polity Press.

Murphy C. (2002) (ed.) *Egalitarian Politics in the Age of Globalization.* London: Palgrave.

Nathan, L. (1998), "The 1996 Defence White Paper: An agenda for state demilitarisation?" in *From Defence to Development,* edited by J. Cock, Cape Town: David Philip.

Nel, P. & A. van Nieuwkerk (1997) "Constructing the nation''s foreign policy mood: South African public opinion and government's foreign relations," A report by the Foundation for Global Dialogue, Johannesburg, and the Centre for International and Comparative Politics, Stellenbosch: University of Stellenbosch.

Nel, P. (1996) "Civil society and the transnational promotion of human rights" in *Through a glass darkly? Human Rights Promotion in South Africa's Foreign Policy,* Foundation for Global Dialogue (FGD) Occasional Paper No 6.

Nel, P. (1999) "The Foreign Policy Beliefs of South Africans: A First Cut," *Journal of Contemporary African Studies,* vol. 17, no. 1, pp. 123-46.

Nel, P., Taylor, I. and van der Westhuizen, J. (eds) (2001) *South Africa's Multilateral Diplomacy and Global Change: The Limits of Reformism,* Aldershot: Ashgate.

Neufeld, M. (1998) "Democratisation in/of Foreign Policy: Critical Reflections on the Canadian Case," unpublished paper.

Neufeld, M. (1999), "Democratization in/of Canadian Foreign Policy: Critical Reflections," *Studies in Political Economy,* no. 58, pp. 97-119.

Nijzink, L. (2001) "Opposition in the new South African Parliament," *Democratization,* vol. 8, no. 1, pp. 53-68.

Nincic, M. (1992a) *Democracy and Foreign Policy: the Fallacy of Political Realism,* New York: Columbia University Press.

Nincic, M. (1992b) "A sensible public: new perspectives on popular opinion and foreign policy". *Journal of Conflict Resolution* vol 36, pp. 772-89.

Nincic, M. (1997) "Domestic Costs, the U.S. Public and the Isolationist Calculus," *International Studies Quarterly,* vol. 41, pp. 593-610.

Nordlinger, E. (1981) *On the Autonomy of the Democratic State,* Cambridge, Mass.: Harvard University Press.

Nossal, K. (1995), "The Democratization of Canadian Foreign Policy: The Elusive Ideal," in, *Democracy and Foreign Policy: Canada Among Nations 1995,* edited by M. Cameron and M. Molot, Ottawa: Carleton University Press.

Nye J. (2001) "Globalization's Democratic Deficit: How to Make International Institutions More Accountable," *Foreign Affairs,* July/August, pp. 2-6.

Nye, A. (1988) *Feminist Theory and the Philosophies of Man.* London: Croom Helm.

Nzo, A. (1999) "Foreign Minister's Budget Vote Address," reproduced in *South African Journal of International Affairs,* vol. 6, no. 2, pp. 217-26.

O'Donnell, G. (1993) "On the State, Democratisation and Some Conceptual Problems: A Latin American View with Glances at Some Post-Communist Countries," *World Development,* vol. 21, no. 8, pp. 1355-69.

O'Neal, J. Lian, B. and Joyner, Jr., J.H. (1996) "Are the American People 'Pretty Prudent'? Public Responses to U.S. Uses of Force," *International Studies Quarterly,* vol. 40, pp. 261-80.

Oldendick, R. and Bardes, B. (1982) "Mass and Elite Foreign Policy Opinions," *Public Opinion Quarterly*, vol. 46, pp. 368-82.

Ottaway, M. (ed.) (1997) *Democracy in Africa: The Hard Road Ahead* Boulder, Colo. Lynne Rienner.

Ottaway, M., 2001 "Corporatism Goes Global: International Organizations, Non-governmental Organization and Networks, and Transnational Business," *Global Governance*, no 7, pp. 265-92.

Outhwaite, W. (1994) *Habermas: A Critical Introduction* Cambridge, U.K.: Polity Press.

Page, B. & Shapiro, R. (1988) "Foreign policy and the rational public," *Journal of Conflict Resolution* vol. 32, pp. 211-47.

Page, B. and Shapiro, R. (1981) "Effects of Public Opinion on Policy," *American Political Science Review*, vol. 77, pp. 175-90.

Page, B. and Shapiro, R. (1992) *The Rational Public: Fifty Years of Trends in Americans' Policy Preferences*, Chicago: University of Chicago Press.

Pahad, A. (1998) "Interview with Aziz Pahad, conducted by the editors of Global Dialogue," *Global Dialogue*, vol. 3, no. 1, pp. 20-22.

Parliament (of the Republic of South Africa) (2001) "Independent groups monitoring parliament," Available at:www.parliament.gov.za/pubs/monitor.htm.

Parry, G. and Moyser, G. (1994) "More Participation, More Democracy?" In *Defining and Measuring Democracy*, edited by D. Beetham, SAGE: London, pp. 44-62.

Parry, G., Moyser, G. and Day, N. (1992) *Political Participation and Democracy in Britain*, Cambridge, U.K.: Cambridge University Press.

Pateman, C. (1970) *Participation and Democratic Theory*, Cambridge, U.K.: Cambridge University Press.

Patomäki, H. Teivainen, T. 2002 "Critical responses to neoliberal globalization in the Mercosur region: roads towards cosmopolitan democracy?". *Review of International Political Economy*, vol. 9, no. 1, pp. 37-71.

Pennock, J. and Chapman, J. (eds) (1975) "Participation in Politics"-*Nomos XVI*, New York: Lieber-Atherton.

Pettit, P. (1997) *Republicanism: A Theory of Freedom and Government*, Oxford, U.K.: Clarendon Press.

Pettman, J. (2001) "Gender issues" in *The Globalization of World Politics: An Introduction to International Relations*, edited by J. Baylis, J and S. Smith, Oxford, U.K.: Oxford University Press, pp. 483-97.

Phillips, A. (1991) *Engendering Democracy*. Cambridge, U.K.: Polity Press.

Phillips, A. (1999) *Which Equalities Matter?* Cambridge, U.K.: Polity Press.

Pienaar, S. (1987). *South Africa and International Relations Between the Two World Wars: The League of Nations Dimension*. Johannesburg: Witwatersrand University Press.

Pityana, S. (2001) "Director-General's Address" (5 June 2000), published in *South African Journal of International Affairs*, vol. 8, no. 1.

Posen, B. R. (1993) "The Security Dilemma and Ethnic Conflict," *Survival*, vol. 35, no. 1, pp. 27-47.

Potter, D.; Goldblatt, D., Kiloh, M & Lewis, P. (1997) *Democratization*, Cambridge, U.K.: Polity Press.

Powlick, P. (1995) "The Sources of Public Opinion for American Foreign Policy Officials," *International Studies Quarterly*, vol. 39, pp. 427-51.

Powlick, P. and Katz, A. (1998) "Defining the American Public Opinion/Foreign Policy Nexus," *Mershon International Studies Review*, vol. 42, pp. 29-61.

Prugl, E. and M. Meyer (1999) "Gender politics in global governance" in *Gender Politics in Global Governance*, edited by M. Meyer and E Prugl, Lanham, Md: Rowman and Littlefield.

Pusey, M. (1987) *Jürgen Habermas* London: Routledge.

Putnam, R. (1993) "Diplomacy and Domestic Politics: The Logic of Two-Level Games". In *Double-edged Diplomacy: International Bargaining and Domestic Politics*, edited by P. Evans, H, Jacobson, & R. Putnam, Berkeley: University of California Press, pp. 431-68.

Pye, L. (1971) "The Nature of Transitional Politics," in *Political Development and Social Change*, edited by. J. Finkle and R. Gable, New York: Wiley.

Raunio, T. & M. Wiberg (2000) "Does support lead to ignorance? National parliaments and the legitimacy of EU governance," *Acta Politica*, vol. 35, pp. 146-68.

Republic of South Africa. 1996, *The Constitution of the Republic of South Africa, Act 108 of 1996.*

Richards, J. (1990) "Why the pursuit of peace is not part of feminism," In *Women, Militarism and War: Essays in Politics, History and Social Theory*, edited by J. Elshtain and S. Tobias, Savage, Md.: Rowman and Littlefield.

Richardson, J. (2000) "Government, interest groups and policy change," *Political Studies*, vol. 48, pp. 1006-25.

Risse, T. and Sikkink, K. (1999). "The Socialization of International Human Rights Norms into Domestic Practices: Introduction." In *The Power of Human Rights: International Norms and Domestic Change*, edited by T. Risse, S. Ropp and K. Sikkink. New York: Cambridge University Press, pp. 1-38.

Risse, Thomas, Stephen C. Ropp and Kathryn Sikkink, eds. (1999). *The Power of Human Rights: International Norms and Domestic Change*. New York: Cambridge University Press.

Risse-Kappen, T. (1991) "Public opinion, domestic structure, and foreign policy in liberal democracies". *World Politics* vol. 43, pp. 479-512.

Robinson, W. (1996a) *Promoting Polyarchy: Globalisation, U.S. Intervention and Hegemony*, Cambridge, U.K.: University of Cambridge Press.

Robinson, W. (1996b) "Globalisation, the World System, and 'Democracy Promotion' in U.S. Foreign Policy," *Theory and Society*, vol. 25, pp. 615-65.

Rosenau, J. (1961) *Public Opinion and Foreign Policy*, Random House, New York.

Rossiter, C. and Lare, J. (eds.) (1982) *The Essential Lippmann: A Political Philosophy for Liberal Democracy* Cambridge, Mass.: Harvard University Press.

Rourke, J., Hiskes, R., Zirakzadeh, C. (1992) *Direct Democracy and International Politics: Deciding International Issues Through Referendums*, Boulder, Colo.: Lynne Rienner.

RSA. (1997) White Paper on Affirmative Action in the Public Service. *Government Gazette*, 18800.

RSA. (1997) White Paper on the Transformation of the Public Service. *Government Gazette*, 16838.

Ruddick, S. (1990) "The rationality of care," in *Women, Militarism and War: Essays in Politics, History and Social Theory*, edited by J. Elshtain and S. Tobias, Savage, Md.: Rowman and Littlefield, pp. 67-81.

Ruggie J. (2001) "Global_governance.net: The Global Compact as Learning Network," *Global Governance*, vol. 7, pp. 371-78.

Rupert, M. (1998) "Democracy, Peace; What's Not to Love?," unpublished paper.

SADC (1999) *Gender Mainstreaming at SADC: Policies, Plans & Activities*, Gaborone: Gender Unit, SADC Secretariat.

SADC (2000) *SADC Regional Development Report 2000—Challenges and Opportunities for Regional Integration*, Harare: SAPES Books.

Sadie, Y. & Van Aardt, M. (1995) "Women's issues in South Africa: 1990-1994". *Africa Insight*, vol. 25, no. 2, pp. 21-8.

Sadie, Y. (1999) "Women in foreign relations in South Africa," *Journal of Public Administration*, vol. 34, no. 3, pp. 33-42.

Sartori, G. (1987) *The Theory of Democracy Revisited*, 2 vols., Chatham, U.K.: Chatham House.

Saul, J. (1997) "Liberal Democracy vs. Popular Democracy in Southern Africa," *Review of African Political Economy*, no. 72, pp. 219-36.

Saward, M. (1994) "Democratic Theory and the Indices of Democratisation," in *Defining and Measuring Democracy*, edited by D. Beetham, London: SAGE, pp. 6-24.

Schmitter P. (1974) "Still the Century of Corporatism?" in *The New Corporatism*, edited by F. Pike and T. Strich (eds.). Notre Dame, IN.: Notre Dame University Press.

Schmitter, P., and Karl, T. (1996) "What Democracy Is and What It Is Not," in *The Global Resurgence of Democracy*, edited by L. Diamond and M. Plattner, Baltimore, Md.: Johns Hopkins University Press.

Scholte, J. (2000) *Globalization: A Critical Introduction*. New York: St Martin''s Press.

Schumpeter, J. (1952) *Capitalism, Socialism and Democracy*. Allen and Unwin, London.

Sevenhuijsen, S. (1998) *Citizenship and the Ethics of Care*. London and New York: Routledge.

Shah, H. (2002) "Journalism in an Age of Mass Media Globalization" www.idsnet.org/Papers/Communications/HEMANT_SHAH.HTM

Shaw, M. (1997) "Crime in Transition," in *Policing the Transformation—Further Issues in South Africa''s Crime Debate*, ed. M. Shaw, Institute for Security Studies, Halfway House.

Shelton, G. (1998) "South Africa''s Arms Sales to North Africa and the Middle East— Promoting peace or fuelling the arms race?'' Foundation for Global Dialogue, FGD Occasional Paper no. 16.

Shroyer, T. (1973) *The Critique of Domination*, Boston, Mass.: Beacon Press.

Sinott, R. 1995, "Bringing Public Opinion Back In," in *Public Opinion and Internationalised Governance*, edited by O. Niedermayer and R. Sinott, Oxford, U.K.: Oxford University Press.

Sklar L., 1997, "Social Movements for global capitalism: the transnational capitalist class in action," *Review of International Political Economy*, vol. 4, no. 3, pp. 514-38.

Smith, H. (2000) "Why Is There No International Relations Theory?" in *Democracy and International Relations: Critical Theories/Problematic Practices*, edited by H. Smith, Basingstoke, U.K.: Macmillan.

Smith, J. (1991) *The Idea Brokers: Think Tanks and the Rise of the New Policy Elite*, The Free Press, New York.

Smith, S. (1996) "Positivism and Beyond" in *International Theory: Positivism and Beyond*, edited by S. Smith, K. Booth and M. Zalewski, Cambridge, U.K.: Cambridge University Press.

Snitow, S. (1989) "A gender diary," in *Rocking the Ship of State*, edited by A. Harris and Y. King, Boulder, Colo.: Westview Press.

South African Department of Foreign Affairs (2001), "New Partnership for Africa's Development," Pretoria, 23 October 2001.

South African Institute of International Affairs (SAIIA). 1996, *Draft South African White Paper on Foreign Policy*, Johannesburg, SAIIA, August 1996.

South African Institute of International Affairs (SAIIA). 2001, *Research News*, no. 2.

Southall, R. (1983). *South Africa's Transkei: The Political Economy of an 'Independent' Bantustan.* New York: Monthly Review.

Southall, R. (2000) "The State of Democracy in South Africa". *Commonwealth and Comparative Politics,* vol 38, no 3, pp. 147-70.

Southern African People's Solidarity Network (2001), "Peace and Human Rights, Democracy and Development in Southern Africa in the context of Globalization," Mangoche, Malawi, 29 November.

Starr, A. (2000), *Naming the Enemy,* London, Zed Press.

Stone, D. (1996) "From the margins of politics: the influence of think tanks in Britain," *West European Politics,* vol. 19, no. 4, pp. 675-92.

Sundar Ram, D. (1998) "Introduction: whither the parliamentary institutions in India" in *Parliamentary institutions in India. Development or Decay?* edited by D. Sundar Ram, New Delhi: Jaipur National Publishing House.

Suttner R. (1996) "Parliament and Foreign Policy," *South African Yearbook of International Affairs,* Johannesburg, SAIIA, pp. 136-43.

Tandon, Y. (1999), "A Blip or a Turnaround?," *Journal on Social Change and Development,* vol. 49, December.

Taylor, I. (1999) "South Africa's Promotion of 'Democracy' and 'Stability' in Southern Africa: Good Governance or Good for Business?," Centre for the Study of Globalisation and Regionalisation annual conference "After the Global Crises: What Next for Regionalism?," University of Warwick, England, September 16-8.

Taylor, I. (2000) "Rethinking the Study of International Relations in South Africa," *Politikon: South African Journal of Political Science* vol. 27, no. 2, pp. 207-20.

Taylor, I. (2001) *Stuck in Middle GEAR: South Africa's Post-Apartheid Foreign Relations* Westport, Connecticut: Praeger.

Taylor, I. and P. Nel (2002) " 'New Africa,' globalisation and the confines of elite reformism: 'getting the rhetoric right, getting the strategy wrong'," *Third World Quarterly,* vol. 23, no. 1, pp. 163-80.

Taylor, I. and P. Vale (2000) "South Africa's Transition Revisited: Globalisation as Vision and Virtue," *Global Society,* vol. 14, no. 3, pp. 399-414.

Taylor, I. and P. Williams (2001) "South African Foreign Policy and the Great Lakes Crisis: African Renaissance Meets *Vagabondage Politique?*" *African Affairs* vol. 100, no.399, pp. 265-86.

Thomas, S. (1996). *The Diplomacy of Liberation: The Foreign Relations of the African National Congress,* London: I. B. Taurus.

Thompson, L. (1985). *The Political Mythology of Apartheid.* New Haven, Ct.: Yale University Press.

Thompson, L. (1991). *History of South Africa.* New Haven, Ct.: Yale University Press.

Thomson, A. (2000) *An Introduction to African Politics,* London, Routledge.

Tilly, C. (1975) "Reflections on the History of European State-Making," in *The Formation of National States in Western Europe,* edited by C. Tilly, Princeton, N.J.: Princeton University Press, pp. 3-83.

Tilly, C. (1985) "War Making and State Making as Organized Crime," in *Bringing the State Back In,* edited by. P. Evans, D. Reuschemeyer and T Skocpol, Cambridge, U.K.: Cambridge University Press, pp. 165-91.

Tilly, C. (1990) *Coercion, Capital and European States,* AD 990-1990, Oxford, U.K.: Basil Blackwell.

Togeby, L. (1994) "The gender gap in foreign policy attitudes" *Journal of Peace Research,* vol. 31, no. 4, pp. 123-34.

Tronto, I and Fisher, B. (1990) "Towards a feminist theory of caring," in *Circles of Care: Work and Identity in Women''s Lives*, edited by E. Abel and M. Nelson. Albany: State University of New York Press, pp. 25-39.

Tronto, I. (1995) "Care as a basis for radical political judgements," *Hypathia: A Journal for Feminist Philosophy*, vol. 10, no. 2, pp. 74-88.

Uys, P-D. (1999) "Kaalvoet in the Karoo," *The Big Issue* (Cape Town), vol. 3, no. 21.

Vale, P. (1989) "Whose World Is It Anyway? International Relations in South Africa" in *The Study of International Relations: The State of the Art*, edited by H. Dyer and L. Mangasarian, Basingstoke, U.K.: Macmillan, pp. 210-20.

Vale, P. (2002) *Security and Politics in South Africa: The Regional Dimension*, Boulder, Colo.: Lynne Rienner.

Vale, P. and Taylor, I. (1999) "South Africa''s post-apartheid foreign policy five years on—From pariah state to 'just another country'?," *The Round Table*, No. 352, pp. 629-34.

Van Aardt, M. (1996) "A foreign policy to die for: South Africa''s response to the Nigerian crisis," *Africa Insight*, vol. 26, no. 2, pp. 107-19.

Van Aardt, M. (1997a) "The Emerging Security Framework in Southern Africa: Regime or Community," *Strategic Review for Southern Africa*, vol. XIX, no. 1, pp. 1-30.

Van Aardt, M. (1997b) "The SADC Organ for Politics, Defence and Security: Challenges for Regional Community Building," *South African Journal of International Affairs*, vol. 4, no. 2, pp. 144-64.

Van Creveld, M. (1991) *The Transformation of War*, New York: Free Press.

Van Creveld, M. (1999) *The Rise and Decline of the State*, Cambridge, U.K.: Cambridge University Press.

Van der Westhuizen, J. (1998) "South Africa''s emergence as a middle power," *Third World Quarterly*, vol. 19, no. 3, pp. 435-55.

Van der Westhuizen, J. (1999) *Malaysia, South Africa, and the Marketing of the Competition State: Globalization and States' Response*, Unpublished Ph.D. Dissertation, Dalhousie University.

Van Wyk, J. (1997) "Parliament and foreign affairs: continuity or change?," *South African Yearbook of International Affairs 1997*, Johannesburg, South African Institute of International Affairs, pp 189-213.

Van Wyk, J. (1998a) "Parliament and the foreign policy process," *South African Yearbook of International Affairs 1998/9*, Johannesburg, South African Institute of International Affairs., pp. 291-306.

Van Wyk, J. (1998b) "The external relations of selected South African sub-national governments: a preliminary assessment", *South African Journal of International Affairs*, vol. 5, no. 2, pp. 21-59.

Van Wyk, J. (1999) "Parliament and the foreign policy process, 1994-99," *South African Yearbook of International Affairs 1999/2000*, Johannesburg, South African Institute of International Affairs, pp. 225-35.

Van Wyk, J. (2000a) *Aspekte van die openbare beleidproses in Suid-Afrika met spesiale verwying na die waterbeleid* (1994-1999), Unpublished MA dissertation, Stellenbosch: University of Stellenbosch.

Van Wyk, J. (2000b) "Power house or rubber stamp? Parliament and foreign affairs," *South African Yearbook of International Affairs 2000/1*, Johannesburg, South African Institute of International Affairs, pp. 83-90.

Van Zyl, A. and Macdonald, H. (2001). *A risk worth taking or missed opportunity: The budgetary implications of the Arms Procurement Package*. IDASA - Budget Information Service: Budget Brief.

Verba, S. and Nie, N. (1972) *Participation in America: Political Democracy and Social Equality*, New York: Harper and Row.

Verba, S., Nie, N. and Kim, J-O. (1978) *Participation and Political Equality*, Cambridge, U.K.: Cambridge University Press.

Verhofstadt, G. (2001), "Protesters ask right questions, yet they lack the right answers," *Financial Times*, 26 September.

Walker, R. (1988) *One World, Many Worlds: Struggles for a Just World Order*. Boulder: Colo: Lynne Rienner.

Wallace, W. (1994) "Between two worlds: Think-Tanks and foreign policy" in *Two Worlds of International Relations*, edited by C. Hill & P. Beshoff, London: Routledge.

Waltz, Kenneth (1959) *Man, the State, and War*. New York: Columbia University Press.

Wendt, A. (1992) "Anarchy Is What States Make of It: The Social Construction of Power Politics," *International Organization*, vol. 46, no. 2, pp. 391-425.

Wendt, A. (1994) "Collective Identity Formation and the International State," *American Political Science Review*, vol 88, no. 2, pp. 384-96.

Wendt, A. (1999). *Social Theory of International Politics*. New York: Cambridge University Press.

Whelehan, I. (1995) *Modern Feminist Thought*. Edinburgh: Edinburgh University Press.

Willett, S. (1995) "The Legacy of a Pariah State: South Africa's Arms Trade in the 1990s," *Review of African Political Economy*, no. 64, pp. 151-66.

Williams, P. (2000) "South African foreign policy: getting critical?" *Politikon*, vol. 27, no. 1, pp. 73-91.

Williams, P. and Taylor, I. (2000) "Neo-liberalism and the Political Economy of the 'New' South Africa," *New Political Economy*, vol. 5, no. 1, pp. 21-40.

Williams, R. (2000) "From Peacekeeping to Peacebuilding? South African Policy and Practice in Peace Missions," *International Peacekeeping*, vol. 7, no. 3, pp. 84-104.

Wittkopf, E. (1981) "The Structure of Foreign Policy Attitudes: An Alternative View," *Social Science Quarterly*, vol. 62, pp. 108-23.

Wittkopf, E. (1986) "On the Foreign Policy Beliefs of the American People: A Critique And Some Evidence," *International Studies Quarterly*, vol. 30, pp. 425-45.

Wittkopf, E. (1987) "Elites and masses: another look at attitudes toward America's world role," *International Studies Quarterly*, vol. 31, pp. 131-59.

Wittkopf, E. (1990) "Faces of Internationalism in a Transitional Environment," *Journal of Conflict Resolution*, vol. 38, no. 3, pp. 376-401.

Wittkopf, E. (1990) *Faces of Internationalism Public Opinion and American Foreign Policy*. London: Duke University Press.

Wittkopf, E. and Maggiotto, M. 1983) "Elites and Masses: A Comparative Analysis of Attitudes Toward America's World Role," *Journal of Politics*, vol. 45, pp. 303-34.

Zalewski, M, 1998, "Where is woman in IR?," *Millennium*, vol. 27, no. 4, pp. 846-58.

Interviews and personal communications

Cassim, R., Trade and Industry Policy Secretariat (TIPS), Johannesburg, 27 July 2000.

Cilliers, J., Institute for Security Studies (ISS), Pretoria, 16 August 2000.

Govindjee, G. & Spiegelberg, H., Ceasefire Campaign, Johannesburg, 26 July 2000.

Kornegay, F., South African Institute of International Affairs (SAIIA), Johannesburg, 27 July 2000.

Landsberg, C., University of the Witwatersrand, Johannesburg, 26 July 2000.

Maloka, E., Africa Institute, Pretoria, (2000).

Mills, G., South African Institute of International Affairs (SAIIA), Johannesburg, 16 October 2000.

Paulecutt, L., Freedom of Expression Institute (FXI), Johannesburg, 24 August 2000.

Schoeman, M., Rand Afrikaans University (RAU), Johannesburg, 8 August 2000.

Van Nieuwkerk, A., University of the Witwatersrand, Johannesburg, 20 July 2000.

Graham, L. Former head of the Foreign Service Institute, Department of Foreign Affairs. Interview, 1 June 1998.

Grobbelaar, T. Head: Women's Human Rights Desk, Department of Foreign Affairs. Interview. 1 June 1998.

Matiwana, M, (2002) Gender Officer, Department of Trade and Industry. Interview, 28 February.

Mazibuko, T. Acting Director-General, Department of Foreign Affairs. Interview. 18 June 1998.

Ngcobo, Z, 2002, Training officer, Foreign Service Institute, Pretoria, 28 February.

Spies, Y, Former training officer at FSI, interviewed in Pretoria on 6 March 2002.

van Nieuwkerk, A. (2001) *Personal electronic communication*, 17 January.

Williams, R. (12 Feb. 2002), Institute for Security Studies, Pretoria.

Crawford-Browne, T. (26 Feb. 2002), Economists Allied for Arms Reduction, Cape Town.

Lamb, G. (26 Feb. 2002), Centre for Conflict Resolution, Cape Town.

Interviews with foreign diplomats (2 – 26 and 27 Feb. 2002), Cape Town.

February, J. (4 March 2002), IDASA, Cape Town.

Index

About the Contributors

Talitha Bertelsmann-Scott is a researcher with Christian Aid, London.

David R. Black is Associate Professor of Political Science and Director of International Development Studies, Dalhousie University, Halifax, Canada.

Patrick Bond is Associate Professor at the University of the Witwatersrand Graduate School of Public and Development Management and a voluntary associate of the Alternative Information and Development Center in Johannesburg and of the Center for Economic Justice in Washington, D.C.

Pierre du Toit is Professor of Political Science at the University of Stellenbosch, South Africa.

Kristen Johnsen is an M.A. student in the Department of Political Science, University of Stellenbosch.

Audie Klotz is Associate Professor of Political Science, University of Illinois, Chicago.

Garth le Pere is Executive Director of the Institute for Global Dialogue, Johannesburg, South Africa.

Philip Nel is Professor of Political Studies at the University of Otago, Dunedin New Zealand.

Yolande Sadie is Professor and Chair of Political Studies and Governance at the Rand Afrikaans University, Johannesburg, South Africa.

Maxi Schoeman is Professor and Chair of Political Sciences at the University of Pretoria, South Africa.

Ian Taylor is Lecturer, Political and Administrative Sciences, at the University of Botswana in Gaborone.

Janis van der Westhuizen is Senior Lecturer, Political Science, at the University of Stellenbosch, South Africa.

Jo-Ansie van Wyk is Lecturer, Political Sciences, at the University of South Africa, Pretoria.

Brendan Vickers is an intern with the Institute for Global Dialogue and an M.A. candidate at the Rand Afrikaans University, Johannesburg.